Dignity from Despair

A Step By Step Guide for Transforming the
Lives of Women and Children—Successful NGO Creation
Using the Maher Model

"Ms. Cunningham has a special ability to synthesize complex issues and writes about them in a clear and easy to follow format. *"Dignity from Despair"* is an excellent guide for any NGO with a goal to impact the lives of women and children that come from a milieu of abuse and neglect. As clearly set out in this book a successful NGO must plan beyond providing just food and shelter to make a long term difference in the lives of the people that are served. This book is easy to follow and is filled with useful tips, start-up documents and real-life case studies that can be used to guide any organization to making a lasting footprint in this often neglected population of women and children."

Gordon Stryker, President
International Women and Infant Sustainable Healthcare Foundation
www.IWISHFoundation.org

Piscataqua Press
142 Fleet St., Portsmouth NH
03801

Ordering Information:

Quantity sales. Special discounts are available on quantity purchases by corporations, associations, and others. For details, contact the publisher at the address above.

Orders by U.S. trade bookstores and wholesalers.
Please contact RiverRun Bookstore: Tel: (603) 431-2100
info@riverrunbookstore.com

ISBN:978-1-939739-20-9

Maher (in the Marathi language) means "Mother's Home":
A haven of hope, belonging and understanding. Our mission is to help destitute women, children and men from all over India exercise their right to a higher quality of life, irrespective of gender, caste, creed or religion.

Dignity from Despair

A Step By Step Guide for Transforming the
Lives of Women and Children—Successful NGO Creation
Using the Maher Model

Darcy Cunningham

PISCATAQUA
PRESS

Dedication

To unnamed millions of women and children around the world who are waiting for the next Maher to come to them ... and to those of you who will carry the light of Maher and Sister Lucy forward.

TABLE OF CONTENTS

Author's Note

Since first agreeing to write this book, two things have heightened my urgency and commitment to this project. One, I have experienced firsthand the amazing unique community that is Maher, I have come to know some truly stellar young people, some from broken homes, some rescued from the streets. Having grown up the last 10-15 years at Maher, they have developed into exemplary young men and women. Women who were at risk of being murdered, or were tossed to the streets, are now vibrantly alive women helping other women and children heal and thrive. Two, I have also experienced worldwide awareness crystalizing in the profound need for all of us to actively engage in protecting and supporting our most vulnerable citizens: women and children, many of whom are trapped in a system that is rigged against them. And that when we truly engage, whole communities are transformed along with the women and children. Everyone's lives are better.

Maher has a 16-year history of proven success for over 2500 women and nearly that many children. Some come for a short-stay, some make Maher their home. Remarkably, these very women and children who are the focus of Maher services, are also soon on the front lines of healing and transforming life in their families and in their communities. This book details, step by step how ordinary committed people can replicate Maher's success, one community at a time. Maher provides part of the answer at least, of how the larger system can change, how people can reclaim dignity from despair.

Note about artwork appearing on the opening page of each chapter: this painting was made by a Maher resident. The design is based on Warli Folk Art Paintings, originating from a tribe indigenous to Maharashtra, India (where Maher is based). A few of the Maher young women have begun creating their own images portraying scenes from daily life, marriages, outdoor scenes and more. These designs can be found hand painted on many of the items sold through Maher's production unit. (See photo on page 287 of one of the artists.)

1 | Introduction

I saw a naked child one day, hungry and shivering by the roadside. I was outraged at God and rebuked Him, "Why do you allow this? Why don't you do something?" But God did not answer. Later that evening, relaxing at home after dinner by the fire, I heard God say quietly, "I did do something: I made you."
—Bahai parable

I first learned of Maher through my friend and colleague Will Keepin (coauthor with Cynthia Brix of *Women Healing Women: A Model of Hope for Oppressed Women Everywhere*). I later met Maher's founder, Sister Lucy Kurien. Sister Lucy and Will asked me to write a book that would detail how to re-create the success of Maher in India, Africa, or anywhere else. It was a request to which my deepest soul answered "Yes!"

As I have traveled to Maher many times now, diving deeply into Maher life and its operations, I have continued to be more and more in awe of what I learn.

And as I follow global events, it is clear that this 'how to' manual is needed *now*.

Sindhu and her children

Dakshesh was four years old when he boarded the train with his mother Sindhu and his baby brother in their impoverished village in rural Maharashtra, India. Desperate for the means to support the family, his mother wanted to go to Mumbai, several hours away, to find her husband; he had left for Mumbai some months earlier in search of work. A few hours later, Dakshesh and his mother briefly stepped down from the train, at what they thought was a rest stop, to buy food from a vendor along the tracks. The baby was sleeping peacefully in their seat on the train, when it suddenly lurched out of the station. In her haste to re-board the train, Sindhu fell and suffered a concussion. After being treated at a nearby clinic, she was dazed and could only remember that she had somehow lost her baby.

Crazy with grief, Sindhu wandered the streets with her remaining son Dakshesh for the next four years; Dakshesh begged food from passersby so that they could survive. When someone finally brought the mother and son to Maher, Dakshesh was so dirty and smelly that the other children wouldn't get near him. His mother had retreated into a mute, almost deadened state.

Slowly, Dakshesh and his mother Sindhu were brought into the loving community at Maher. Over time Dakshesh excelled at school and also immersed himself in the other activities at Maher, including tae kwon do and classical Indian dance. Currently in college, Dakshesh was recently chosen to attend a leadership institute in the United States for high-potential disadvantaged young people from around the world. Sindhu still lives at Maher. She is still mentally disturbed but has recovered enough to perform simple work and to smile again.

This case history demonstrates that impoverished and deeply disadvantaged children can grow into vital, contributing members of society if they are given basic opportunities, love, and support.

Sindhu and Dakshesh

Absolute Poverty

In 2008, the World Bank estimated that 1.29 billion people were living in absolute poverty, deprived of food, water, shelter, clothing, sanitation, health care, and education. Of these, about 400 million people lived in India and 173 million people in China. In Sub-Saharan Africa, 47% of people lived in absolute poverty. The United Nations reports that in India, every third person lives below the poverty level, every second child is malnourished, and every third girl child is unable to complete eight years of schooling ("Millennium Development Goals"). This deprivation is a global challenge; it is observed in all parts of the world, including the developed economies. Furthermore, according to a recent study by the United Nations Charter on Children, the most vulnerable group is the worlds' children. Every day nearly 30,000 children die, largely from hunger, treatable diseases, and natural calamities. Some decrease in levels of absolute poverty has been achieved since 2008, but there is still a long way to go.

Impacts of Absolute Poverty

According to experts, many women become victims of trafficking (most commonly prostitution) as a means of survival.[1] Children are often compelled to abandon school in order to contribute to the family income, putting them at risk of being exploited.[2] This author visited a slum in India where the only work available to families of the lowest castes was for young girls to become prostitutes.

Poverty affects many more women than men. Diana Pearce coined the phrase "the feminization of poverty." According to her research, two-thirds of the poor over age 16 are women. As a consequence of lack of access to education and of gender bias, women suffer from a poverty of choices and opportunities.

Violence Against Women

Violence against women affects a broader range of society than even poverty, and knows no caste, religion, or ethnic boundaries.

Surveys suggest that about one-third of all women worldwide face beatings in the home. Women aged 15 through 45 are more likely to be maimed or die from male violence than from cancer, malaria, traffic accidents, and war combined. A major study by the World Health Organization found that, in most countries, between 30 and 60 percent of women had experienced physical or sexual violence by a husband or boyfriend.[3]

Every year in India, thousands of women are doused with kerosene and set ablaze. Unwed mothers are abandoned on the streets to starve, and often commit suicide. Teenage girls are brutally raped and banished from their families. Many wives are routinely battered by their husbands; other women are rejected for belonging to the 'wrong' caste.[4]

What the World Needs Now...

A new consensus is developing in the international community that the most effective projects to address absolute poverty and its effects will focus on women and girls and be community based.

---

[1] "Experts encourage action against sex trafficking" *voanews.com*. May 15, 2009. Retrieved 2010-10-24, as found on Wikipedia 2013-06-15.
[2] "Child sex boom fueled by poverty" Deena Guzder, *Globalpost.com*. Oct. 28, 2009. Retrieved 2013-04-23.

---

[3] Nicholas D Kristoff and Sheryl WuDunn, *Half the Sky* (NY: Vintage Books 2009), 61.
[4] *Women Healing Women*, William Keepin, PhD and Cynthia Brix, M.Div (Prescott AZ: Hohm Press, 2009), x.

Why Focus on Women and Girls?

Women perform 66% of the world's work and produce 50% of the food, yet they earn only 10% of the income and own only 1% of the property. Whether the issue is improving education in the developing world, fighting global climate change, or addressing nearly any other challenge we face, empowering women is a critical part of the equation.[5]

It is becoming clear that international aid targeted to help women and girls benefits all of society with a multiplier effect. Investments in gender equality yield the highest returns of all development investments.[6] "Investing in the potential of the world's women and girls is one of the surest ways to achieve global economic progress, political stability, and greater prosperity for women — and men — the world over."[7] Examples of how women's economic empowerment accelerates growth include:

- Higher female earnings and bargaining power translate into greater investment in children's education, health, and nutrition, which leads to long-term economic growth.

- In India, GDP could rise by 8% if the female/male ratio of workers increased by 10%.

- Total agricultural outputs in Africa could increase up to 20% if women's access to agricultural inputs was equal to men's access.

- Women-owned businesses comprise up to 38% of all registered small businesses worldwide. The number of women-owned businesses in Africa, Asia, Eastern Europe, and Latin America is growing rapidly. That growth directly impacts job creation and poverty reduction.[8]

The Organisation for Economic Co-operation and Development (OECD) Development Assistance Committee (DAC), a unique international forum where donor governments and multilateral organizations come together, has concluded:

- It is time to increase targeted investments in women and girls. In the current financial environment, investments need to focus on those areas which have proven to have a catalytic impact on poverty, development, inequalities and on future generations—girls' education, family planning, control

[5] Former President Bill Clinton addressing the annual meeting of the Clinton Global Initiative September 2009.
[6] OECD Policy messages from the DAC Network on Poverty Reduction, OECD, Paris. 2010.
[7] Hillary Rodham Clinton, US Secretary of State, International Women's Day 2010.
[8] United Kingdom Department for International Development (2010), Agenda 2010 - The turning point on poverty: background paper on gender.

over productive and financial assets and women's leadership.

- It is time to confront and overcome the cultural and social norms which hold back women and girls. While women and girls continue to face discrimination and prejudice on the basis of their sex, many also face additional barriers to their development through social exclusion on such grounds as ethnicity, race, and caste.

- It is time to put women and girls front and center and to move beyond empty promises. Making the world a better place for women will make a better world for all.

The Need for Community-Based Action

There is a growing consensus that governments and large institutions are proving incapable and/or unwilling to solve the world's social, economic, and environmental problems. Government revenue is diverted away from basic services by corrupt officials. Foreign aid is often poorly designed and targeted.

As concluded by Kristoff and WuDunn in *Half the Sky*, "projects that have made a stunning difference...are all grassroots projects with local ownership, sometimes resembling social or religious movements more than traditional projects. Often they have been propelled by exceptionally bright and driven social entrepreneurs....[9] Maher is a remarkable example of one such project.

Maher: A Uniquely Effective Model of Community-Based Action and Social Change

Maher (meaning "Mother's Home" in Marathi, the local language of Pune India) is an interfaith, caste-free refuge for battered, at-risk, and destitute women and children. Founded in 1997 by Sister Lucy Kurien, Maher is centered at Vadhu Badruk, about 32 kilometers from Pune in Maharashtra, India. Over the years its activities have spread to the surrounding rural villages and to other states in India.

To date, Maher has provided refuge to nearly 2500 women and just over 2000 children, many of whom might otherwise have been murdered, committed suicide, or starved to death. Many of the women flee in the night and arrive accompanied by their children. Some women and children are literally picked up off the streets, saved from starvation, abuse, trafficking, crime, and death. At Maher they are all welcome, irrespective of caste, creed, color, or social status. Efforts are made while at Maher to bring them into the social mainstream. Depending on the desires and needs of the individuals, Maher provides love, support, life skills education, training for self-employment, and help reuniting with families. In time, many of the women

---

[9] Nicholas D Kristoff and Sheryl WuDunn, *Half the Sky* (NYC: Vintage Books 2009), 229.

work at Maher as housemothers, helping others as they themselves were once helped. The children attend school and are supported as needed until they are either married or employed and self-sufficient.

While the initial goal of Maher was to rescue women in imminent risk of death, the work quickly expanded to improving the lives of the women and children, including reevaluation of some of the traditional values of Indian village life. Maher's services have increased greatly over the years and now include care for mentally disabled and elderly women and unwed mothers, education of slum children, and help with health care hygiene, and economic wellbeing. Women and children remain at the center of Maher life.

The genius of Maher: seven areas of uniqueness

1. **Women healing women; children passing it on: together creating a new India.** All Maher housemothers and many of the other staff themselves sought refuge at Maher. They understand the harsh realities of many women's lives and can offer compassion beyond measure. Part of their healing comes from helping the next to arrive. Maher's children, as they become young adults, volunteer their time to teach other disadvantaged children dance, music, self-empowerment,

nonviolence, and more. They are learning a whole new set of values which will guide them as adults creating a new future.

2. **Core values drive operations and leadership.** Without being beholden to any particular church, philosophy, or group, Maher overtly upholds universal spiritual values, including unconditional love and respect for all; social justice for all; and truth, transparency, and fairness in all interactions. A values-based NGO is a living, breathing culture of core values shared among all employees and residents. This distinguishes Maher from the traditional institutional feel of other organizations which have a more machine-like business approach and which rely on authoritarian relationships.

3. **Holistic individual development.** Maher's programs respond to the physical, social, mental, and spiritual needs of women and children seeking refuge. All of the women and children have opportunities to learn the skills and self-confidence to prepare them for independent lives in their communities, whether with family members or on their own. The women and children, even those deeply traumatized, are made whole through unlimited love, nutritious food, regular exercise, education, artistic expression, and leadership and human development

training. Many of the children choose to go on to college and university with Maher's continuing support.

4. **Needs-based support for healthy family and village life**. Maher will intervene at the woman's request to reunite families where this can be done, changing the fabric of family life for the better. Maher also works to re-knit the fabric of village life through village awareness meetings, classes on overcoming alcoholism, establishment of local self-help groups, and other projects, thereby bringing improved health, well-being, dignity, and opportunities for all. Maher staff act as resources and guides, rather than as bearers of "the one way."

5. **Small home-like living centers as part of a larger community**. The women and children live in small "homes," generally no more than 30 children and three to five housemothers, within the larger Maher community, so that children grow up in a family-like environment rather than in large, impersonal, "efficient" institutions. Each child is treated as a unique individual, lovingly supported and brought up as parents would their own children. Daily operations, family life, and discipline are all heart-centered.

6. **Addressing the roots of violence and despair**. While starting with a focus on women and children, Maher has developed organically to address a broad array of interrelated social problems. Every one of Maher's now 24 programs (full list in Appendix) has a community outreach and educational component to help respectfully challenge and bring change to traditional norms that engender violence and despair.

7. **Anticorruption**. Maher has done all this without surrendering to the corruption that is prevalent in Indian society, thereby demonstrating the value and courage needed to bring change to the corrupt system that so undermines Indian growth and sustainability.

How to Use this Book

Intended Audience

This book was originally conceived for Indian and Western people who desire to start Maher-like projects in India. However, the oppression of women, domestic violence, and the destitution of women and children are worldwide. Because organizations such as Maher are needed and can be transplanted anywhere, it is hoped that the following groups will also find the book useful:

- Foreign NGOs or individuals who wish to begin Maher-like efforts outside India, whether in Africa, Southeast Asia, or South America.

- People seeking to bring community-based services to women and children in the West in new forms, either independent of government funding and limitations or by adapting existing models.

- Staff at Maher and like-minded organizations as a staff development resource, such as for new employee orientation.

Finally, this book is offered to individuals worldwide, perhaps battered women themselves, who are each trying to do what Sister Lucy has done. The challenges are many. If this book can shorten the learning curve for some of these courageous souls, they will have an even greater chance of success.

A Guide to Action

You may already know about the magnitude of the needs of women and children and be filled with horror and frustration; you may have a story that makes the statistics real and personal. Or you may have stumbled upon Maher or organizations like Maher and want to be part of spreading hope and salvation. Many different experiences may compel you to action, and yet you may feel overwhelmed about how to start. This book is a practical tool to help channel your energy and commitment so that you can become part of this global

movement to emancipate women and girls and in so doing improve life for everyone.

Steps for moving forward

Dignity from Despair serves as a companion to the earlier book, *Women Healing Women*, by Will Keepin and Cynthia Brix. *Women Healing Women* provides an introduction to Maher's work and should be read first. Next, if you have not already, visit Maher. Then this book will serve as a guide to creating your own Maher.

Step 1:

Read *Women Healing Women* for the stories of some of the women and an overview of Maher. As the introduction to the book explains, much has been written on the plight of women in Indian society, but this book presents an effective practical response to the appalling injustices—and a model of hope for agencies and programs for oppressed women around the world. *Women Healing Women* recounts the true story of Maher, a remarkable project and center for battered women and children located near Pune, India. Maher is an interfaith community that honors all religions and "strongly repudiates caste distinctions" making it a "rare beacon" shining new hope upon some of the gravest problems in India and around the world. The book is rich with stories—poignant first-hand accounts by women and children whose lives have been transformed by the Maher project.

Step 2:

Live at Maher and experience it first hand. In the words of Maher, "see how it is." Stay for a month or longer, participate in daily life, and get to know some of the women, children, and staff. See how they bring in new residents and handle challenges that arise. Ideally, visit not only the main site in Vadhu Badruk and perhaps one of the Pune homes, but also some of the standalone sites in other parts of India. Overviews of some of these sites are found at the end of this chapter.

You should also visit some more traditional institutions in some of the bigger cities and compare what Maher offers. You might also visit NGOs run by others who have inspired you. Note elements of each that really speak to you. Whatever you learn will support you as you move forward.

During these visits, here are some things to pay attention to:
- What is the target population that is being served at this site? How is this similar to or different from what you plan to do?

- What is the range of services provided? Are some more critical than others?

- What challenges come up and how are they managed?

- What are your observations about the staff?

- What are the qualities of the site, the buildings, the furnishing, and the arrangement of space that are helpful?

- How do you see Maher's values reflected in everyday life?

- At Maher, focus on the population you intend to help. Live with them at Maher, watching what the social workers and housemothers do and questioning why.

Step 3:

Read *Dignity From Despair*, a detailed guide to creating new Maher-like projects.

If you are inspired to begin a Maher in a new location, or if you already operate a similar program, read this manual to learn how Maher has been developed and how it is run. This manual includes everything from how to create a charitable organization, to how to set up a house (including floor plans, space requirements, and budgets), to the "art" of Maher: the values and leadership that make it unique. Brief case histories, tips, and photos are interspersed throughout the text. This book is full of practical information and is designed so that you feel like you have Sister Lucy and her seasoned staff to turn to for questions and guidance. Ideally, read it through once for an overview, then go back and work through all the steps relevant to your imagined NGO. The result will be inspired by Maher, but not a replica.

Cases and Tips

Interspersed throughout this volume are cases, tips, and more that offer examples and supporting information regarding the accompanying content. These are drawn from observations of, and conversations with, Maher staff and residents over multiple visits. They are included to add texture and color, and to provide examples that can open up possibilities in your own thinking and actions. All of the names (except Sister Lucy) have been changed to protect people's privacy.

Book website

www.replicatemaher.wix.com/tools

As an additional resource there is a website dedicated to this book, and maintained by the author. All of the templates, including documents such as job descriptions, spreadsheets for budgets and admissions records, will be found there. Access is free. The intent is to make content available that is ready for use and easily adaptable to individual NGO needs. Additional material may be added in the future, possibly including information offered by similar NGOs willing to share their experience and best practices.
Visit www.replicatemaher.wix.com/tools for more information.

Scope of the current volume

This book focuses on Maher's first two projects: homes for battered and destitute women and homes for orphans and children from broken and/or impoverished homes.

Following this introductory chapter, Chapter 2 describes how to start an NGO, from defining your vision, mission, and values, to forming a governing body and selecting trustees, to licensing and registration. Chapters 3, 4, and 5 focus on the financial aspects of starting and running a business, including step-by-step guides to creating startup and annual plans, formats for budgeting and financial reporting, and fundraising.

Chapters 6 and 7 cover running and staffing the homes, from daily operations to recordkeeping requirements, policies for residents and staff, staff roles, and hiring, training, and managing staff.

Chapters 8 and 9 consider working with individual women and children, from admission until departure from Maher. Chapter 10 addresses the "art" of Maher including how to infuse your own values into an organization, leadership, and more about recreating Maher's genius.

Chapter 11 will help you reflect back on all you have read and thought about, and assess where you are in your own process. It then briefly looks ahead to ways you might later expand operations, such as developing community awareness projects and self-help groups. Each chapter is supported with tables, charts, samples, and templates, including financial reporting spreadsheets, job description templates, a list of interview questions to help in hiring staff, admission and other client records, and much more. All of these documents are easily adaptable to local requirements and are freely available at www.replicatemaher.wix.com/tools.

As described above, this book provides both the science and the art of Maher,

with the hope that you can learn from Sister Lucy and her staff, reflect on the values underlying what they do, and in turn apply your own gifts and inspiration to achieve results with your own undertaking.

CASE The beginning of Maher

While Sister Lucy was living in a convent and working in nearby villages, she found herself helpless to prevent a pregnant mother from being burned to death by her husband. Greatly distressed, she wanted to do more and talked with Sister Noelene, a sister from the same order who founded Hope Project in Pune and with whom Sister Lucy worked for eight years. Sister Noelene tried renting a room for battered and abused women. This was not successful. Sister Lucy recognized that these women needed responsible staff to work and live with them. About this time, her mentor, Father D'Sa, met an Austrian man who desired to help women in India. This man traveled to India to meet Sister Lucy and then financed the first building and land for the start of Maher.

Things began quickly. The doors first opened in February 1997 and women and children began arriving immediately, referred by other people. By May there were 30 to 40 children, some orphaned and some with their mothers. Sister Lucy bought food supplies, cooked, cleaned, and did the counseling and teaching. She would often get Maher's vegetables by scavenging at the village marketplace after market day ended, vying with goats and cows for food items. She then began teaching the women how to buy, prepare, and cook vegetables, since most of them had not been able to afford to buy them in the past. She also taught the women about hygiene. Slowly they were able to help with more of the work of caring for their 'Maher family.'

By July Sister Lucy was able to hire the first professional social worker, Marcy, who worked as a combination social worker/housemother. Soon Marcy started training some of the women to become the first housemothers. Sister Lucy next saw the need for a Production Center. Here women learned skills and produced items for sale such as hand sewn cards, candles, cloth purses, painted tribal designs, and more. By year three, a woman was hired to develop and run the Production Center.

Names and Places

Two names are referred to again and again as they provided a great deal of the source material from their first hand knowledge and experience. Below is a brief biography of each of them relevant to their contributions to this volume, beginning with their respective roles.

Sister Lucy Kurien

Founder and Executive Director of Maher. Born and raised in India, Sister Lucy is a Catholic nun, although Maher is completely independent of the Catholic church. Sister Lucy left school after the 8th standard to enter the convent. She has had no official training in running an NGO, in social work, etc. She learned as she went, always guided by her heart and her faith, and by mentors such as Father D'Sa and Sister Noelene. Even so Maher is uniquely her vision, and others who have joined embraced that vision whole-heartedly.

Chaya Pamula

Founder and Executive Director of SOFKIN (Support Organization for Kids in Need) and Trustee of Maher. Chaya was born and raised in India, and is herself an orphan. She currently lives and works in U.S. Wanting to "give back" to other orphans as she was given to, she took a six month leave of absence from her job to return to India and found SOFKIN. She then returned to her job and family in the U.S. and now

oversees SOFKIN from afar. She returns to India one or two times a year. However she is actively involved with all the children and staff, talking to them via phone, email, and Skype daily. For example the children know they can call her any time of the day or night to talk about a school project, or a personal issue, or whatever they need. Once a year she organizes a fundraising event in the U.S. and raises nearly all of the funds for SOFKIN, and is able to contribute to Maher as well.

Several Maher sites and SOFKIN, a Maher-inspired site, are referenced throughout the text. Therefore each of these (Vadhu, Bakori, Ratnagiri, Apti, Kerala, and SOFKIN) are briefly described below.

Vadhu original building (left). Later added dining hall with one home (middle), and Production, dance hall, etc.

Vadhu Badruk

This is Maher's first home, built with the expectation of expansion. It began in 1997 with one small building. As of 2013 this site now houses nine children's homes, a block of staff quarters, guest quarters, the Production Center, an office, and classrooms for dance, music, and art. A short-stay women's home is incorporated here as well. It is located in Vadhu village, about 40 km from Pune office.

Vadhu Annex - 9 Homes plus guest rooms

Bakori

Maher began work in this area with a kindergarten and self-help groups, later adding a small home in a tiny rented building for some of the poorest children. Bakori village is a remote area with almost no access to public transportation. Most of the adults are illiterate, and there were few opportunities out of poverty before Maher. The new Bakori building was designed and built for Maher in 2003 on land donated by Weikfield Company, with construction funded by Friends of Maher in Europe. Bakori is two separate homes within a single building, with shared garden, office, social worker rooms, guestrooms, and play space. One home is for boys, the other for girls. Each home has space for 20 to 30 children, its own living area, kitchen area, storage areas, and washing area plus space for two housemothers. Sometimes local women seeking refuge live there as well, helping the housemothers, even as they themselves

are helped. During the days, while the children are at school, there is a kindergarten for the children of workers from Weikfield, and also assorted classes for village women such as tailoring. A number of self-help groups are also supported by the two resident social workers. The building is new, modern, has solar hot water, Internet, and has rooms for guests: often European social work interns are on hand at Bakori for periods of two to six months.

Bakori site (2 homes)

Ratnagiri

This is a single home for 30 girls (with land for future boys' home) in Ratnagiri, a medium-sized city south of Mumbai and a full day's travel from Pune office. For seven years Maher operated this home in a building provided by the Jesuits for an orphanage. In 2013 Maher purchased a large family home to renovate, plus a nearby empty plot of land for future expansion so they may at last add a home for boys here. The social workers and most of the housemothers have come from Maher's Pune sites.

Ratnagiri home (2012), residents and staff

Apti Village and Krupa House

Apti is a small village of less than 2000 people, located about 10 km from Vadhu. Maher began with outreach projects and then a small rented home. Later, a local resident donated land, and Krupa House was built in 2007. Now a Maher social worker oversees Krupa House (25 children and 2 housemothers), as well as approximately 20 self-help groups, including a group for teenage girls. Toilets were built for the local school, a well and water storage tank provided for the village, and other needs of the village are supported. Recently a program to honor village elders was held.

Apti Krupa House with staff and residents

Kerala Project

Kerala project began when ten boys, orphaned by the 2004 tsunami, were taken in by a swami and his ashram. Later the ashram turned the boys and the building over to Maher to run. Because of Kerala state laws, this project has its own trust, although Sister Lucy is Executive Director. As of 2012, 44 boys live there, with 6 staff. Kerala is the southernmost state in India, nearly 30 hours by train from Pune. In 2011 a second building was built on adjacent land for a girls' home.

Kerala project veranda and some of the boys who live there

SOFKIN (Support Organization for Kids in Need)

SOFKIN is located in Hyderabad India. This children's home was inspired by and modeled after Maher. Most of the children are orphans, although some come from families unable to send their children to school. SOFKIN began in a small rented home with seven children. Housemothers to date have all come from Maher in Pune. As the number of children grew, and as their ages necessitated separating girls and boys, they rented a new larger space. After seven years, there are now 22 children and 3 housemothers. Chaya Pamula founded and directs this home, and continues in the roles of director and social worker, while living in the U.S. Chaya is beginning to consider buying a permanent home (or building) for SOFKIN.

SOFKIN (Hyderabad)

Additional Photos

Maher-constructed home in Thakar Wasti tribal area

Bakori Project roof: solar electricity & hot water system

Mogra House residents (in Vadhu Annex)

2 | *Visioning & Creating Your Organization*

Unless someone like you cares a whole awful lot,
nothing's going to get better.
It's not.

--Dr. Seuss, *The Lorax*

The focus of this chapter is on creating the framework within which your organization will operate. This critical groundwork includes defining your overall purpose, vision, mission, and values, as well as taking the steps necessary to legally incorporate as a charitable organization. The work in this initial planning stage will support the many decisions that come along later and the process of finding like-minded people to help you, seeking donors, securing funds, and acquiring land and buildings. At the very least you must create and register the nongovernmental organization (NGO) and obtain the relevant licenses before you can begin any operations.

The material in this chapter is presented in seven steps:

Step 1: Conceptualizing the organization

Step 2: Creating an NGO: overview and types

Step 3: Forming the governing body and selecting trustees

Step 4: Preparing the incorporation documents and supporting materials

Step 5: Choosing and registering a name for your organization

Step 6: Registrations and filing NGOs

Step 7: Licenses, tax exemption, and other issues

The majority of the information applies to creating a nonprofit organization anywhere in the world. While the specific legal entities and forms may vary, the process will be quite similar.

Step 1: Conceptualizing the Organization

The first step in your planning process is to systematically think through why and how you want to create an NGO. Essentially you need to define *why* this organization should exist, *what* is being offered, and to *whom*, *where*, and *how* it will be done. This important preparation work is absolutely critical and will guide all subsequent decisions, regardless of the country in which you will operate.

You will need to address:

• Overarching purpose: What is the passion that drives you to create an NGO?

• Vision: What is the picture of the future your organization aims to create?

• Mission: What is your organization's current core purpose?

• Values: What essential qualities will guide your work?

• Objectives: What specific activities will you do to accomplish your mission?

• Annual plan: How will you allocate your resources each year to accomplish your objectives?

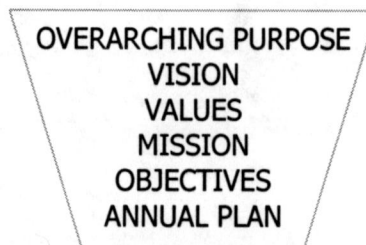

OVERARCHING PURPOSE
VISION
VALUES
MISSION
OBJECTIVES
ANNUAL PLAN

This diagram shows the narrowing specificity from overarching purpose to vision, mission, values, objectives, and finally to the annual plan. The time frame for each also becomes shorter as the funnel narrows.

Overarching Purpose

Each Maher-inspired NGO will take on its focus based on the passion of the founder and the needs of the local area. For example:

• Sister Lucy gained experience working with women in a day program where the women had access to counseling and some training, but that was all. A woman asked for shelter and Sister Lucy had to tell her no. To Lucy's horror, the woman was murdered by her husband that evening. So Maher began based on Sister Lucy's desire to help battered and threatened women, both to provide shelter, and to help them create new and fulfilling lives. Being a nun, at first she did not think about these women coming with children. So she added care for

18

children, and is now passionate about this part of the work as well.

- SOFKIN is an NGO serving orphans and at-risk children, located in Hyderabad, India. It was started by Chaya Pamula, who was inspired by Maher and also by Chaya's own experience as an orphan in India. Chaya was given assistance and an education; she now lives with her family in the U.S. She wanted to give something back to other Indian children like herself.

- Kerala Project is an NGO in southern India, which began with 10 boys orphaned by the 2004 tsunami. A swami took them in, using an empty building at his ashram. While he had the space, he soon realized that he did not know how to run an NGO or raise the boys. Therefore, he asked Maher to take over, donating the land and the building. Because boys and girls cannot live together in Kerala, the organization grew by adding only boys. In Kerala, a major concern is alcoholism, and this further influenced the organization to take in children endangered by alcoholic violence and poverty. The Kerala Project includes a major outreach program, "Alcohol Free Kerala." Recently a new building was constructed next door to house girls from these families, in addition to the boys.

As you reflect on and identify your purpose, consider these questions: what event(s) or circumstance(s) compel you to start this NGO? What will your focus be? What would your story be, if your paragraph were added to the ones above?

Next, consider whether you will focus on women and children, orphan and at-risk children, pregnant teens and their babies, or mentally disturbed women? Below is a list of some possible ways you could begin, each representing a small step. If you have been to visit Maher you will have seen each of these options. Maher gradually grew to the complex and broad service organization that it is today. Where will you start?

- A single home taking in orphans and at-risk children who are unable to attend school or receive proper food and care and lack a safe, loving environment. Example: SOFKIN.

- A single home taking in battered or at-risk women with their children. Example: How Maher began.

- A single home taking in orphan and at-risk girls only or boys only. Example: Kerala Project or Ratnagiri Project.

- A single home in a tribal or small village offering care and education for orphans or children whose parents cannot afford it, and also supporting village development. Example: Apti village and Krupa House.

- Kindergartens or crèches offering preschools and daycares for poor, working, or slum parents, where the children learn hygiene, basic school-related behaviors, and the value of education, making it more likely that they can enter school and succeed. (This may be a simple way to begin, requiring less staff and resources. While the organization startup is the same, the daily operations are not part of this manual. Sister Lucy also learned that offering one of these smaller programs can be a first step in gaining the trust of residents, especially in slum or tribal areas, who may initially be suspicious or hostile to outsiders.)

- A single home taking in unwed mothers helping them to have safe, healthy births and then to give their children up for adoption or to raise them properly. Example: Maher's Aashai project[10]. In this case, it will be important to have a plan for the women after their children are born. If the mothers keep their babies, how long will they stay at your NGO and how will the mothers live and support themselves and the child?

Ultimately you must decide your overarching purpose based on what is in your heart. As you develop your mission and vision statements, leave open the possibility to expand in directions you feel you might need to or like to in the future.

---

[10] Aashai Project cares for unwed mothers. See Maher "Rainbow of Services" in the Appendix.

TIP Sister Lucy advises: Please do not open homes for children and women just to give them food and shelter. They can survive without you. If they are hungry they will find some food. They may look in the dustbins, rob, or loot, but they will eat. If they are sleepy, they will find a place under a tree or on a shop veranda. What they need from you and me is to give them love, care, and education. Not only academic but also values-based education. This is what is important for them to thrive.

Mission Statement

Although the logical next step is to develop a vision statement, many organizations find it easier to begin with a mission statement, focusing on the foreseeable future. A mission statement is a clear and succinct representation of the organization's purpose for existence. It draws a boundary between what is included in the organization's aims, target population, and core activities and what is not. It helps trustees and members focus limited resources on their main objectives. It also gives potential participants and donors a "snapshot" of the organization and what it hopes to accomplish.

Writing a mission statement

To write a mission statement, a useful first step is to identify your stakeholders – people and organizations who have a part to play in the success of your organization. This may include key community leaders, potential clients and staff, other organizations serving your target populations, district welfare office personnel, government officials, potential donors, etc. Then conduct a simple needs assessment by asking your stakeholders questions such as:

- Approximately how many potential clients are there in the area where you plan to locate?

- What are the unmet needs of those you are hoping to serve? How would they prioritize these needs?

- Who else is providing a similar program or service in your target area? Are there potential areas of collaboration?

- How could/should potential clients be referred to you?

Talking with stakeholders reflects a core Maher value of respect: "we see how it is," learning first, building trust, and then working together for the best long-term outcomes. While one of your greatest strengths may be your passion for helping others, there is the risk of missing critical needs or offending key people without this vital step.

TIP A stakeholder conversation might go like this: Introduce yourself and say you are beginning a project to establish a home for orphans and children at risk or whose families cannot send them to school. Tell them you want to provide a stable loving home life, where the children's needs are met and they receive good educations and are prepared to enter society as responsible adults, prepared for work and marriage. Ask the above questions. Learn as much as you can from their experience and about their interests. You are beginning to build a relationship!

There are several other advantages to gathering stakeholder information, including:

- To help your mission be more effectively focused;
- To begin to develop relationships with people who can help you later, such as with funds or startup equipment or as sources of political or community support;
- To guard against working in a vacuum and avoid missing critical needs, duplicating efforts, or making other errors.

Sample mission statements

Mission Statement	Comments
Maher • Develop and deliver services to address the root causes of violence and despair and their effects, so women, children, and families are healthy, happy, and self-reliant. • Where possible, support family reunification, providing services as needed to support healthy and stable homes. • When family reunification is not possible or desirable, provide safe and loving residential educational, and developmental services for children and women. • Enable sustainable communities by addressing economic, education, health, and environmental issues focusing on villages and slums.	Note that this mission has evolved and broadened over the last 16 years.
SOFKIN To support the upbringing of underprivileged children irrespective of name or nationality, caste or creed, or race or religion, by providing basic amenities, education, and medical aid in a secure and healthy environment.	This mission purposefully reflects a narrower scope of operations than Maher.
ActionAid To work with poor and excluded women, men, girls, and boys to eradicate poverty, discrimination, and injustice.	This is a very broad mission for a large NGO working in many states of India, as well as other countries. It does not specify certain populations of excluded people; indeed, they work with a huge range of people. This is broader than Maher's mission and likely broader than you will begin. Your mission must be narrow enough to reflect the necessary focus for your work.
Pathfinder International To ensure that people everywhere have the right and opportunity to live a healthy sexual and reproductive life.	This organization works all over the world, focusing on sexual and reproductive life. Its mission is broad geographically, yet narrow in terms of the type of work it does.

Once you have collected and analyzed stakeholder information, begin to write your mission statement. The statement should answer these questions: (1) "Why are we creating this organization?" (2) "Who specifically do we wish to help?" and (3) "How?" (that is, with what core services and programs?). The mission statement should describe what you will do and for whom. It should be general enough to guide future choices. For example, ask yourself if building a school for local children or opening a clinic for immunizations would be included or excluded in the organization you are creating. As with Maher, the mission may start narrowly and later be expanded.

You will probably need to write several versions of your mission statement, trying to be clear and specific in a minimum of words. Show it to your key stakeholders to see what they think.

Vision Statement

A vision statement is a picture of the future the organization aims to create. Broader and more future oriented than the mission, it is designed to inspire organization members and to guide strategic business planning and resource allocation. A vision sets the overarching direction, not the details of how the organization will get there. To help articulate the vision, try asking a question like, "If we are successful, in 10 or 20 years how will village life in India be different for women, for children, and for everyone?"

TIP
Use phrases and words of stakeholders to help shape your vision. Father Francis D'Sa (Maher trustee) said many years ago "There is a huge task awaiting us, the task of changing the attitude of society, especially of men towards women. This is a gigantic task. Maher is therefore not just a project, it is a vision of a new society where men, women, and children have opportunities for growth, education, and happiness." See the links to Maher's vision below.

Maher's vision

No matter who we are, we walk together toward wholeness. All have the opportunity for a decent life, dignity, and happiness irrespective of caste, gender, or religion. There is no longer any work for organizations such as Maher.

Writing vision and mission statements

As you develop your vision and mission statements, you might go back and forth between them as you refine your ideas. The larger view of how will things be different is your vision and will be something you work towards for 20 or more years. The more narrow consideration of what you will do and for whom over the next five to ten years is your mission statement. Do not make the vision so big that it is undoable (for example, ending wife battering in India). Be willing to start small and then expand. If you foresee expansion, will your expansion be more of the same (such as more homes)? Or will you seek to broaden services to include other population groups or to address other issues? You will want to consider the future when creating your formal documentation.

Organizational Values

Values are essential ways of being, deeply held driving forces. They define how the organization will behave with clients, customers, donors, surrounding communities, and governmental and NGO groups, as well as how people behave with each other within the organization. Value statements represent the living enactment of the fundamental values held by the founder and the people within the organization. They will be broad but embody specific actions. For example, "basic ethical values" is too vague, while "embracing all regardless of caste, creed, or religion" or "truth,

transparency, and fairness" are specific ethical values.

Generally between four and ten is a good number of core values. If you have more, then likely some are really restatements or corollaries to others. After you develop your initial list, you should check to see if there are any missing or if some overlap too much. Values can be discussed at trustee meetings, house meetings, and staff meetings and can be further refined as the organization begins to operate.

Below are Maher's core values, to provide you with inspiration and to help you develop your own. Do not just take this list because it is a quick answer; your values will be unique to you and your context. If some of these values resonate deeply with you, then they may become part of the guiding values of your new NGO.

Maher's core values

- *Embracing all people of all faiths, regardless of caste, class, or ethnicity*

- *Spiritually infused interfaith daily life and operations*

- *Unconditional love and respect for all*

- *Social justice for all, regardless of caste, class, or gender*

- *Truth, transparency, and fairness in all interactions and in distribution of resources*

24

- *Reawakening our personal relationship with Mother Earth and treating her as the Body of the Divine*

- *Lifelong learning and continual reevaluation and change*

Each of these values is expanded upon in Chapter 10, The Art and Genius of Maher.

All members of the Maher community are expected to demonstrate these values in their daily interactions with everyone else, including staff, clients, residents, family members, and village people. Values are not only for employees but also for the women, children, and other clients to learn as guides for their lives, even after they leave Maher. Government officials and villagers learn about Maher's values as they interact with the organization. For example, in India, paying a bribe is so standard it is not seen as unethical. Maher's refusal to pay a bribe may cause others to think about the correctness of this value. Slowly, over time, this is how values help achieve a vision.

How a core value extends to policies and behaviors

Values provide the foundation for all decision making. For example, rewards and recognition presented to clients, employees, and guests should reflect the organization's values. All hiring decisions should bring in people who already embody these values or who can embrace and demonstrate them. Values,

therefore, lead directly to a whole range of policies, practices, and behaviors on the part of leadership, staff, residents, and guests.

For example, Maher's first value, "Embracing all people of all faiths, regardless of caste, class, or ethnicity" is reflected in the following policies and behaviors:

- Displaying Maher's "circle of religions" banner in all Maher buildings;

- Celebration of major holidays of each faith represented in the community, with discussions of the positive values that the holiday stands for;

- Daily prayers, prayers to welcome guests, prayers at events, etc., that are all "generic" (they do not address a particular name or form of God, and so are interfaith);

- Declining donations that come with stipulations in favor of any one religion.

Maher's circle of religions banner

25

The result is that Maher is not devoid of spirituality, but actively creates space for each person to follow her or his own beliefs and practice.

Here is another example. "Unconditional love and respect for all" is reflected in:

- Practice of heart-centered action in dealings with women, children, families, men, donors, and guests;

- Practice of "we see how it is:" listening and learning before intervening;

- Emphasis on guiding and teaching children (and women) after "mistakes" rather than on punishment, with second and third chances to "get it right";

- Seeking responsibility and reconciliation instead of blame;

- "Always room for one more" philosophy (doors are open 24/7);

- Thank you letters, usually handmade, for all donors and benefactors; these are uniquely written, with warmth, and are not form letters;

- Willingness to match caste and religion when arranging weddings in recognition that whole families need to be able to live well together, and that not all share Maher's values.

Chapter 10, "The Art and Genius of Maher," covers all of Maher's values with examples of policies, behaviors, and actions. Maher staff and residents could easily write a whole page for each core value, listing ways that value is in evidence in Maher daily life and administrative practices. This would be a great staff meeting exercise for any organization.

After you develop your own list of core values, when you come across other references to "Maher values," think instead of your own values. In this way you can begin to define how your values will be incorporated into your organization's policies and behaviors.

```
OVERARCHING PURPOSE
VISION
VALUES
MISSION
OBJECTIVES
ANNUAL PLAN
```

Developing Objectives

Once you have identified your overarching purpose, vision, mission, and core values, you can determine the specific projects and programs with which you will begin. Objectives are more immediate than the mission and focus your energy and resources in the near future. They help you clarify your target communities, the activities you will undertake, and possible local partners.

Your first choice: women and children or just children?

Identifying your passion and overarching purpose most likely will answer this question. But if it does not, consider the following: Taking in women with their children takes more skills than if you take in only children. On the other hand, having the women to help take care of and mother the children also makes care of the children easier. And with the mothers in residence, boys and girls can live in one home instead of separately. In India, women's homes have only short-stay licenses, allowing women a maximum stay of three months. Mothers arrive with children ranging in age from newborn to teenagers. Their children may stay with them, but without specific children's licenses, the children must leave when their mothers do. As Maher has found, often even if the women can return home in that time frame, it may better serve both the children and the parents for the children to remain longer. This is only possible with separate children's license.

You can also read ahead to the chapters on working with women and working with children to get an idea what will be required.

Further choices regarding children

If your mission focus includes serving children specifically, then you will have to consider which groups of children you will accept. There are many layers of need: street children, children already in trouble with the law, orphans, different age groups, etc. What you decide will influence what kind of site you choose and where, how many staff members and with what level of experience you will need, the programs you offer, and more.

Age and gender considerations

If the NGO will be accepting only children, you will need to decide what age groups to take in, and whether to take both boys and girls. Remember that if you begin with younger boys and girls who can be housed together, as they grow up you may need to expand your facilities to comply with laws and changing age-related needs.

Separate licenses are required for different age groups. Up to five years old is one license, ages six to eighteen is a separate license. Maher has both licenses. According to Indian law, and indeed in many countries, at age eighteen children become classified as adults and are no longer eligible for NGOs licensed for only children.

Notes about specific ages

Younger children require more housemothers since they need more assistance than older children. For example, 20 toddlers need 5 housemothers, while 20 middle school children require only 2 or 3 housemothers.

Kindergarten through about 6th standard boys and girls can usually be housed together. When boys reach 7th standard they will move to their own home. Some of the older girls may remain to help out with the younger children. Often meals and large common spaces are still shared. (Check individual state laws to be sure. For example, in Kerala it is not permissible to house boys and girls together at any age, and they may not share meal space.)

Young people, from 10th through 12th standard and on to university, are not only quite self-sufficient, they often help with the younger children's care and act as role models. Many college and university students still live at Maher. After age eighteen, to enable them to remain at Maher while they complete their studies, these young people also become part-time staff, earning a small salary. They may teach classes such as dance or tae kwon do, perform office work, or do other work.

What about just boys or just girls?

Sister Lucy and Chaya Pamula both have said that they dislike separating siblings. One reason is that, because of the low status of girls in India, many families would only send the boys and not educate the girls at all, keeping them at home, essentially as slaves. In Kerala, where children are at risk due to alcohol-related violence, it was heartbreaking to take only boys and leave the girls at risk. Too often, separating siblings adds to the trauma these children experience. Sister Lucy says that she will never again agree to a home for all boys. Some of the reasons include:

- Families flee together, including both boys and girls. How can you help part of a family and send away others?

- Ideally boys and girls growing up together at Maher learn new ways of respecting and valuing each other as individuals, a part of Maher's vision of India's future.

- Educating and supporting girls leads to the greatest hope for real social change and improving the lives of families and communities, as you read in Chapter 1.

Children's circumstances

You will also have to decide whether you will take only orphans, or also children whose families cannot afford to send them to school. Will you rescue children off the street, or take children the police bring or that other institutions throw out? Will you choose to help slum or tribal children? In some areas, caring for tribal children or those of other protected groups may require additional licenses.

Children who have been on the streets, possibly for years, or with criminal records, are generally the hardest to work with, and require seasoned staff and much patience. Children from poor but intact families who need education and support and orphans who have not yet had to learn to survive on the streets are generally the easiest to work with and require fewer and less experienced staff. Children from slums or tribal areas will often lack most basic hygiene skills and will require extra time and attention to settle into a structured routine and school. The more extreme the poverty these families live in, the greater the likely cultural adjustment the children will need to make. The younger the children, the easier their adjustment.

Chaya of SOFKIN lives in U.S. while supervising the housemothers from afar. Therefore she has decided not to work with the police because she does not want to take in the children already in trouble on the streets. Her staff is not ready for the troubles these children may bring. Instead, SOFKIN's children are mostly referred through word of mouth by neighbors or friends. Sometimes Chaya approaches local organizations such as churches or temples. These children are mostly orphans, although some come from poor families.

While children from the streets or the police or those who other institutions throw out have many more disadvantages and are more challenging to work with, it can be deeply rewarding as well. For many of these kids Maher is their last hope (or really their first hope) as Maher is now known to be able to make a difference even with some of the most difficult children. Maher's ability to take more children from broader circumstances grew out of the capacity built by the women who originally came seeking shelter and stayed as housemothers.

You might apply for several licenses covering a broad segment of children, but start smaller and simpler. As you develop experience yourself, and develop experienced staff, you can take in children from more difficult circumstances. Whatever you choose, this will be reflected in your objectives. And of course, a child may show up and you know you cannot say no, so you expand and grow as fate offers.

Referrals

Once you select a certain population of women or children, you will have to develop a referral network. How will women, children, or families in need know to come to your NGO? How will parents become willing to entrust you with their children? One important tool is to develop relationships with other related NGOs, governmental units such as CWC (Child Welfare Committee), and especially the local community.

Sample objectives

Maher has written objectives which clarify exactly the kinds of projects and actions they will focus on as they fulfill their mission:

- To give shelter to destitute women and children by establishing centers at various places

- To provide for all the basic needs in such centers

- To arrange training for women, children, youth, and, if need be, for men too

29

- To make efforts for finding jobs for women, children, and youth and if need be for men too

- To promote, execute and encourage schemes of social upliftment with the express purpose of the betterment of society at large and for the establishment of a consciousness of social ethics, morality, and basic ethical values

If you are starting with a home for orphaned children, then your objectives will be something like:

- To give shelter to orphaned children by establishing a single home

- To provide for all the basic needs, including providing education, a loving environment, and services as needed so the children thrive

- To develop staff and experience in dealing with children from difficult circumstances
- To develop relationships within the local community to strengthen families health, happiness, and wellbeing

If you will be taking in women and children, your objectives will incorporate the women's needs. If you plan any community development, (whether awareness meetings, self-help groups, etc.) those will be included as well. Your objectives will grow as your NGO does, but all within your mission.

Annual Plan

An annual plan, the last step in your planning process, is where you get down to specifics. Here you outline what will you do in the coming year toward your organization's objectives. Chapter 3 covers detailed information to guide you in developing and implementing your initial start-up plan and budgets. Chapter 4 focuses on securing donor support to fund NGO operations. Chapter 5 includes ongoing annual planning, budgeting, and reporting. Being able to document how you wisely used resources to accomplish specific achievements is critical to securing donor support.

One more question to begin to think about now, in preparation for the next chapter: will your strategy be to start

Case Story

Sister Lucy began Maher working under the Trust of the Sisters of the Holy Cross, since it was illegal for her to take in women without a trust within which to operate. This later became a problem and she had to hastily create her own trust. She now advises—form your NGO first! And be sure to find like-minded people to serve as trustees, people who agree with and are inspired by your vision and values.

small and grow slowly as you gain experience, adding a second small site perhaps a few years later? Or will you seek to have a larger site full of women and children (25-40) within the first year? Will you rent or buy space? These questions and more will be addressed in Chapter 3, after the NGO is officially created.

Step 2: Creating an NGO

Overview

What is an NGO (Non-Governmental Organization) and do I have to form one?

Generally, NGOs are not-for-profit organizations that are largely independent of government and work for one or more humanitarian issues. Being a legal, registered NGO is required to secure governmental and foreign funding and helps you acquire other funding, as well as quality staff, trustees, and community support.

What type of NGO?

There are likely several legal forms your NGO can take. In India, a society, a trust, a cooperative society, and a not-for-profit company are all options. All of these come under separate government acts, some are national, some are state-based. You will need to seek specific information for your state, or country if you are outside India. The steps listed in this chapter for creating an NGO are

similar almost anywhere, but some of the details will vary, such as where to register, the minimum number of trustees required, and governance rules.

Maher, located in the state of Maharashtra, was required by state regulations to register both as a society and a trust. Sample society and trust documents are available on the book's website. These can be useful guides in terms of general information, as well as the language employed in incorporation documents.

Get appropriate legal assistance

It is highly recommended that you consult a lawyer who specializes in registering non-profit organizations in your state and country. The laws are often a confusing array of sometimes overlapping or contradictory choices and actions. Even in the U.S., lawyers who do not specialize in this can, and do, steer clients incorrectly. Trying to fix these errors after you have registered can turn into a great deal of unproductive time, effort, and money.

Intended as an overview, below are the main differences between a Society and a Public Charitable Trust in India[11]

---

[11] Adapted from information from Mathew Cherian, Director CAF India with additional information from Maher. CAF is an 80 year old, U.K.-based, not-for-profit organization. CAF network offices are located in UK (Head Office), India, Australia, Bulgaria, Russia, South Africa, USA, and Brazil.

Differences between Society and a Trust in India

	Public Charitable Trust	Society
Statute/Legislation	Public Trust Act like Bombay Public Trust Act, 1950	Societies Registration Act of 1860
Jurisdiction of the Act	Concerned state where registered (Operating in multiple states requires registering in each state)	Concerned state where registered (Operating in multiple states requires registering in each state)
Authority	Charity Commissioner/Deputy Registrar	Registrar of Societies
Registration	As Trust	As Society (and by default also as Trust in Maharashtra and Gujarat)
Main Registration Document	Trust deed	Memorandum of Association and Rules & Regulations
Stamp Duty	Trust deed to be executed a non-judicial stamp paper, varies from state to state.	No stamp paper required for Memorandum of Association and Rules & Regulations
Number of persons needed to register	Minimum two trustees; no upper limit	Minimum seven, no upper limit
Board of Management	Trustees/Board of Trustees	Governing body or managing committee
Mode of succession on board of management	Appointment or election	Election or appointment by members of the general body
Requirements	At least 3 meetings per year Bylaws	At least one meeting per year Bylaws
Decision Making	Majority or consensus	Majority rule
Role of Body as Maher uses these	Governing Body	Advisory body, although it elects the trustees

> **TIP** Registration documents require a listing of the objectives of the NGO. These will likely be different from the current objectives to fulfill the NGO mission. For example, the objectives listed in Maher's Society document cover a wide range of objectives that could be applicable to the vision, but that Maher is not currently engaged in. However if a need arose, Maher is formally structured in a way to allow later pursuit of these projects without having to amend its trust documents. It may be useful to think about activities you might include as you expand your work; including them in your incorporation documents leaves the door open for adding projects and services in later years without amending these documents.

Step 3: Forming the Governing Body

All NGOs need to have a governing body in place that will be ultimately responsible for all activities and decisions of the organization. This body will be involved in all matters of strategic relevance, including strategic planning, financial management, human resources and networking.

Carefully selecting governing body trustees who embrace your vision, values, and mission can provide a good support base from which to work. Note that you can begin to gather like-minded people early on, as potential trustees, to help in the formation process. You will get a chance to see how this group works together, if values are truly shared, and whether egos are getting in the way. It is never good to have trustees who use their role to feed their egos—this must be about serving something larger than themselves.

Responsibilities and Obligations of Trustees

- Able to fully commit to, and actively support, the mission, vision, and values of NGO

- Willing to do work on behalf of organization (whether meetings, planning, networking, fundraising, site visits to potential building sites to review and meet neighbors, appearance at festivals and holidays, encouraging the staff, etc.)

- Assist the executive director in leading the NGO

- Make a significant donation, and/or ask their contact networks for donations.

Trustee Qualities

- Passionate about the vision, mission, and core values of the NGO

- Some applicable professional skills such as legal, business, IT (information technology) or fundraising (or significant contact network for fundraising). Each trustee should have at least one area of expertise so that these skills do not need to be hired from the outside

- Respect for executive director and staff

- Understanding that more than housing is needed, that the core of what is offered is hope, love, care, and deep relationships with women and children

- Operate from the heart and from a passion for helping people; truly want to be part of, and gain personal satisfaction (not fame or prestige) from, this kind of work

- Desire to protect and use wisely NGO resources

- Able to participate in meetings productively, offer ideas, and opinions; willing to compromise and balance the need to run a business with need for heart-centered action

- Open and respectful to people of all faiths and backgrounds

- Love for all children

> **TIP** "If you don't love children then there is no place for you at Maher."
>
> —Father D'Sa

Step 4: Formulation of Bylaws

Most charitable organizations the world over are required to file bylaws with their incorporation documents. Bylaws, which are the set of rules under which the organization will operate, often have no prescribed format. However, they typically include such items as:

- Legal status: society, trust, corporation etc.

- Trustees: conditions/qualifications, term length, procedure to become a trustee, rights, responsibilities, obligations, and termination of trustee position

- Officer roles, selection, responsibilities, and powers

- Meetings: types, frequency, rules of operation, and decision making

- Committees: types, member selection, and term length

- Fiscal year and accounting cycles, raising of finances, acquisition and disposal of property

- Methodologies, tools, and strategies for monitoring and evaluation etc.

- Organization functions and structure

- Location and contact address

- Rules for dissolution of NGO if needed

- Method for amendments, modifications, and revisions of bylaws

A sample set of bylaws can be found on the website of this book. (www.replicatemaher.wix.com/tools)

Step 5: Choosing and Registering a Name for Your Organization

Your registration documents will need to reflect the name of your organization. While this may seem simple, you will have to ascertain that the name is not already in use, nor too similar to another organization. You will have to actually register your NGO's name.

The name you choose should be simple, easy for people in your area at least to remember, and also capture an essential idea of your mission. It might be a word in the local language such as *Maher* (mother's home), or it might be an

acronym, that is, a made up word from the first letter of each word of a phrase. An example is SOFKIN from Support Organization for Kids In Need. While the word is made up, its letters are reminders of two English words (most of the donors as well as the founder live in the U.S.) "soft" and "kin" (which means family) so the new word is easy to remember. Hope House is the name of the home run by one of Sister Lucy's mentors. Be creative! Try out lots of names—suddenly one will just sound right.

The catch is, of course, that the name has to be unique. And since you will also want to develop a website for your new NGO, creating and registering your domain using your proposed NGO name is a good way to find out if the name is unique. Domain registration includes a free search that takes a few seconds. I recommend a site called "godaddy" but there are many others. If you select another site, just be sure it is registered with ICANN (Internet Corporation for Assigned Names and Numbers). At the above site, you can do a search on your name for free, and if it is already taken, try another, or perhaps a variation. You can purchase your domain name for a few dollars, renewable each year, or you can buy several years at once for a discount. This name will then be yours all over the world, registered so that no one else can take it. You can also create a quick and simple website here hosted for free. You will also be able to create an email address for your organization and begin to use that immediately in your correspondence. Another way to

TIP Sometimes your name will be taken in the YOURNGO.com format, but by an organization in another country. In this case, try a different ending to your name such as YOURNGO.org; there are a number of different endings possible and the site will help you. The .org ending is most often used by non-profits. Another variation idea is what Maher did: their domain is maherashram.org (ashram is an Indian word for hostel).

check out your intended name is to simply do an Internet search on it: type it into any major search engine (such as Google) and see what comes up. Maybe the name you are considering means something bad in another language, or is associated with a very different kind of business but which has a bad reputation. Sometimes there are many places with a similar name, in which case you might want something more unique. An example is "Hope House" in the US. Because there are several unrelated organizations with this name (as evidenced by a quick Google search), each has had to add some variation to their domain name for example hopehousemaine or hopehouseboston, etc. This can become confusing, and is not recommended. If you are based in one country and expect to work only there, then as long as there are not

duplicates in your country (or even nearby countries), then you should be fine.

Step 6: Registration

Registering a Society or a Trust in India

The application for registration of a society or a trust should be made to the relevant government body having jurisdiction over the region/sub-region of the state in which the NGO is to be registered. In India, a typical set of documents to be submitted includes (be sure to verify local requirements):

- Cover letter requesting registration of the society (The letter needs to state the various documents annexed to it. All the subscribers to the memorandum of association need to sign the letter. A person duly authorized by all of them to sign on their behalf is also permissible.)

- Society memorandum and/or trust deed

- Rules and regulations and bylaws, in duplicate, certified by at least three members of the governing body

- Report of activities to date

- Funding sources (This a list of types of funding you anticipate such as Indian individuals, Indian corporations, government grants, Indian service organizations, such as Rotary, or foreign individuals.)

- Financial reports

- Sources and pattern of income and expenditures (such as a list of your donations to date, including what or how much from whom and whatever may not be in your financial reports)

- Minutes of the governing board meeting that endorsed the setting up of the NGO

- Letters of support

- Other items such as a business or annual plan, proof of existence of a physical site, or other documents

Note that in some situations, (for example, you are given a building to use and clients are pre-existing), operations may begin on a small scale before the actual registration while you gather supporters, demonstrate what you can do, clarify details, and develop experience.

Planning documents, funding records, and financial reports are discussed in Chapters 3, 4, and 5 respectively.

Step 7: Licenses, Tax Exemptions, and Other Government Filings

The following sections pertain to India, but wherever you are, you will have similar requirements for government filings. You can use this list as a starting place for your own research, or to seek legal counsel.

Permanent Account Number (PAN)

Every nonprofit organization that is required to file the return of income under section 139(4A) of the Income Tax Act, has to apply for allotment of a permanent account number (PAN). The application should be made using the prescribed form to the income tax officer. Outside India this may be known as a Tax ID number, or something similar.

Licenses

Regardless of where in the world the NGO will operate, you must file for any relevant licenses before you open. Which license depends on which segment of people will be served and the type of services delivered. In India, separate licenses are required for very young children and older children up to the age of 18 (generally school age is the division but this varies by state and country). Taking in women requires a different license, (a short-stay women's home in India), as do other activities, such as running a school, kindergarten, or clinic. Multiple sites can require multiple duplicate licenses. Again, local government officials will be able to specify which licenses you will need and where to get them. You may also want to apply for several licenses all at once, for example for several different populations of women and children even if you plan to start with only one of these groups.

Registration for Income Tax Exemption

Income tax exemption means that the NGO will not be required to pay tax on donations and other income it receives. An application for income tax exemption can be made only after an organization has been registered and the registration number and certificate obtained. Then, in order to qualify for exemption u/s 11 of the Income Tax Act (that is, to exempt the income of the organization from tax) the NGO must apply to the national income tax authority using the prescribed form.

Generally the following documents can be filed for all tax exemptions: NGO income, as well as 80(G) exemption for donors discussed below:

- Certified copies of society and trust deeds, registration certificate and registration number
- A description of the organization's purpose and programs, including who the organization serves and why, location and area covered, examples of training materials,

workshops, and other services (Most of this will be in the registration deed.)

- Financial information, sources of funding, financial statements (revenue and expense statement and balance sheet) for two or three projected years, including years to date

- Proof that if the organization undertakes any commercial or revenue-raising activity to sustain itself, the purpose is only for fundraising and no part of such profits would be distributed to trustees, staff, etc.

Registration for Income Tax Exemption for Donors

In India, as in most other countries, many institutional and some individual donors look for a tax exemption, in whole or in part, for their donations.

80(G) certificate under the Income Tax Act

In India, all registered non-profits, set up for a charitable purpose, are eligible to apply for an exemption under Section 80(G) of the Indian Income Tax Act, 1961. The local income tax authorities need to be approached for this purpose, and these authorities generally need the above list of documentation. Generally the NGO will apply for this after it has had at least one year of operation.

A donor is entitled to a 50% tax rebate for donations made to a nonprofit organization having 80(G) certificate.

There is also a 35(AC) Certificate under the Income Tax Act, but this is complicated to file, undergoes rigorous screening, and difficult to come by. Seek professional guidance if you wish to pursue this.

Registration for Seeking Foreign Funds

If you intend to accept foreign contributions in India, you must have a FCRA certificate (Foreign Contribution Regulation Act). The application for obtaining prior permission of the Central Government to receive foreign contributions should be made using the prescribed form FC-1A. The application for registration of a nonprofit organization for acceptance of foreign contributions should be made in the prescribed form FC-8. It is also suggested that you have a separate bank account for foreign funds.

Author with residents of Pardi Wasti village

3 | *From Dream to Manifestation*

Hold fast to dreams,
For if dreams die
Life is a broken-winged bird,
That cannot fly.
— *Langston Hughes*

Overview: From Dream to Manifestation

This chapter and the next two focus on planning and financial matters. How do you manifest your dream? You will be introduced to the concept of planning, a theme that will appear in several contexts in this manual. This chapter will guide you as you develop and implement your NGO start-up plan. You will identify what you need to do to set up your first site, and break this down into a step-by-step process. This will help you organize your thoughts and time. The planning

process will also help you project NGO resource needs, plan how to acquire them, and then report to trustees, donors, and other stakeholders on plans, donations and goods received, and results achieved. Planning supports you as you direct the work of the NGO and builds transparency and credibility for your donors, community, and other stakeholders.

Many grassroots organizations start out "on a wing and a prayer," as we sometimes say in the U.S. Maher began this way, finding an "angel" in a man from Austria who had a dream to do something for the women of India. Serendipitously, he met Sister Lucy,

41

believed in her vision, passion, and commitment, and gave her enough money to buy land and construct the first building. This original site has now grown into the large Vadhu Badruk campus. Most NGOs, however, start with little more than a dream and passion; they must seek support in small contributions, person by person. The information in these three chapters will help you through your first start-up plan and your first fundraising cycle, and in the process build credibility and gather needed support for the NGO. You will also learn how to manage resources wisely in the coming years, as the NGO grows and expands.

Chapter 3 From Dream to Manifestation:
> Preparing a start-up plan, implementing the plan, and estimating start-up costs

Chapter 4 Fundraising: Finding Partners to Participate in Your Vision:
> Fundraising plans and activities and stewardship of donors

Chapter 5 Annual Planning and Financial Reporting:
> Annual planning, tracking, budgeting, and reporting

Introduction

Chapter 2 helped you create the NGO, at least on paper. You likely have at least a few supportive followers. You have completed statements of vision, mission, values, and your near-term objectives.

Now it is time to give your dream structure, answering hard questions and providing details, such as how much it will cost to acquire land, build or renovate a building, and furnish it. You will develop your start-up plan and walk through much of its implementation. This includes weighing options and estimating costs, and creating both capital and operating budgets. Additionally, the plan will help you systematically make many necessary decisions so that you are ready to open your doors to your first residents.

Your objectives (Chapter 2) will define the scope of your project services and activities for the first few years. You will want a site that can accommodate growth of NGO activities and projects, even as you start small and simple. As an example, if you are starting a home for orphans, some of the details to address include:

- How many residents do you expect to have by the end of the first, second, and third years of operation?

- How soon do you expect to need more space or a second building (to separate boys and girls, or simply to take in more people)?

- What will you be offering residents in addition to a bed, food, clothing, and school? (Music classes, computer classes, counseling and emotional development, outings, etc.)

- Will you be doing it all or will you hire staff to help? If you plan to hire staff, how soon?

- What outside services might you need to use, how often, and at what rates?

- Do you plan to begin other programs for the local area, such as awareness programs or self-help groups? If so, when?

You will need to answer similar questions about the NGO's focus population(s); each group will have unique needs. For example, battered women may need special medical and counseling support, plus possible legal guidance and family mediation.

About Planning

Dreams are necessary as a starting point, as is faith in yourself and in Grace (or luck) that your dreams will come to fruition. However, "luck favors the prepared soul." When planning, you look realistically at what is true now, compare that to where you want to be in a year or two years' or five years' time, and then determine what kinds of activities will carry you from now to this future place. You must be both realistic and specific. Goals and activities must be clear and measurable. Looking at results lets you know whether you have succeeded or need to try something different. If your plans are not clear, you have no way to tell how well you did and what changes you need to make to do better in the future. Donors and trustees also want to know that the best outcomes possible have been achieved, given the resources invested. Each year you will learn and improve on your operations.

The planning process helps organizations stay realistic about what can be accomplished in one or two years. Many organizations fail because they try to do too much at once, spreading their resources (time, staff, or money) too thin, ending up doing nothing well. If Maher had started all 24 projects (or even one-half of them) in the first year or two it would have been unable to do anything well and would never have developed its solid reputation for excellence.

Planning, the process of identifying goals and activities to achieve them, translates across your organization. The most successful organizations do an annual plan for total operations; subunits or departments do a plan for their part of the organization; and each staff person completes an annual plan for her or his work duties and professional development. All of these plans are linked: Individual staff work plans support the department, and department plans support the organization's plans. Social workers do annual case plans for each client. In this way each person and team in the organization, whether staff or client, has a clearly articulated focus for the year, including activities to complete and a list of resources needed. This will bring about the achievement of your highest potential as well as organizational goals.

Planning is a lot of work to start with but will save future time and problems, and possibly avoid disastrous mistakes that might threaten the NGO's existence. Planning is an investment in the future of your NGO.

> **TIP** If all this is new to you, then it may be a good idea to seek out a mentor or two who can offer advice, answer questions, and listen. A mentor should be someone who has some experience in starting or running an organization, with nothing personal to gain from any of your choices. Ideally he or she will share your passion for the NGO objectives.

Creating and Implementing a Start-Up Plan

Your start-up plan and your start-up budget are closely linked; your plan describes *what* you need to accomplish and *how* and in what *timeframe* you will do it, and your budget will detail what you expect to *spend* to do all this. The plan is the narrative, and the budget is the numbers. Together they tell the story of what you will accomplish, as well as when and how. This will be very helpful when you go to prospective donors to ask for their help.

Working out all these elements up front will help you plan your time and set expectations for your funders, if you already have some. As you demonstrate that you can write a plan *and* meet that plan, you will build your own self-confidence and the confidence of your early supporters.

The NGO needs a building somewhere to be able to house and provide services to the chosen client population. You need to rent a building (and possibly renovate it), or you need to buy (or be given) land and on this land either build a new building or renovate an existing one.

Renting or Buying

Before you begin your plan, it will be helpful to know if you will be (a) renting a building and starting small, (b) acquiring land with an existing building that needs renovation, or (c) constructing a new building. The options encompass significant differences in costs and complexity, and your start-up plan will look quite different depending on your choice. For example, time and funds required to prepare for occupancy will differ for each option.

Renting

Renting a space may be a good way to start, especially if you plan to start small. The cash and work needed up front are much less than when buying a site.

Costs at a glance
Based on Maher's and SOFKIN's experiences, the following is an estimate of costs to rent and set up one home for 12 children plus 2 staff and to operate for one year:

Furnishings and set up	Rs. 1,09,200
Operations: (Rs. 3000 per child per month)	Rs. 4,32,000
TOTAL	**Rs. 5,41,200**
	U.S. equivalent: $9046

Sample rental rates and deals

Maher has tried all sorts of rental agreements over the years, ranging from a few rupees per month as a token, to a rent of Rs. 4000 per month in Jharkhand (more rural, housing 25 people), or Rs. 5000 per month in the city of Pune for a small house for 20 children, with almost no outside space but close to excellent English-medium schools.

SOFKIN in Hyderabad paid Rs. 7000 per month for only 12 children, then they expanded to a larger site (3000 sq. ft.) and now pay Rs. 11,000 per month. This site is in the city where rent is higher and also near very good English-medium schools. Rents farther out of cities where the only schools are government schools are generally less.

Other rental considerations

Renting, even if that rent is donated to you, may come with strings attached. Owners can make demands, such as which women and children to accept or turn away. Landlords can also threaten to evict the NGO if they do not get rent increases or other demands met, and they can raise rent without much warning. A landlord might be seeking to enhance his or her personal reputation through connection with the NGO, possibly even misrepresenting the NGO. Even with a standard lease agreement, sometimes landlords refuse to fix a building, possibly putting the NGO's license at risk. You also risk fixing the building at your own cost and then being asked to leave. In Sister Lucy's experience, such rental arrangements may not be worth the apparent savings in time and money; owner demands end up being too costly and restrictive in the end.

On the other hand, Chaya Pamula has made renting work for SOFKIN. Serving mostly orphans, SOFKIN began in one small rented home with three children. After about five years, with fifteen children, it rented a larger home. Only now, after eight years, is SOFKIN considering buying its own site. In the meantime it has developed a wonderful reputation, a strong base of donors, and an experienced staff.

If you decide that renting is your best option, be aware of the possible risks going in. Be sure you know what is in the agreement you are signing and get everything in writing, being clear about who is responsible for repairs, whether you may renovate, etc. You may be able to get a long-term lease (at least five years) and lock in your rent rate for that time period. This will simplify your financial planning and avoid surprise rent increases.

Buying land and a building and renovating

Maher homes in the city of Pune were started using this option. Homes in neighborhoods near schools, utilities, and services were purchased and renovated to meet Maher guidelines. The original home in Pune included the main office space, until the numbers of

children and the office needs grew. A separate office building was then purchased next door to a small house that is now another Maher home. This second option generally takes less time than buying land and building a home, your third option. It is also a more likely choice if you are operating in or near a city where open land may be scarce.

> **TIP** Smaller homes are preferred: Chaya suggests no more than 15 children, and Sister Lucy no more than 25. This allows for more care and attention for each child and gives more of a family feel, two of the defining characteristics of Maher and SOFKIN.

Costs at a glance

Based on Maher's experiences, below is an estimate of costs to buy land with a building and renovate it, to set up one home near a city for about 20 children with 3 staff and to operate for one year. (It is not cost effective to buy a site for only 10 or 12 residents. Note too that sometimes buying and renovating can cost more than buying land and building new, depending on the location.)

Land and building purchase	Rs. 28,50,000
Renovations	Rs. 8,50,900
Furnishings and set-up	Rs. 1,10,200
Operations: (Rs. 3000 per child per month)	Rs. 7,20,000
TOTAL	**Rs. 45,31,100**
	U.S. equivalent: $75,733

Buying open land and constructing a home

This third option can be ideal, allowing you to construct a sturdy building designed specifically for your needs, with new plumbing and electricity. While this may take longer to complete and require more funds at the outset, you will likely have fewer problems later on.

Costs at a glance	
Based on Maher's experiences, what follows is an estimate of costs to buy land and construct a simple building in a village setting, and to set up one home for about 20 children with 3 staff and operate for one year. (It is not cost effective to buy a site for only 10 or 12 residents.)	
Land purchase	Rs. 10,38,782
Building construction	Rs. 24,35,063
Furnishings and set up	Rs. 1,30,200
Operations: (Rs. 3000 per child per month)	Rs. 7,20,000
TOTAL	**Rs. 43,24,045**
	U.S. equivalent: $71,189

> ### *CASE Be Willing to Think Creatively*
>
> *Maher creatively negotiated a land donation to develop two homes. The donation came from the Weikfield Company, a company with which Maher has developed a good relationship. Weikfield hires some of Maher's people (women, school graduates, self-help group members) and donates food and equipment. The company has a number of migrant and construction workers at a remote plant site who would often miss work due to child care issues. So Weikfield donated a plot of land across the street from their plant for a large Maher building to provide daycare programs for the children of their workers. Built with money from European donors, the building also holds two Maher homes for orphans and at-risk children. Four housemothers and two social workers live on-site. The more than 40 Maher children go off to school during the day, allowing Maher to devote staff time to daycare and other programs, such as tailoring and craft classes for village women. One of the two large halls is also available to Weikfield to use during the days to sponsor classes or meetings for employee groups. Both the company and the village, which is too remote for women to go elsewhere for clothing, are served and enriched.*

Generally land in a city is more expensive per square foot than it is in surrounding villages, and the more remote the site, the cheaper the land. (This is also generally true for buildings and rent.) However, in remote sites there will likely be less access to utilities, good schools, medical services, etc. Land with a dependable water supply is very costly now in India. These are things to think about as you consider alternate sites.

When assessing how much land to buy, remember that you will need space not just for the building but also for outdoor activities such as clothes washing and drying, for a play area, and for a septic system for site drainage. Ideally you might also have space for a vegetable, herb, or flower garden and perhaps for vermiculture pits. Also, when deciding about potential plots of land, consider road access, drainage, and options for future expansion.

Summary: three primary considerations

Ultimately whether you rent or buy or buy and build will depend on three primary considerations:

1. Limits of funding and time. How much money can you raise and in what timeframe?

2. Estimated target population size in geographic area. Sister Lucy had nearly 25 women and children within a few months and

nearly 50 after one year, because the needs were so great near that site. If the NGO will be located in an area where the need is great, then starting small and slowly may be difficult, as you will have to turn away many in need.

3. Staff skill and experience. Will you be in residence full time? What are the combined skills and experiences of you and those who will be working with you at start-up time? For example, are you hiring a social worker with experience working in a residential setting?

Opening a big facility in a high-needs area will require significant funds as well as significant experience. Finding the ideal land and a dream building may be stage two in the NGO's life, after getting started in a rented space and building relationships, credibility, and experience.

> **TIP** Do not build on land that you rent. The landowner could take away your right to access the land, and you would lose the building.

Rent: Ratnagiri
(note that whole top floor is
a large open room plus
toilets and showers)

Buy and renovate:
Prem Sagar

Buy and build: Apti Krupa
House
(See also Bakori in Chapter 1)

Creating a Start-up Plan Narrative

To create your start-up plan narrative,
list all of the goals you need to
accomplish to get the NGO from where it
is now to fully operational. At a
minimum you will include the five goals
listed below. You can start with a blank
page for each goal you identify. Write
one goal on the top of each page in big
letters.

Here are some universal goals for
starting an NGO:

1. Select and secure a site (land and
   building) (requires a capital budget,
   funds, and trustee approval).

2. Prepare the site for occupancy.

3. Raise all necessary funds to meet all
   goals.

4. Prepare to admit residents.

5. Begin daily operations, serving
   clients.

Note that you will be working on some
of these goals at the same time. You
may also have additional goals, such as
selecting and hiring a staff before the
first year is complete.

Next, make 4 columns on each page,
labeled with:

- Activities

- Timeline (starting date to
  completion deadline)

- Who is responsible

- Resources needed (funds,
  expertise, time, goods in kind)

Activities: Expand each goal by listing
the major activities you will need to
accomplish to meet this goal. Number
each activity using a number and a
letter, the number for the goal and the
letters for the activities. So the first

activity for Goal 1 would be 1A. See sample below.

Timeline: Estimate the dates on which you will start and finish each activity. Remember that you will be working on some of the goals simultaneously, and some of your completion dates will be deadlines you will have to meet for other activities to begin. If you want to have children living with you by the start of the school year, then you can work backwards from that deadline, with some idea when, for example, construction must be completed, and therefore when it must start, etc.

Who is responsible: Write the name of who is overseeing the activity's primary work. Also note if the trustees must approve this action.

Resources needed: For each activity, give a brief description of what will be needed. Include the dollar amount and the funding source.

You will, of course, be able to adapt your plan as you go along.

Each goal will have a page that looks like the sample below.

Goal 1 Select and secure a site (land and building)			
Activities	**Timeline**	**Who is responsible**	**Resources needed**
Activity 1A: create a list of basic requirements any site must meet	Complete by date x	Founder with trustee approval	Time for trustees meeting
Activity 1B: develop a list of possible sites	From date x to 3 weeks later, on date y	Founder	Transportation
Activity 1C: rate each site according to your requirements list	Date y	Founder	May require expert advise (such as engineer to assess renovations)
Activity 1D: create lists, with prices, for required furnishings		Founder	
Activity 1E: create capital budget		Founder	Research Engineering firm
Activity 1F: select site	By x date	Trustees	Trustee meeting, donor(s) Completed capital budget for each site being considered
Activity 1G: get legal consultation and sign written agreements	By x date	Trustees	Legal consultation List Rs. required at signing

TIP If you plan to rent a small space and begin, then you can skip many of the steps of the start-up plan below (pages 51-67) which deal with purchasing land or constructing a building. The steps in this box represent a "key" to a shortened process for renting.

Simplified start-up plan to rent a small space and begin

Goal 1
- Complete Step 1A
- Consolidate Steps 1B, 1C, review possible sites, rate according to your list in 1A
- Complete Step 1D
- Step 1E, simply read the introduction and follow the first example for the rental capital budget.
- Complete Step 1F

Goal 2
- Skip Steps 2A-C
- Complete Step 2D

Goals 3-5 remain the same.

The next section of this chapter will walk you through implementation of many of the steps in a universal start-up plan based on the five sample goals above. You can use the information there to help you create your own start-up plan and as well get a good idea of details you will need to sort out as you work on your plan. Do your best to complete writing the start-up plan, with its goals, activities, and timeframes, before you begin implementation.

Once you have a good outline of the start-up plan, show it to the NGO trustees, a few supporters, and a mentor. Ask if they notice activities or resources you forgot to list. See if they think the timeline is realistic. They might also notice areas where they can offer assistance. Perhaps they know a lawyer who would be willing to offer their services for free. Then you are ready to begin implementation. Trustees should approve the plan at this stage.

Implementing the Start-Up Plan

The following pages walk you through a step-by-step implementation of each of the five universal goals and their activities. Use this example to help you implement your own start-up plan. Some steps will obviously not be relevant, and can be skipped. For example if you are buying land and building, no need to worry about rental deals; or alternatively if you are renting, then skip the steps regarding purchasing land or a building.

Goal 1: Select and secure a site (land and building)

Activity 1A: Create a list of basic requirements any site must meet

Having a list of specific requirements will help you when you look at possible sites. You will be able to immediately eliminate some sites that do not meet your requirements. Most importantly, you will have a list of what information to gather and what questions to ask at each site. This list will also help you identify what renovations will be required for each building you see. Trustees should see and approve the list when it is complete.

Modify the sample list below to meet the needs of the NGO, taking into account the objectives from the previous chapter and local regulations. Later (Activity 1C) you can use this to make a chart with the criteria listed down the left side and a column for each property you like. This will help you compare sites logically.

Sample List of Basic Requirements

Rental site check-list and minimum site requirements

Generally you cannot renovate a building you do not own, nor do you want to. Therefore, any building you rent must meet these requirements as is. Buildings you will renovate or build must also meet these requirements, as well as the additional requirements in the second list. This list is based on a maximum of 15 children and 2 staff and can be adapted as needed for a larger group.

- Large open multi-purpose room (eating, gathering, activities such as schoolwork and exercise, even sleeping)

- Spacious kitchen and storeroom

- Can be made into a home in which the children can be comfortable

- Outside space for the children to play games and sports and exercise

- Security of area: Is the neighborhood safe? Can the entrances all be controlled and locked? (some governments require that children be housed in a gated area, and that boys' sleeping areas are separated from girls' sleeping areas)

- Distance to good schools, especially English-medium and private schools (ideally close enough that no transportation is required, or you will need to add this to your costs)

- 1000-sq.-ft. minimum indoor space (based on requirement of 55 sq. ft. per child for most of India; check local governmental regulations; Kerala state detailed requirements as of 2011 are on website www.replicatemaher.wix.com/tools)

- One lockable office room for secure conversations, admissions, and record storage

- Sick room

- Storage sufficient for bedrolls and children's clothing and schoolbags

- At least two toilets and two bathing rooms

Note that if the NGO will be located in a more remote area you will also need to consider access to utilities such as water, electricity, gas, phone, and Internet; access to shops for fresh food and basic supplies; and access to medical care.

> **TIP** If you have not done so already, now is a good time to look at other institutions with a similar purpose (or visit Maher) and note what you like and do not like about the different places. Whatever space you consider, see it with your heart: can you see it becoming a warm and inviting home, full of love?

Additional requirements and considerations if purchasing or constructing a site

Any building you either build new or renovate calls for the following additional considerations:

- Estimate the minimum square feet of land you will need to include a building, areas for outdoor use, drainage, etc. For example, 4000 sq. ft. of land allows for a single-story home for 20 children, a staff room, office space, outdoor play space, a well, and a small garden. (This also allows expansion, as you can later add a second floor.)

- Calculate the minimum square feet of building space (based on 55 sq. ft. per child). If you are buying, remember to think about how many residents you expect in five years, and in ten years.

- Toilets and bathing rooms: in India, the government requires one toilet per seven children and one bathing room per ten children, although this may vary by state. Requirements are similar for adults.

- Possible additional rooms could include: guest room, sick room, prayer/meditation room, and staff room.

- Site drainage: Sister Lucy estimates that each child uses approximately 7 to 9 liters of water per day, so multiply this by the number of residents you will eventually have. Note that you will need significantly more drainage than a family would need, so most family homes will require modification. Check if plumbing and septic tank is adequate or will need changes.

- Area for clothes washing and drying.

- Possible additional space for composting, a garden, vermiculture pits, or biogas production.

Keep this list of requirements in mind as you assess existing buildings, knowing that you may have to get creative as you consider them. Use it as a guide for what information to gather and what questions to ask at each site. This list will also help you identify what renovations will be required for each building you see. If you will be constructing a new building you can provide this list to an architect, along with photos or videos showing how the spaces will be used and the feel you want the building to have.

Activity 1B: Develop a list of possible sites

Look around your local geographical region, seeking sites that meet your list of requirements. Depending on your plan, look at open land, land with buildings, or buildings for rent. Find out costs for the ones you may be interested in. Assess each site's local community, both in terms of its need for your NGO's services and for the wellbeing of future NGO residents. Be sure to have your requirements list with you as you look at possible sites. You will be able to immediately eliminate some sites when they do not meet your requirements.

Activity 1C: Rate each site according to your requirements list

In this step you will begin to narrow the list of possible sites to those two to four which seem to most closely meet all your identified requirements. In Activity 1D you will estimate costs to furnish each site for occupation. Finally in step 1E you will assess the complete funding requirements of each of these top sites. Only then will you have enough information to present to the trustees for a final decision.

Rating rental sites
If you plan to rent, simply use the rental checklist from activity 1A. Any site you rent must meet all those requirements. Sometimes a landlord might agree to make a small modification or addition in return for a longer-term lease. If there is more than one good option, consider the

> ### CASE Think to the future
>
> *When the Ratnagiri home was informed that their lease would not be renewed, Sister Lucy had to look quickly for a building to house the nearly 30 girls who lived there. Her license was for 50 children and she had always wanted to build a home next door for boys, so that she did not have to separate siblings. Therefore any building to be purchased must have room to build this future boys home. She told this to the family whose home she was considering, and he brought over a neighbor who owned an empty plot of land across the small street that was also available to buy. She did all the negotiations at once to buy both properties.*

best combination of access to schools and services.

Rating sites for purchase

Comparing sites that you are considering for purchase, especially if some have a building already and some do not, is more complicated. An easy way to compare the sites against your requirements is to make a comparison chart: take the requirements lists above, list them down the left side of a page, and then make columns, one for each property you are seriously considering. (Turning the paper sideways will make it easier if there are more than three sites to compare.) Some items on your list may be rated as yes or no, such as access to utilities or space to expand, while other items may be rated numerically, such as the number of kilometers from different types of schools. Some items, such as distance to schools, may require a bit of

explanation, as in the hypothetical example that follows.

Some renovation/adaptation considerations, all of which will require funding:

- Extra toilets and bathrooms

- Removal of wall(s) to create the large multi-purpose room, or to enlarge the kitchen

- Additional rooms may to meet other requirements and/or to create the required sq. ft. per child

- Site drainage may require an extra septic tank, for example

55

Requirements	Site #1	Site #2	Site #3
Sq. ft. of land	X sq. ft.	X sq. ft.	X sq. ft.
Sq. ft. of building	0 (no building)	X sq. ft.	X sq. ft.
Space to expand?	Yes	Yes	No
Site drainage	Easy to create	Needs work	OK
Outside play area?	Needs clearing	Yes	Tiny
Clothes drying place	Yes	Yes	Yes
Distance to schools	English-medium 8 km; govt. school .5 km;	English Medium 2 km; govt. school 3 km;	English-medium .5 km; govt. school 1 km;
Bathrooms & toilets needed	New construction	Add 2 toilets, 1 bathroom	Add 2 toilets, 1 bathroom
Other renovations needed* (specify these)	New construction	Move one wall for large room, add new room for office and increase sq. ft. by x	Add 3rd floor to create necessary sq. ft. and large room?
Etc. (rest of requirements from activity 1A)			

*Note: for buildings you are considering for purchase and renovation you will need to estimate which renovations will be needed to meet your requirements list.

How to tell if a building is a good selection:

Hire a trustworthy engineer to assess the building's structure, water, plumbing, drainage, and electrical systems. The engineer will also be able to advise you whether the modifications needed can be safely completed (for example, some walls cannot be removed without compromising the stability of the building) and how much these modifications might cost.

TIP Find someone who is familiar with construction who will be willing to advise you, and whom you can trust. This person will be able to provide you with cost estimates, for both materials and labor, or will be able to suggest several trustworthy contractors for you to interview. This consultant will also be able to help monitor the work to see that you are not cheated. It might be someone in the community whose family or neighbors or friends will benefit from your services. Over time you may also develop a good working relationship with a contractor or engineer who will advise you on this project and future ones.

Activity 1D: Create list, with prices, for required furnishings

Develop lists of all the items you will need to purchase to furnish the building for NGO use. Price the lists in the local area. Use the information below as a guide to help you make your lists. The kitchen equipment table below can be a model for listing and estimating costs for all your supplies. The results will enable you to develop a capital budget in the next step. Note that furnishings will not vary a great deal from site to site. The major difference is that in some rental or purchased buildings some of the kitchen equipment or shelving may already be present.

1. Kitchen and storeroom for food and supplies (capital costs)
Sample kitchen list with approximate costs: (for twelve children plus two staff, increase quantities for more residents; based on average prices in India in 2012)

Item	How many	Cost each	Total Rs.
Plates, bowls, spoons, glasses (steel)	20	250	5000
Other common big utensils, pans, containers, knives, peelers, cutting boards, serving spoons, rolling pin, etc.			5000
Water tank	2	900	1800
Gas stove	1	3000	3000
Gas cylinders	2	1250	2500
Mixer	1	2000	2000
Fridge	1	15,000	15,000
Rack for utensils	2	1600	3200
Buckets, sweepers, towels, etc.			1500
Total			**Rs. 39,000**

TIP Create a list of furnishings as soon as possible. Once you do, use it as a "shopping list" for potential donors. List how many you need of what items, by what date, and their approximate cost. This list can be supplied ahead of time to local groups, businesses, and other interested people who may supply you with the needed items. Then you will not need to purchase them.

Here is a list from one home: (Ratnagiri, based on 2011 costs)

Item	Estimated cost in Rs.
1 computer	30,000
2 steel cupboards	7,500 each
2 steel racks	2,500 each
20 blankets (wool)	Approx. 10,000 for all
20 thin cotton blankets	Approx. 5,000 for all
10 mattress pads	Approx. 5,000 for all
20 bed sheets	Approx. 3000 for all
20 towels	Approx. 1000 for all
Slide, seesaw	5000-10,000
20 metal trunks (for children's clothes)	Approx. 12,000
Food rations (rice/dal/oil, etc.)	Approx. 10,000 per month
Toothpaste/toothbrush/soap/hair oil	
Notebooks, story books, games, and toys	Approx. 3000
Clothes (girls ages 5-10)	
"Charging battery" to use when power is out	Approx. 2500

2. Bedding for residents expected in first year (capital costs)

Bedding per child: Rs. 1000-4000, depending whether bed is laid out on floor at night and rolled up during the day or left out on cots or full beds.

- Mattress pad, covered with a hand-sewn thin cloth made at Maher
- Thin cotton blanket
- Bed sheet
- Wool blanket
- Cotton carpet (1 x 2 meter for under the pad)
- Pillow and pillowcase

3. Office furniture and supplies, including computer (capital costs)

- Computer, printer/copier, power storage battery/surge protection, phone, desk, four or more chairs, file cabinet (locking), shelving, TV/DVD player or at least music CD player (Supplies such as paper and pens, which are operating costs.)

4.Furnishings and other household goods (capital costs)

- Additional storage and shelving for children's clothing, schoolbags, bedrolls, donated items, etc.

- Household goods such as buckets, tables and chairs, and ceiling fans.

5. Initial stock of personal items for residents (capital costs)
(replacements and additional items are operating costs)

- Toiletries such as toothbrush, toothpaste, towel, comb, hair elastics, soap, shampoo, hair oil, nail cutters, and sanitary pads for women and girls

- School supplies such as book bags, rulers, pencil boxes with at least a pencil and a pen, chalk, and notebooks, plus chalkboard/slate for younger children

6. Remaining finish work (capital costs)
Leave a little time and a contingency fund for items you may have forgotten in your planning.
- Examples: painting, extra cleanup work, a sign for the front of the building, and window coverings. Make sure the house is clean and welcoming, both in appearance and feel.

Activity 1E: Create capital budget

Capital and operating budgets, if well done, will tell you what funding the NGO will require to prepare and furnish the site, and to operate for the first year. This information will be necessary to help NGO decision makers choose a final site and to have accurate numbers for funding requests.

Difference between a capital budget and an operating budget.

Capital budget: Capital costs are distinguished from operating expenses in that their useful life is expected to be several years (at least four or five). Examples:

- Land and buildings (including all construction costs)
- Furnishings: refrigerators, stove, tables, chairs, etc.
- Initial stock of household goods when setting up a new home, such as bed linens, pillows, blankets, etc., things you buy all at once so that you can open your doors
- An addition to a building (such as a new room or area requiring construction, that is then used over and over for many years)

Operating Budget: This will detail your costs of daily business, including items that are used up either right away or will wear out and need to be replaced periodically. These are called operating expenses. Examples:

- Rent and utilities (electricity, Internet, phone, etc.)
- Food, clothing, toiletries, school supplies and fees
- Household goods (bedding, cleaning supplies, dishes, etc.) As these items are worn out and replaced, replacement purchases are considered wear and tear and part of operating expenses
- Office supplies (paper, pens, notebooks, etc.)
- Staff salaries and benefits
- Medical expenses
- Transportation costs (train, bus, petrol, etc.)
- Costs for celebrations or outings

How to create a start-up operating budget is covered later in this chapter.

A capital budget for each site on your semi-final list will include:

- Cost of land OR land plus building
- Cost of construction OR renovation
- Cost of furnishings

Three sample capital budgets

Note:

- Prices will vary by country, region, and current market prices: the budgets below are samples and guides only. Prices are generally higher in cities, and the schools are better. Villages and more remote areas will generally be less expensive, but access to schools, medical facilities, counseling services, etc. may also be limited. You will have to research local costs and services in the areas you consider.

- Often, 5% is added to the total as a contingency fund for unplanned additional costs.

- Furnishing costs are taken from the previous step (1D).

Follow the hypothetical capital budget for the option you are considering:

1. Rent

2. Buy land with a building and renovate

3. Buy empty land and build

Option 1: Hypothetical capital budget to rent
(Start-up for 12 children and 2 staff, based on 2011 costs.)

Item	Quantity	Cost (Rs.)	Cost (U.S.$ at Rs. 60 Per $)
Building preparation	Includes: • Painting and cleaning • NGO sign	2000	34
Furnishings and goods required to begin operations	• Furniture and bedding • Kitchen (refrigerator and dishes) • Office equipment and furnishings	26,200 39,000 42,000 107,200	 1792
TOTALS		**Rs. 109,200**	**$1825**

The next two capital budgets will require calculation of land and construction costs, along with other fees needed to acquire and occupy each site.

Option 2: Hypothetical capital budget to buy land with a building and renovate
(Based on a new home for 30 girls and 5 staff in Ratnagiri in 2013. Note that this is an expensive city, and there was not enough time to buy open land and build. Timeframe: six months from selection to occupation.)

Item	Quantity	Cost (Rs.)	Cost (U.S.$ at Rs. 60 Per $)
Land with house	4500 sq. ft. of land with 2620-sq.-ft. building	Rs. 33,50,000	$55,992
Building renovation	Includes: • Add 4 toilets and 4 bathing rooms • Add 3 rooms • Site drainage improvements • Other miscellaneous renovations	14,99,955	25,070
Engineering and design fees	2.5%	23,887	399
Furnishings and goods required to begin operations	• Furniture and bedding • Kitchen equipment • Office equipment and furnishings	31,200 70,000 42,000 Rs. 1,43,200	 2393
TOTALS		**Rs. 50,17,042**	**$83,855**

Option 3: Hypothetical capital budget to buy empty land and build

(Based on Maher's experience, in a village setting, in 2013: sample land and construction costs for 20 children and 3 staff. For illustration only.)

Item	Quantity	Cost (Rs.)	Cost (U.S.$ at 60 Rs. Per $)
Land	3500 sq. ft. Acquisition costs, franking fee, land registration, advocate fee, etc.	Rs. 10,00,000 Rs. 38, 782	$16,714 648
Building construction	1535 sq. ft. Includes: • Large multipurpose room • Kitchen and storeroom • Office and counseling room • Staff room • Toilets and bathing rooms • Storage • Sick room	(Rate: Rs. 1500 per sq. ft.) 23,02,500	 37,907
Engineering and design fees	2.5%	57,563	948
Other	• Electrical installation • Bore well	15,000 60,000	250 1003
Furnishings and goods required to begin operations	• Furniture and bedding • Kitchen equipment and dishes • Office equipment and furnishings	28,200 60,000 42,000 1,30,200	 2174
TOTAL		**Rs. 36,04,045**	**$59,336**

TIP In India all land sales must be registered with the government, and there is a registration fee equal to a small percentage of the selling cost. Some sellers will want to do the sale "off the books" to avoid this fee. While this might be tempting, Sister Lucy explains that then, even if the amount was paid in full, the seller could claim they still owned the land. Because the sale was never registered, the land and the money paid would be lost. It is a big risk and also illegal. Sister Lucy, according to Maher values, does it legally.

Activity 1F: Select site

Present the result of your work in the prior steps to the trustees. Include comparison charts, alternative budgets, etc. Provide them with all the information they need to make wise choices for the NGO's future. The trustees make the final site selection and this decision must be recorded in an official meeting report.

If you find a perfect piece of land or building but do not yet have the funds, you might be able to put a deposit down on it and take a couple of months to gather the funds. You can use the chapter on fundraising to quickly develop a plan to gather the necessary funding. Most of the information you need to explain to prospective donors about what they will be investing in, how much you need, and exactly how it will be accounted for will have been gathered by your work to date.

Property pre-purchase check-list

- All land and building ownership documents should be clear. Be sure to check the government listings for the property for clarity and to see that there are no loans outstanding. (This loan balance could become your responsibility.)

- Land should be approved for residential use (non-agricultural).

- Town planning office and local (village) office must approve your intended use of the building.

TIP Borrowing money: In India (and likely in many developing countries) securing a loan for a new NGO is very difficult and interest rates are outrageously high. Sister Lucy and Maher have always avoided loans for these reasons. Therefore, this option is not addressed in the current volume. Sometimes a foreign aid or donor group provides low-interest loans to NGOs. Searching the Internet and asking other local NGOs might uncover such opportunities. Be sure the source is reputable before you get started. They, like any donor, will require the planning and budgeting documentation before providing a loan.

- Obtain building tax exemption and property tax exemption from government land management office.

Activity 1G: Sign written agreements and seek legal consultation

Prior to signing anything, consult a lawyer to help you with the formal agreements. Perhaps you have a trustee who is a lawyer. Be sure you fully understand the written agreements and the conditions for completing the purchase or getting your money back.

The NGO Memorandum notes who must sign documents to purchase major assets (such as land or building) and perhaps to sign a lease. At least one trustee and the executive director (usually the founder) should sign on behalf of the NGO. Make sure you are each both signing your name and stating your role with the NGO, so it is clear that you personally are neither the owner nor the renter.

At the time of signing you will be expected to make either a full payment or a partial payment with an agreement to a schedule of regular payments.

The timeline for Goal 1 will vary depending on how quickly you wish to open, how much time you need to do the research, and access to funds. Be sure to note in your plan who is responsible and what resources you will need for each activity.

Goal 2: Prepare the site's building for occupancy

Activity 2A: Select an architect or engineer

Select an architect or engineer (or both) to assist you with building construction or renovation. Sometimes a construction engineering firm will have architects on

> **TIP** Deeds, titles, and other important paperwork should be kept in a safety deposit box at a bank in case of fire. Include copies of the NGO's trust documents, licenses, and financial statements.

staff and one firm will manage the whole project. You will have consulted at least one or two companies as you were assessing possible sites. If you felt comfortable working with one, and if they were responsible (returned calls and provided what they promised when they promised), then you might choose one of these. Or you may interview others. You must be able to build a good, respectful working relationship with this person. It is always a good policy to get at least two bids for the work you plan to have done.

Activity 2B: Building design or renovation plan

Develop an initial design with an architect, who will consult with an engineer about the structural integrity of the design. To help design the building, you might take them to Maher (or show some Maher videos) so they can get a feel for the future use of the building as a home. You should also provide the list of requirements developed earlier in activity 1A.

Renovations may still require the assistance of an architect, or you might go directly to an engineering firm, depending on how complex the renovations are and the skills of the firm. Be sure to have a written time schedule of the stages of work and the finish date, including all costs and a payment schedule.

TIP Selecting trustworthy and competent builders and architects can be challenging. They may be very nice but lack experience, or they might be charming but planning to cheat you. If you are a woman, be sure they can work respectfully with a woman, listening carefully to your ideas, concerns, etc. Ask to look at other projects they have completed. Ask the owners of these projects if the work was completed correctly and on time, if the final cost was as promised, if were there any surprises and how these were managed. This might take a little extra time in the beginning but will save you future problems. A Maher trustee tells of choosing a woman architect, on principle, and then finding she was not competent. This cost Maher significant money and time.

Activity 2C: Construction

Constructing a new building
Construction will most often be done using fairly standard materials and design, with concrete block structure and re-bar support. Construction costs are often estimated in terms of Rs. per square foot, making bid comparison fairly easy. The engineering firm you hire will likely develop your designs with you and then present a project summary with building costs, including labor and materials, and a timeframe. The fee for

design engineering is often a percentage of the total cost. This will be a contract that you both agree on, and there should be a payment schedule (how many payments you will make, for what amount, and on what dates). There could also be penalties specified for late completion or cost overruns, as long as there were no design changes on your part. The trustees should formally approve this contact.

You will need to oversee the work, be it renovating an existing building or constructing a new building. Go to the site several times a week, noting progress, seeing how problems are handled, and asking questions if something doesn't look or sound right. You might ask for a brief weekly report to keep you up to date regarding how construction is faring compared to the time schedule and budget. You do not want any surprises at the end of the project.

Activity 2D: Furnish the building

Do any final painting, and thoroughly clean the entire building. This will be

TIP Start with very clear, written contracts that outline cost and time to complete the work they propose to do for you. You might even try the Western practice of specifying financial penalties for failure to meet contracted deadlines or budget limits.

much easier before furnishings are delivered. Then, using the furnishing lists developed earlier, purchase all of the items you need to furnish the building for NGO use. Save all receipts and keep careful records of all expenditures.

Before your Grand Opening make sure the house is neat, clean, and welcoming in appearance and feel.

The entire timeline for Goal 2 could be anywhere from one to twelve months, depending on whether you are doing a new construction, renovating, or renting.

Goal 3: Fundraising

Here you plan how to raise all of the necessary funds and other resources to meet your goals as well as your normal operating expenses, once you open. Fundraising, the process of seeking investors and stakeholders to share this dream with you, is addressed in the next chapter. This goal will require completion of your first capital budget (above in Goal 1, activity 1E) and your first operating budget (addressed below).

Goal 4: Prepare to admit residents

Activities will include obtaining the necessary licenses and creating the necessary recordkeeping processes to comply with government orders. Licenses are mentioned in Chapter 2 and recordkeeping is addressed in Chapters 6, 8, and 9. You should also begin to

establish relationships with institutions who might refer clients to you (such as other NGOs, police, hospitals, village leadership, etc.).

Goal 5: Begin daily operations, serving clients

Admit new clients and get to work!

Summary

Note that you will be working on several of these goals at the same time. If you plan to hire staff, that might become Goal 6. The information you need in order to hire and train staff is in Chapter 7. If you have not completed registration of your NGO, completion of this process will be in your start-up plan as well.

Start-up Budgets

Budgets are estimates of what you expect to spend during a given future period (generally one year). A budget always follows the plan that specifies what the NGO will be doing for that year. A budget, which is a future projection, is distinct from financial reports or expense reports that are produced after the reporting period is over. The budget and the reports are then compared to see how close the projections were and what factors caused differences and whether these factors were preventable, reproducible, predictable, or otherwise. The point is to learn how to better project needs and how to use and manage your resources better. Donors also like to see how their investment has been used, and to be sure it was used responsibly. Financial and expense reporting will be covered in the next chapter.

As you read earlier, there are two general kinds of budgets: capital and operating. You will have to do both kinds of budgets to start up and then again each year. Budget preparation for a start-up is quite different than for an NGO with some history of operations. Guidance and samples for creating a start-up capital budget were provided earlier, as part of Goal 1E in the NGO start-up plan.

Preparing a Start-up Operating Budget

This will be your most challenging operating budget because you will not have a record of what things cost in the previous year.

Each section of your operating budget will require research into local costs. Some costs (such as electricity) will not vary much based on number of residents, while other costs will vary directly based on how many residents you have (such as food). You will have to make some assumptions to complete this budget. It is very helpful to write out your assumptions, both to remember them and to use the same assumptions for the whole budget and also so that, at the end of the year when you compare your budget to what you actually spent, you can see if a variance was due to an

inaccurate assumption or to other factors. More about this analysis follows in Chapter 5.

How to estimate your first year's operating costs

Costs will generally fall into four categories:

- Housing expenses (rent, utilities, Internet, etc.). These won't vary much, whether you have 7 or 15 residents.

- Direct expenses (food, clothing, school fees, annual medical exams, etc.). These will vary directly based on the number of residents you have, and can be calculated on a per person basis for budgeting.

- Staff expenses (wages, training, etc.). These are "step" expenses. For example you might have 2 staff for 5 to 12 children, and then when you add a 3rd staff member for the 13th child. This is a 50% increase in your staff expense.

- Other expenses (small items like toiletries, medicines, outings, transportation, etc.). These are either small amounts or miscellaneous expenses that occur and may vary quite a bit from month to month.

Step 1: Make your budget assumptions

You can group these to mirror the four categories above. Do your best to estimate both costs and timing of costs. For example, school fees are payable in which month?

Housing:

- Check with local utility providers to learn the average electricity cost and water cost for a large family home. If you will have a well, you will not need to buy water.

- Check with providers for monthly phone cost, Internet set-up and monthly costs, etc.

- If you are renting, you will have a monthly payment, or if you paid for part of your land or building with a loan, you will have that monthly payment. (Technically monthly payments for assets such as land are considered a capital expense, but you can include the payments in your operating budget for planning purposes.)

- Household goods are things for common use, like dishes, cleaning supplies, buckets, etc. You will buy some to start out (listed in your start-up capital budget), but make an estimate of what you think you might need to replace later in the year.

Direct Expenses:

- How many residents do you expect to have after three months, six months, nine months, and one year? You might start with six children, so food costs, school fees, etc. will be for six, then over the months, as you take in more children, these costs will rise.

- Check the costs of milk, rice, flour, beans, and basic vegetables and fruits in your area. Look at some sample menus (meals you might prepare), and see how much it would cost to make that meal for the number of people you estimate. Also, included at the end of this chapter are some estimates for daily food costs per child at Maher; keep in mind that food prices tend to vary a great deal by both region and season. (Remember to include yourself and staff in your daily food calculations.)

- For clothing and school uniforms for the children, research costs at local markets. (Most clothing beyond school uniforms may be donated.)

- Which schools will children attend, at what cost per child per school (for example, four children at a private English-medium school, and four at a government school)

- Will the children need transportation to school and if so what is the cost? (Find out cost per day, then you can calculate per month, for eleven months a year.)

- What do schoolbags, books, and stationary supplies cost locally?

- Medical exams are required as each child arrives; find out what the local clinic will charge per child.

- Will you be providing teachers for extra classes such as dance, tae kwon do, etc.?

Staff expense:

- How many staff will you hire and when do you expect to hire them? Will they eat meals with you or live on-site?

- List other staff expenses, such as training, transportation, and any other expenses you expect to pay so they can do their job. Include payments to contract services such as counselors.

Other expenses:

- Estimate usage and replacement of things like toiletries, general first aid supplies, and office supplies.

Who your residents are, where they come from, and what their circumstances and needs are will affect your budget. For example: women have no school fees and related expenses like books and uniforms, but they require other training and development. They may also require more counseling, plus

legal counsel. Unwed mothers require a great deal more medical care, and sleeping on a bedroll on the floor is not an option. Do your best to anticipate the needs of your proposed client group.

Step 2: Build your budget month by month

On page 71 is part of a budget template for demonstration purposes. Two months have been copied into the left side of the page. The notes on the right explain how to complete the different parts. The remaining ten months will need to be completed as well, and then you will have annual totals. A downloadable template for your use is available at the book's website. The templates have rows and columns labeled, ready for you to enter data. They also have formulas embedded in them so that they do all the math for you—both the subtotals and the totals. Note that this sample is for a house with children only. It may be adapted as needed for other client groups (for example, add a section for women's care). School and child costs are grouped to allow easy calculation of per child costs for reporting purposes.

Month by month budget worksheet
Use the information you collected in step 1 above to fill in the budget worksheet. Note that a full budget worksheet is on line at www.replicatemaher.wix.com/tools.

There are further instructions for its download and use. The online spreadsheets have all the formulas embedded that will add subtotals and calculate averages for you.

YOUR NGO - Monthly Budgeted Expenses - YEAR 20xx

Category		Jan	Feb	March through December	ANNUAL
	Staff				
	Women				
	Children				
Category					
HOUSING	House Rent				0
	Electricity				0
	Telephone				0
	Gas				0
	Water bill				0
	House goods				0
					0
	subtotal	0	0		0
FOOD	Groceries				0
	Vegetables				0
	Milk				0
					0
	subtotal	0	0		0
CHILDREN	Admission fees				0
DIRECT	School fees				0
	Special fees				0
	Exam fee				0
	Books, supplies				0
	Uniforms				0
	Clothing				
	Annual Medical				0
	Extra curricular				
					0
	subtotal	0	0		0
OTHER	Medical - other				0
	Misc Expense				0
	Travelling				0
					0
	subtotal	0	0		0
STAFF	Housemother 1				0
	Housemother 2				0
	SW/part time				0
					0
	subtotal	0	0		0
	TOTAL	0	0		0

Top rows: refers to how many clients and how many staff are in residence for each month.

ANNUAL column: in the full spreadsheet you will have all 12 months, then the annual totals here.

Housing category:
- If you pay no rent, leave this blank.
- Household goods include cleaning supplies, bedding, replacement kitchen items, and office items. (A new stove or computer would be in a separate capital budget.)

Food category:
- Indian government requires vegetables and milk to be tracked separately.

Children direct category:
- Fill in the amounts in the correct months. For example school admission fees are due just before school starts, while school fees are monthly.
- Annual medical is for initial medical exam at time of admission, and then their annual exam after that.
- Clothing is all children's clothing and footwear, other than school uniforms.
- Extracurricular is for teachers and tutors who come to teach dance, tai kwon do, help with studies, etc.

Other category:
- Medicines and other medical expenses beyond annual exams.
- Misc. expenses include toiletries, other stock replacements, and house repairs, plus picnics or special events, staff training, etc.
- Traveling includes all transportation expenses.

Staff category:
- Monthly wages, plus contracted services such as bookkeeper, counselor, etc. (HM = housemother)

Note: School fees vary widely based on type of school. (For example from Rs. 2200 per child to Rs. 4800 per child per year.) Types of schools in India (all kindergarten through 10th standard) include:

• English-medium schools, generally the best and the most expensive

• Private schools, often run by religious institutions, although, in India, they are not allowed to teach any particular faith

• Government schools, the least expensive

Girls ready to go to private school

Higher education institutions (college, vocational schools, universities) have different costs.

Generally children are age 16 by the end of 10th standard, so two years of college or vocational school take them to age 18. The Indian government declares them adults and independent at age 18. Maher has arranged for partial and full scholarships with many schools, both government and private, including some higher education institutions. Ideally you will want to help these children gain as much, and as good, education as possible, so plan and budget accordingly.

Girls lined up to go to government school (Ratnagiri)

72

Taking the time to complete the above budget worksheet keeps your annual summary and budgets from being merely wild guesses. From this completed worksheet you will create:

1. Average monthly budget by category: divide the annual subtotals for each of the five subcategories by 12. You will use this to report and compare your actual expenses to budget, covered in Chapter 5.

Average	Housing	11,200
Monthly	Food	14,700
Budgeted	Children direct	2360
Amounts	Other	1800
	Staff	5100

This box is at the bottom of the online version of the Monthly Budget Worksheet

2. Annual budget summary: again use the totals from this worksheet to create an annual summary for ease of viewing. (Step 3 below)

Step 3: Create an annual summary of your start-up operating budget
(12 children and 2 staff in a rented building based on 2011 data.)

Fill in the "Annual cost Rs." column with data from the budget spreadsheet you just completed. To calculate "Avg. monthly cost Rs." (avg. = average) divide the "Annual" column by 12. Annual cost in U.S.$ is only relevant if you have foreign donors. The "Notes" column is for any notes that will provide useful explanatory information.

Start-up Operating Budget

Item category	Avg. monthly cost Rs.	Annual cost Rs.	Annual cost U.S. $	Notes
Housing				
Rent	7000	84,000		
Utilities: phone/elec/water/fuel	4000	48,000		
Household goods	200	2400		
Children direct				
Food	14,700	1,76,400		Monthly equivalent (14 people x Rs. 35 per day x 30 days)
School fees, books, stationary, etc.	1400	16,800		Mostly due in June
Clothing, footwear, & school uniforms	960	11,520		
Other				
Miscellaneous & medicines, toiletries	1200	14,400		
Medical	100	1200		
Transportation & taxes	500	6000		
Staff				
Housemothers (2)	5000	60,000		
Social worker	100	1200		Contract services as needed only
TOTAL	**35,160**	**4,21,920**		
Total cost per child	**2930**	**35,160**		

Note that this budget is for a rented building. If the NGO buys land and builds and payment is at the time of building, this requires a large amount of funding at the start but then no monthly rental costs. (If the NGO has loan payments, these can be included in your operating budget to demonstrated monthly cash requirements.)

SUMMARY: Projecting Total Estimated Costs

Now that you have a complete capital budget and an operating budget, you can tell prospective donors exactly how much you need, for what, and by when. For example, in our hypothetical case above, add your capital budget (refer to activity 1E) to your operating budget above to provide for the first year of care and schooling, for a total of funds required to begin and operate for one year. Below is a sample of a chart showing summary costs. These numbers can be inserted into the "case for support" that you will create in the next chapter to present to potential donors. Listing the costs in foreign currencies is only useful if you intend to contact foreigners for donations.

Hypothetical case for renting a home, furnishing and operating for one year:

Item	Est. Cost Rs.	Euro €	U.S. $
Furnishings and building preparation	1,09,200	1394	1825
Cost to operate for first year for 12 children	4,21,920	5385	7052
Total funding required	**Rs. 5,31,120**	**€ 6779**	**$ 8877**

For the other two options, buying and renovating or buying and building, you will go through the exact same process to build a month-by-month operating budget. The budget spreadsheet will create annual totals, including your estimated cost of operation for the first year for the number of children you project. You can then complete a similar summary table to the one above, simply adding the line items for land and building and your operating projections. Below is a sample.

Item	Est. Cost Rs.	Euro €	U.S. $
Land	10,38,782		
Building construction	9,55,490		
Furnishings	1,30,200		
Cost to operate for first year for x number of children.			
Total funding required			

4 | *Fundraising: Finding Partners to Participate in Your Vision*

Charity is the heart speaking. Giving is what happens when people listen. And philanthropy is the systematic application of giving for the betterment of humanity…. [The idea behind philanthropy] is loving humanity and wanting to see it improve.

—John Yemma, "Philanthropy Unbound," *The Christian Science Monitor Weekly*, November 19, 2012: 5.

Fundraising [12] may be the part of the work you feel least prepared to do, but it can be just as rewarding, given the long-term relationships you will develop. In this chapter we will seek to demystify this activity and present straightforward steps to help you develop a plan of action. Do not become stressed by wondering where the money will come from! As Sister Lucy says, based on experience, "When the work is good and managed well, the funds will follow. Do not be afraid. Trust in the goodness of God and people."

Instead of thinking that you are begging people to give you money, approach them as investors—connect with them as people who share your passion for the NGO's mission. This NGO is the vehicle through which a shared vision and dreams are met. Help them feel a valued part of what you are doing.

Think about inviting people to join you in a shared passion to make the world a better place, one person at a time. Be sure to remember that money is not the only form of investment: time, goods, skills, and contacts are all important contributions too!

---

[12] Grant writing is another source of funds for NGOs. However, grant writing is an art, often requiring a lot of effort with little result, especially if one is not skilled in the process. Grant writing, therefore, is outside the scope of the current volume.

77

Steps to Fundraising Success

- Vision, Mission, and Values

- Start-up plan and budget (a simplified strategic plan)

- List of current, specific resource needs

- Case for philanthropy investment and support

- Fundraising plan

- Fundraising activities

- Stewardship of donors

The previous chapters guided you in the development of a clear vision, mission, values and start-up plan and budget. This plan and budget contain the details of what you expect to accomplish and the specific resources you require to do so. The first three points above are the foundation of what you need to plan and complete your fundraising. This chapter will focus on generating the income necessary to get started and then maintain the NGO, beginning with writing the case for philanthropy investment and support. The discussion of a fundraising plan, activities, and stewardship of donors that follows will give you strategies for generating funds to maintain your organization.

Writing a Case for Philanthropic Investment and Support

A case for support names a social *need* investors care about and states how

your NGO will meet that need responsibly and creatively. It is a short written document that will be given to people interested in supporting your work. Its purpose is to identify what you are doing and help people believe that you can do what you say you will do. It outlines the NGO's vision, mission, values, plans, and strengths and the required resources. The case for support gives the reader a way to see the NGO, as well as a new view of their own place in the larger community. It should inspire them to want to join you.

Trustees should ratify the case for support, confirming agreement on the part the NGO Trust with the goals, benefits, strategies, programs, and funding priorities. The case for support will then become the basis of each future request for support by you, the trustees, or staff.

The final case will be a written document of two to four pages and may include photos and perhaps a short one- to two-minute video.

Elements will include:

- Summary inspirational statement about the project

- Success story that captures importance of the project

- Project outline placed in the context of an urgent need (that is, what is the need and what you will do about it)

- Brief background of NGO or founder, to encourage confidence that the project will be successful (for a new NGO, providing background of founder and other key people is critical)

- NGO's vision, mission, and values

- Funding requirements: explicit detail about what is needed, when, at what cost, and with what expected outcomes

- Invitation to invest

Sample case for support

Below is a hypothetical case for support, based on a Maher project in Jharkhand state. (Note that the photos are missing, but you will adapt for your own project.)

MAHER IS NOT JUST A PROJECT; IT IS A VISION OF A NEW SOCIETY

"There is a huge task awaiting us, the task of changing the attitude of society, especially of men towards women ... Maher is therefore not just a project, it is a vision of a new society where men, women and children have opportunities for growth, education, and happiness."   Father Francis D'Sa (Maher Trustee).

Lila's story: when I was 8 years old my father got very angry at my mother and threatened to kill her. I was very scared and could hear their fighting from my place hiding in the corner of our one-room house. I wanted to protect her. She ran from the house to try to get help.

Later my mother came home and my father was even madder and he did kill her. So I had no mother and because I was a girl I had no importance to my father; he stopped allowing me to attend school and sent me out to work so he could drink. This was how I learned how fragile life is for a woman in India. Then a woman told me about a special place where women and children would be protected from men when they were angry. She helped my younger sister and I get to Maher and Sister Lucy.

Now my sister and I both attend school. I want to be a social worker like the ones at Maher. Sister Lucy provided a home for my sister and me, and supported us as we were growing up and in getting an education. Her work is so important, and there is still so much need.

(cont.)

A Case For Support: A New Shelter in Jharkhand

Jharkhand is one of the poorest states in India, with one of the highest rates of maternal and infant mortality. In this state, poverty has reached unimaginable proportions, with a very high population density; there are just too many in the streets and railway stations. This leads to despair, violence, and delinquency. Jharkhand also struggles with all the problems of poverty, including health issues, lack of medical care, poor nutrition, and family violence. Mothers have little say in the affairs of their family or their children.

Five years ago Sister Lucy, Maher's founder, heeded a request and began to provide shelter and services to women and children in Jharkhand, in a small rented space. Because Maher's efforts always go beyond immediate assistance to those in most need, staff also sought to address the roots of the poverty, violence, and despair that they found. The need is much greater than the space available. As word spread, Maher very quickly outgrew the small space they were given. Right now women and children in great need and holding great hope are being turned away. It is heartbreaking for staff to have to turn away women and children in dire need due to a lack of space.

Today, Sister Lucy is positioned to build a larger facility to change the lives of women and children. You can help Maher build a safe place for this region of Jharkhand. You can make no greater investment than to provide quality of life for children and women who have been abandoned or fled to the streets. Without philanthropic investment Sister Lucy cannot reach out to these people.

Maher seeks to change life in Jharkhand by offering the following:

- Maher will provide shelter, care, and services to thirty women and their children

    o women and children will live in this safe haven in peace and dignity

    o women will be provided with vocational training and become self-sufficient

    o when possible and desirable there will be efforts made for family reconciliation

(cont.)

- children who cannot return home will receive complete care, including an education that provides for their intellectual, professional, and spiritual development and teaches them general life skills in preparation for self-sufficient adulthood

> Sabita arrived at Maher with her two small children in the middle of the night. Her husband, an alcoholic who beat her regularly, went too far and nearly killed her. She was bleeding, her sari was torn, and her children were clinging to her with wide frightened eyes. She was so terrified she barely spoke a word that night. Now, three years later, both children are in school and doing well. Sabita is a housemother and is particularly effective at village awareness meetings about alcohol—helping other women and families like her own. Her husband is trying hard to stop drinking. He has a regular job now, and he comes to visit her and the children. Perhaps the family will even be reunited one day.

- For children who have no families to care for them and are wandering the streets Maher will provide for up to 50 children

  - they will live in a loving home environment, receiving food, clothing, and care

  - they will receive an education that provides for their intellectual, professional, and spiritual development and teaches general life skills in preparation for self-sufficient adulthood

At 8 years old Asha was discovered nearly naked in a railroad station, without family; she had never attended school. She was destined for a life of prostitution and early death. Today she is a bright and cheerful 11-year-old. She loves to read and is doing very well in school. You can find her making up stories entertaining other children. She aspires to become a teacher to help others learn to read.

(cont.)

A Short History of Maher

Maher is an interfaith, caste-free refuge for battered, at-risk, and destitute women and children. Founded in 1997 by Sister Lucy Kurien, Maher is centered at Vadhu Badruk, about 32 kilometers from Pune in Maharashtra, India. Over the years its activities have spread to other states in India, including Jharkhand. This chart shows the accomplishments of Maher in India as of 2013:

• Over 30 homes for women and children	• 165+ staff
• 2333 women and 2215 children helped to date	• Over 400 self-help groups
• 720 children and 240 women currently in residence	• 85+ rural and urban communities served in 3 states

(Insert NGO photos—at least 1-2)

The vision, mission, and values of Maher provide the foundation for all of its work and services.

(Insert here your NGO's Vision, Mission, and Values.)

(cont.)

The Plan for Meeting the Need in Jharkhand

Land has been identified that is appropriate for building two homes that would better meet the needs in Jharkhand. (Note that state laws require that boys and girls be housed separately.) Maher has paid a down payment to the current owner with a plan to pay the remainder as funds are raised.

The budget for completion of this shelter is as listed below:

Particulars of the Project	Cost Rs.	Euro €	USD $
Land, registration fee, etc.	20,00,000	25,526	33,428
Construction cost (boys home)	31,40,000	40,075	52,482
Construction cost (home for girls & women)	40,90,000	52,200	68,360
Combined cost to furnish the 2 homes (50 children + 30 women)	3,58,100	4570	5985
Totals	**95,88,100**	**122,371**	**160,256**

Annually we will require the following funding to care for the women and children:

	Cost Rs.	Euro €	USD$
Cost to operate 2 children's homes (50 children)	18,00,000	22,973	30,085
Cost to operate women's home (30 women)	7,92,000	10,108	13,238
Totals	**25,92,000**	**33,081**	**43,323**

An Invitation
There could not be a more important investment for Indian people right now. Maher will apply its vast experience in Jharkhand to expand services, helping more women and children, if you will consider making a gift. Your investment in Maher is one that will provide real lifelong change for women and children. By giving women and children the opportunity to develop, they will give back to help the next generation.

Adapting the case for support to your NGO

If you do not have historical experience to relate, then describe what in your personal past (and in that of your staff and trustees) has provided you with the skills and credibility this project plan requires. If you have done the work of defining the NGO vision, mission, and values, registering it, and creating the detailed start-up plan, this in itself will reassure donors that you are serious and skilled. If you have even one year of operation, talk about all that you have accomplished. You will need to have both capital and operating budgets developed and available to demonstrate exactly where any numbers you use have come from. Use stories and photographs that capture people's attention and their hearts. For example, you may have a photo of a child who has no one to help her. Detail how your NGO will transform her life.

You will need to supply all of this information whenever you (or anyone else) talk about the project or ask for funds. Preparing some version of this will save you a great deal of time later, and will make you appear prepared and credible to people who may not know you.

Print up your case for support on good quality paper, in color if possible, especially if you have photos.

Developing a Fundraising Plan

Step 1: Do your homework

Write the case for support, or at least have all of the elements clearly defined. If you are just starting, you will have objectives, a start-up plan, and budgets developed, as described in Chapters 2 and 3. After at least a year of operation (and for all following years) you will be able to report on NGO performance (income, expenses, and results in terms of people helped) and explain any

TIP If you feel uncomfortable or hesitant asking for money, this will be communicated, and people will also be hesitant to give. Money is simply one form of energy, energy you need to fulfill a shared vision and mission: energy they can invest to make a difference in the world, by giving to your NGO.

deviations from your plan. Prospective donors want to see evidence that the NGO exists and what it has accomplished.

Step 2: Develop your funding plan

Your fundraising plan will proceed directly from the homework above. From your current year's plan, list each goal, including all financial and material requirements.

- List all possible sources of funding. Look to your relationships to find donors.

  o Friends—who do your trustees and staff know? Look to friends, family, neighbors, church/temple/mosque members, etc.

  o Community—people benefiting from your services (for example, local businesses will have access to more stable employees) and people who care about your mission may want to invest.

  o Consider service organizations such as Rotary Club.

  o Consider international contacts (individuals or foundations).

  o Once you have started operations, look to people who already know your NGO from personal experience. This will include former clients and staff, families of former clients, former trustees, people who have volunteered for your NGO, local businesses, etc. Even families with a moderate income who have benefited from your services may wish to contribute as they become able.

TIP For Maher, initial support received from Europeans has been critical. As European volunteers came to Maher, they spread the word, and funding followed. Once Maher grew strong and proved itself, then Indians came along. Indians have seen so many fake charities, started by con artists for their personal gain, that they are understandably very hesitant to support Indian charitable organizations. Once they see an NGO's successful results, and most of all its transparency, they want to give.

- For each person on your list, note specific interests (for example, children's education), and make a guess about how much he or she might be able to give.

- Prioritize this list in terms of who is mostly likely to be able to invest *right now*. (This is based on how much they already know about you, whether they have made a gift before, their access to money, etc.) Have a "short list" to start with, and focus here. You can grow the main list and come back to the other names on the list later.

- Estimate what you expect from each donor on your short list and add this up. This will be your first fundraising target. Expect about 60 to 65% of that amount. If this is not sufficient to reach your projected needs, you will need to either simplify your plans or come up with new funding sources.

- Select a strategy for how to approach and develop each priority resource identified above.

    o Personal face-to-face invitation

    o Small group gathering by invitation to present your story

    o Online, followed up with phone call

- Develop a timeline: include all events, visits, and meetings for the year (what your timeframe is, who is going to contact which name on the list when, and for events, who is responsible for what).

- Provide support and coaching to volunteers or trustees who will help you fundraise.

- Keep records about what worked and what did not work to monitor progress and evaluate performance.

TIP *Five I's*

- **Identify** people, businesses, and organizations that are most likely to have interest plus capability.

- **Inform** people of the community need and your plan to meet that need.

- **Interest** people and find out what their interest is. In what ways do they care about your work? Find out what they want to learn and how would they like to help.

- **Involve** people who are interested: use tours, meetings, and volunteering opportunities.

- **Invest** At this point people will make an investment. First investments are often smaller; investments will increase as people better understand the need and how the NGO is addressing that need.

Step 3: Develop relationships

People give to people: relationships are the heart and soul of fundraising. Whether you are meeting a potential donor one-to-one, on the streets, or at a formal fundraising event, it is useful to think of everything you do as building relationships.

Step 4: Create a database for all donors

It is vitally important to develop and maintain a database of donors. You can start this as you begin to meet stakeholders while you are gathering information for your initial site. For each prospective donor, complete a form that summarizes what you know about them, their interests, any connection to your organization members, etc. Add notes each time you contact them, when you

send letters, thank you notes, etc. Note what they say is important to them and what/how much they contribute. Either file these forms alphabetically or enter the information into a computer. Keep this information current over the years of your relationship with them so you can easily look up individuals to remind yourself of their special interests, history of support, and more.

SAMPLE FORM (you may add blank space for data)

PROSPECTIVE DONOR FORM

Date_____

Name of Prospective Donor_____
Phone_____ Email_____
Fax_____

Postal Address (city & codes)_____

Spouse_____

Employment_____

Title/Responsibility_____

Business Postal Address_____

Phone_____ Fax_____ email_____

Secretary/Assistant Name_____

- Connection to NGO, or trustees, or staff
- Boards they serve on or organizations in which they are active
- Professional affiliations and interests
- Personal and leisure interests, lifestyle
- Observations and notes

You must record every donation received. This should include from whom, the amount of cash or items received, and the date it was received, at the least. At the year's end you will need to report annual totals of domestic and foreign cash donated, as well as the value of goods in kind if these are capital goods (such as land).

A donor spreadsheet has been created and is on the book's website — (replicatemaher.wix.com/tools)— for your use. This spreadsheet has three parts. The first is to enter every donation transaction, including personal information for each donor and each gift. A second part of the spreadsheet calculates and displays the total, by year, of the cash donated and the approximate value of goods in kind donated, both of which you will need for annual reporting. A third part of the spreadsheet reorganizes the information to create a list of donor names and contact information. This can then be used to create a mailing list.

TIP Why people choose to give

- They appreciate the NGO's mission and value to the community

- To give back to the community or society

- To make a difference in the world

- The project or program mission and values inspire them

- The geographic location has special importance

- To be recognized or to belong to something larger than themselves

- A desire to get involved

- To honor or memorialize someone

- The right person asked them to

- To take a tax deduction (see Chapter 2 for more information) .

Weikfield family honored by Sister Lucy at Maher Day

Fundraising Activities to Build Relationships and Generate Support

There are infinite activities that can be used to reach out to possible donors. These will vary from large events to one-to-one contacts. Face-to-face is always better than purely written contact, especially when you do not have a longstanding relationship. Following are a few suggestions for ways to reach potential donors and investors.

Know your prospective donor before you contact him or her:

- Is he a current donor?

- What is her relationship to your NGO? (Such as, friends with staff or trustees of the NGO.)

- What is his involvement in the local community?

- What are her charitable and social interests?

- What is his giving potential?

Ways to contact prospective donors
Individually

1. First you will want to contact him or her, usually by phone, to set up a meeting:

  - Tell him who you are and why you are contacting him.

- Tell her you would like to meet with her to discuss your NGO or to invite her to an event.

- Tell him how much time you might want to take and offer choices (For example, in his office or home. Is Tuesday or Wednesday better?)

- If she says she is not interested, ask if she would like any relationship with your NGO, such as a newsletter or a future contact.

- Once you have obtained the appointment, *end the call!* Tell him you look forward to talking with him again.

TIP When people are not interested you most likely will not get beyond informing them about your work. That is fine— just move on!

2. Preparation for the meeting:

  - Plan your strategy, tailored to this prospective donor.

  - Confirm your goal for the meeting and a follow-up plan.

- Know the *Case for Support*, the financial and program information, the urgency of the need, and the impact on services and the local area if funding goals are not met.

3. At the meeting:

- Discuss the most relevant points to your need for support and the urgency of your case. Link this to what you know about this prospective donor and his or her interests.

> **TIP** When you talk to a prospective donor, look for her eyes to light up in resonance when you talk about the NGO's vision, mission, values, or specific projects. Look for ears that perk up at stories of hope and dreams of better lives. These are good signs of interest and fertile ground for your work. What is impossible for one person to do becomes possible when others join: this truth is at the heart of philanthropy.

- Discuss your NGO's competencies:

  o Describe what your NGO does effectively. (Remember to include qualifications of founder and trustees if the NGO is just beginning.)

  o Recount any recognition received for providing this service.

  o Confirm the impact of service with facts and stories.

  o Discuss benefits of service to the community.

- Ask for support:

  o If the answer is yes, thank her or him.

  o If the answer is no, or not yet, ask if you may follow up with her, provide more information, etc.

  o You can leave of copy of the case for support with him.

- Follow-up:

  o Write a letter thanking her for her time and interest (whether or not she made a donation). Call and visit for follow-up (seven to ten days after sending the letter) if appropriate.

  o Update your database about this donor.

Note: Trustees play an important role in fundraising. They may do some or all of the following:

- Make a gift that represents a stretch but is within their means

- Participate in fundraising activities and events

- Host small gatherings for family, friends, and neighbors

- Help writing an annual fundraising plan and case for support

- Participate in identifying, cultivating, and educating potential supporters

- Help recognize and celebrate donors

Small Group Gatherings

Alternatively, to build relationships you might invite small groups of people together for a presentation to learn about your work and to have an opportunity to join you as a donor/investor.

- Select a group of 30 to 40 people to invite, with the expectation 6 to 20 will attend.

- Have each group of people be compatible with each other in some way.

- Select one to three special guests that will inspire others in this group to attend.

- Write a specific statement as to the purpose of the meeting (if it is to inform, to invite donations, or both).

Sample agenda for a small group gathering:

- Length of meeting is about 1½hours.

- First 40 minutes: socialize and share food or snacks and beverages. Have NGO staff and trustees prepared to meet and talk with specific guests to learn more about interests and potential connections.

- Next 20 minutes: present the story of the NGO, current status, and perhaps have someone speak who has personally benefited from your program or show a video. Ask for questions.

- Last 30 minutes: socialize and offer more food, or perhaps sweets. Have NGO staff and trustees reconnect with guests to learn their response and whether they have questions.

- Debrief: it is important that you, NGO staff, and trustees who attended share what you have learned. Be sure information on attendees' interests and connections are recorded. Use the "Prospective Donor Form."

- Send thank you letters for attending.

- Send "sorry we missed you" notes to those who did not attend.

- For those attending who seemed to have strong interest, follow up within a week to learn if they would be interested in investing.

Alternatively, if the event is one in which people will be asked to invest right there, provide information on how they do that. Have volunteers in the room assigned to connect with people to discover their current interest and help them make the investment. Have something for donors to put their investment in, such as an envelope. Collect full contact information so you may provide each donor with a receipt and thank you letter, as well as have this information for your database.

> **TIP** Have ready a list of suggested donation amounts and what each will cover. For example: a list of furnishings needed and the cost of each, the average cost to feed, clothe, house, and educate one child for a year.

Asking via email or the web

Generally, you might consider the option of email or online contact for donors beyond your local geographic area. These will still be contacts who have some link to you, your staff or trustees, or your mission (for example, friends and relatives of staff and trustees or visitors who have come to see what you are doing and want to follow your work and continue to be a part of what you are doing). Your case for support will still form the basis for the content of either an email notice or a web-based posting. Use photos and graphics to capture viewers' attention as well as data showing success, and make sending a donation easy. For example, include a "donate now" button on your website. Be sure to include complete information for mailing a donation, perhaps directly to your bank. If you are hoping to attract foreign donors, it may be worthwhile to set up a way people can make a secure credit card payment over the Internet, using a vehicle such as PayPal. You might also create a short one- to two-minute video for YouTube that is compelling and might draw people to contact you.

Donations beyond money

Always have a ready list of other ways people can become part of your NGO's success. Examples include:

- Donation of beds, blankets, computer, school supplies, etc.; be specific about your needs such as: 20 wool blankets, or 10 school book bags or backpacks

- Donations of food, such as bags of rice or tins of cooking oil

- Donations of clothing and fabric in good condition (specify the age and gender of children)

- Visiting with the children, perhaps sharing songs or dances (interfaith of course)

- Taking the children on an outing (planned with, and supervised by, staff)

- Time in office to help type records, or prepare a mailing of the newsletter

- Produce a short educational video about your organization to post on YouTube (with staff approval)

TIP Get creative! Maher has a program in which local families will come to Maher to celebrate their family member's birthday by bringing a big cake (and even dinner) and serving all the children. The children welcome them with songs, aarti ceremony, flower garlands, and big smiles.

Large events

These take a lot of planning, work, and funds to organize, publicize, and carry out and are beyond the scope of this book. However here are three tips that may help create some of the energy and reach of larger events:

1. Have a table or booth at a large public event with similar goals and values. For example there might be a big program for International Women's Day, or a march or rally to end violence against women and children. Be there with signs and lots of printed information you can pass out.

2. When you celebrate some of the interfaith holidays or national holidays, make it a pageant not only fun for your residents, but invite family members, neighbors, village leaders, etc., to join you. They will have fun and also learn a great deal about your work by experiencing your community.

3. You might sponsor one large event annually that is designed to celebrate the accomplishments of your residents, NGO programs, and staff, to thank trustees and major supporters, and to invite continued support. SOFKIN raises most of its funds through such a once-a-year event. There is music, dancing, performances, awards, and more. By SOFKIN's seventh year there were 750 people in attendance!

Stewardship of Donors

Again it is crucial to remember that the key to success is building long-term relationships with people who share your passion and commitment. Even if an initial gift is small, you are building a relationship that will last years, and hopefully their support will grow as you do. You need to develop and maintain your database of donors, even including those who expressed interest but have not yet made a gift.

Every donor would like:

- prompt acknowledgement of a gift – within three to five days
- confirmation that his or her gift is working as you promised
- measurable results on the gifts-at-work *before* being asked for additional support

Thank you letters should be personalized to the donor, acknowledge how his or her gift will be used, and signed by you. These letters may also be handwritten, on cards made by the children, or signed by a trustee. At Maher these are never form letters, but rather heartfelt notes, a reflection of Maher core values. Donors have written back to Sister Lucy thanking her for her thank you letter to them, saying it felt like a hug from Sister Lucy! Include something personal about their visit, or an interaction with them, or an acknowledgement of their particular interest, etc. (An exception might be after a large event with several hundred people. But be sure the thank you letter following these events contains photos and highlights of the event and celebrates all the contributions, repeating again what the investments will make possible.

Keep people updated on progress toward your goals. This may take the form of a newsletter, or a blog on the NGO's website, perhaps with a thermometer image that shows the progress in raising funds toward a goal. Keep your blog up-to-date and interesting to keep people coming back to it. Include inspiring stories and photos of people helped by the NGO, and reminding readers that their support is what allows the work to happen. Provide an updated list of resource needs to encourage future donations.

Maher also sends out holiday cards (Christmas, Divali) that are hand made by staff and residents—over 4000 each holiday!

Values Start Here

Accept and pay no bribes or "kickbacks," make no promises you cannot keep, and accept no gift if it comes with strings attached. Making a donation does not grant control or privilege within the NGO. Fundraising does require gratitude and warm personal thank you letters. Transparency is critical.

TIP A good fundraiser

- Must believe in the cause

- Should be innovative

- Should be an effective communicator

- Should be persistent and determined.

Other Notes and Tools

Have just one story:
Stick to the agreed case for support: this is what we do, how we do it, what our values are, etc. This way people helping fundraise for you do not make promises that you cannot keep.

Web-based tools and video tools:
"Pictures speak a thousand words" is a time-honored truth. Short videos can be made even with a simple camera or smartphone, edited on a computer, and posted free on YouTube and on your website. Links to a few examples (Maher's and others') are on the book's website.

Consider noting larger donors on your website with words of thanks. For corporate donors, include their company logos.

Volunteers:
Volunteers who come to visit, work with you, and meet your clients personally can be some of your best ambassadors, telling the NGO's story and successes to their circle of family and friends. In this way you can expand your friends, even around the globe

Dr. Sharma & Father D'Sa, trustees, Sister Lucy

5 | Tracking, Reporting, and Ongoing Planning

The test of our progress is not whether we add more to the abundance of those who have much; it is whether we provide enough for those who have too little.

— Franklin D. Roosevelt

Now that you have:

- A start-up plan of what you will do when

- A budget projecting financial resources required to complete that plan

- Some donations to begin the work

- A site selected and work begun

What is next?

You now need to think ahead to when the NGO must report regarding the goals in your plan, the money you collect and spend, and how that compares to your projected budget. As you hire contractors and buy furnishings you will need to begin right way to track exactly what you purchase from whom, for what, when. Government, donors, and trustees all require that you account for the funds you are given. And as the NGO's first year draws to a close, you will need to prepare for the next year by planning, budgeting, reporting, and fundraising all over again.

This chapter is divided into two parts:

- Tracking, analysis, and reporting

- Creating annual plans and budgets for continuing operations based on previous years' experience.

Part One: Tracking, Reporting, and Analysis

- Why track, report, and analyze?

- How to track income and expenses

- What reports to generate

- How to analyze and use these reports

Why Track, Report, and Analyze?

Tracking and measurement is not an end in itself: this work is an active part of how your NGO operates. This cycle of related activities serves four purposes:

- To meet government and licensing requirements

- To earn the trust of donors and other stakeholders as they see clearly the efficient and effective use of resources achieving intended outcomes

- To demonstrate transparency

- To help the organization plan better and decrease the risk of monetary crisis management, as needs are better anticipated and met

Generally a planning cycle is one year. Just as your plan and budget are for one year, you will need to track what happened over that year, and then report and analyze those reports. Before you can report results, you must have systems to track as you go.

The following map shows the relation of all these parts at a glance. All of the elements in the map will be addressed in this chapter.

TIP If all of this financial management is making you worry, you might want to consider hiring a part-time bookkeeper to help monitor your tracking systems, enter all the paper records into the computer, assuring they match, and create reports. For a new organization, two to three hours a week should be sufficient. This does not mean you can ignore all the financial data. You have to supervise this person to be sure all is done legally and accurately. If you have little financial background, selecting a trustee who has these skills and shares your passion for the NGO may be a brilliant move. The trustee can help with setup and do the tracking and reporting, at least for the first year or so. Then, when the NGO is larger and has more funds, she or he can help you hire someone to do this job. Another potential source for bookkeeping assistance is local companies who become early supporters. They might allow one of their employees to help you a few hours a week. Be creative!

Following the Money

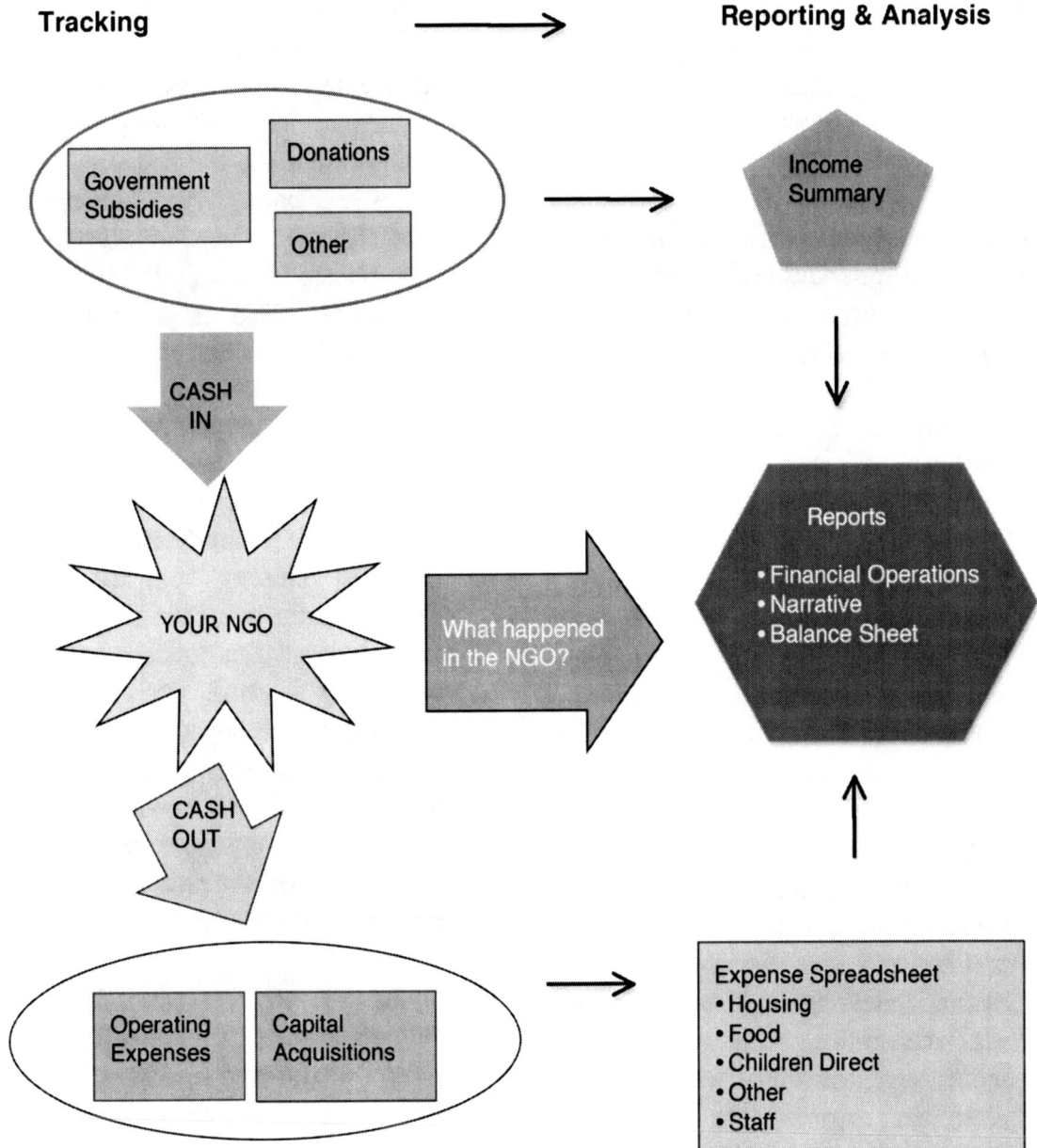

Tracking ⟶ **Reporting & Analysis**

Government Subsidies

Donations

Other

CASH IN

Income Summary

YOUR NGO

What happened in the NGO?

Reports
- Financial Operations
- Narrative
- Balance Sheet

CASH OUT

Operating Expenses

Capital Acquisitions

Expense Spreadsheet
- Housing
- Food
- Children Direct
- Other
- Staff

Tracking Income and Expenses

For useful reporting, all income and expenses must be tracked very carefully and accurately. It is best to take the time now, when things are relatively simple, to set up these systems. Trying to switch recordkeeping processes after a few years is difficult.

There are three ways to manage tracking and reporting of this data. You will have to choose which method, or combination of methods, is right for your NGO. Factors in your decision will include your own comfort with computer spreadsheets, the NGO's financial ability to purchase software and/or professional assistance, and local regulations for tracking data. These three methods are:

1. Purchase and use an all inclusive software program, such as QuickBooks. Then, once you set it up, you can simply enter in each separate transaction and the software will track income, expenses, cash balances, etc. Whenever you want a report, whether month-end or year-end, you just ask for that report. Unless you are comfortable with computers, you may need professional assistance to set it up. After this, entry of data is easy to learn and do. While this solution will cost more up front, it will save much time and effort later as well as accommodate future growth.

2. Design or modify computer spreadsheets, based on the models in this book. (Downloadable templates can be found on the book's website.) Here too, once the spreadsheets are set up, data entry is quite easy. This solution is simpler and much cheaper. However, if your NGO grows in complexity, as Maher has done, you will likely need a system more like the first one. Most of the data from computer spreadsheets can be read by QuickBooks, so making the transition is feasible. This is exactly what Chaya at SOFKIN has done.

3. Create all the paper registers that Maher uses and keep these daily. Anyone can enter the data easily. Then you or a bookkeeper will pull the data together from the many paper sources to create any reports for analysis. This option is fairly simple for a small operation with only one or two houses. As the NGO grows, however, the process becomes very time consuming and leaves a lot of room for errors. Backup copies in case of fire are cumbersome and impractical.

You must also consider what the local government requires. If your NGO is not receiving payments from the government for child support, then often the paper records required are fewer. This book provides basic spreadsheets and a complete list of paper registers, based on Maher's experience, for you to use and customize as needed.

CASE Computer records are not yet accepted everywhere

In India, many local government agencies still require separate paper ledgers for all records; no computer records are acceptable. There are nearly thirty paper registers at each home, and compiling them into complete, accurate, and meaningful reports is very challenging, especially as the organization grows and has multiple locations. Historically, as individuals have tried to sort through the registers for multiple houses and report results for Maher as a whole, these reports vary by who has collected the data; there is little consistency. Maher is trying to now create more accurate records that meet international (and even Indian large donor) standards. This is proving challenging. Start now with an integrated system instead of waiting.

SOFKIN uses some of the paper registers for daily receipts and transactions. These are easy for the housemothers to complete. Then these notebooks are totaled at month's end for entry into spreadsheets, and now QuickBooks. You may choose the same.

A system of checks and balances

Reports of income and outgo must balance with the bank's cash records, so you will need to be careful and accurate. Funds coming in must be recorded and reported at least monthly and annually as income. You will also have to report how NGO income compares to NGO expenses, showing how the money was spent. Every rupee must be accounted for. In India, Africa, and elsewhere corruption is common. You will need systems that do not allow opportunities for staff, trustees, or residents to pocket funds or any resources intended for the NGO's use.

Bank accounts

The NGO will have both savings and checking accounts with the same bank. If the NGO accepts foreign donations, there will be a third account for those funds. Check signing and withdrawals should require two signatures. Both of the signatures will be registered with the bank.

You should know how much money is in all accounts at any time. Monthly, you should check balances in the NGO checking and savings accounts, making sure your totals match the bank's totals.

Maher pays staff salaries by making transfers from the Maher account to each individual staff person's account. It is much safer to handle these as transfers so no one needs to carry the cash. Staff members need to have their personal accounts at the same bank as Maher for this to work. Additionally, if you follow the Maher practice of opening bank accounts for women residents, these will be at the same bank and handled as transfers as well.

Tracking income

Any resources that come in must be tracked and recorded carefully. Income will be from three general sources:

- Donations of cash or goods in-kind

- Government subsidies for residents' support

- Other

Other includes income from goods your residents make for sale (tailoring, crafts, etc.) and other miscellaneous income.

In the last chapter, on fundraising, you developed a system for tracking donors and donations. If you use donor forms and enter all the information on computer spreadsheets, unless the government has further requirements, you may not need further records for donations.

Samples of Maher's income registers

If you do not use the computer spreadsheets, or if the government requires paper registers for donations, you may wish to use the following two registers. Both can be created using the ledger paper notebooks available at most office supply stores.

Cash Donation Register
The headings for all necessary information can match the donor spreadsheet fields (columns). Be sure that the year-to-date donations of cash match both the bank records and the daily cash register, described below.

In-kind Donation Register
This is a list of donations of clothes, blankets, rice, shelving, equipment, etc. It will have all the same columns as the cash donation register.

> **TIP** Column headings for both of these paper registers may be the same as on the computer donor spreadsheet, or simplified if you are using a combination system. Examples:
>
> - Year, First name, Last name, Postal address, Email address, Cash amount OR item donated, Check number (or other reference number), Type of donor, and a Notes column.
>
> - A minimal list for government requirements may include Date, Donor name, Cash amount OR items donated, Check number (or other reference number).

Tracking other income

In addition to tracking donations, if your NGO receives government subsidies for residents' care, you will need to create a register to record these payments. However you track donations and other income, your annual records must match the "cash in" records below.

Tracking cash in and out

All cash income ideally should be deposited directly into the bank for the most transparent tracking. Keep all your bank deposit records in one file.

You will also need a daily written summary of "cash in" and "cash out." This will yield a daily cash balance. You will match this monthly with the bank statements. You can also calculate a total "cash in" for each day, week, and month, noting subtotals for donations and government payments. If you use a computer spreadsheet, monthly totals for "cash in" donations can be compared to the donor spreadsheet totals.

Tracking "cash out" means accounting for every purchase the NGO makes, plus any other payments such as salaries for staff. "Cash out" includes cash payments, bank transfers (including staff salaries), and checks written.

If you keep cash on hand for daily small purchases (such as bus fare, milk, toiletries and other small purchases) you will also have a register to account for every rupee in and out of this petty cash fund. Get written receipts where possible. Organize and save all NGO receipts by expense category (housing, food, children direct, staff, other).

TIP Ask merchants for a receipt if they do not normally provide one. If you give them a blank piece of paper, they can write their name, shop name, a summary of your purchases (you can fill in details later if needed), and the total money received.

Daily Cash Register

Maher's Daily Cash Register is a simple way of collecting all the daily data, organizing both cash in and cash out, and showing a daily cash balance. Cash out is also tracked by expense category. Below is an example. You can purchase ledger paper notebooks with the columns already drawn. This is part of the system of checks and balances: the total cash on hand on any given day must match both the Daily Cash Register and the bank statement.

Left page – Cash Flow: bank balance, cash flow, statement balance. Each day there is an opening balance, cash in, cash out, and a closing balance. You can note whether the cash received was a donation (and so will be recorded in the donor spreadsheet or paper register) or from the government (and so will be recorded in that register).

Right page – Expenditures: by category, matching the expense of the NGO budget (utilities, groceries, etc.). All expenditures each day are listed, accounting for all cash spent. The right and left pages should match: expenditures on the right page must match "cash out" on the left page *each day*. Note that "Expense types" match the categories in your budget.

Tracking Expenses

If you are using the Daily Cash Register (below) from Maher, then you will also have a daily record of expenses. Each month these expenses need to be subtotaled by type. In the example below, you find Rs. 600 in the GROCERIES category, Rs. 50 in the HOUSEHOLD GOODS category, and Rs. 1000 in the UTILITIES category. Each

month you will have thirty days' worth of such entries to add up by type of expense. Each month the summarized expenses need to be collected so you can create a month-by-month report, and also annual reports.

Expense tracking spreadsheet

Tracking expenses on a computer spreadsheet is one option. The monthly summaries from the Daily Cash Register can be entered directly into the expense tracking spreadsheet (template on line, sample below under "Reporting expenses"). If you are relying on a paper system you can use the described example registers below. Or you may choose a hybrid system as described in the accompanying tip (See page 106).

Following is an example of the expense tracking spreadsheet for one year.

Daily Cash Register

(LEFT PAGE) Cash Flow Rs.

Opening balance Rs. 3500

Date	Balance	Cash In	Kind	Cash Out
1/1/2014	Rs. 3500	400	D	600
		200	G	100
	Rs. 3400			
1/2/2014	Rs. 3400	1000	D	900
				150
	Rs. 3350			
D= donation G = government O= other				

(RIGHT PAGE) Expenditures Rs.

Date	Items purchased	Expense type	Amount	Subtotal
1/1/2014	dal, rice	groceries	450	
	vegetables	vegetables	100	
	dish soap	house good	50	600
	gas cylinder	utilities	100	100
1/2/2014	electric bill	utilities	900	900
	oil	groceries	150	150

Entering data each month shows you exactly where the NGO is, especially if you also look at income to date. The expense tracking spreadsheet also lists at the top how many women and how many children are in residence each month. This information comes from the admission files (see Chapter 6). At the

bottom left of the expense tracking spreadsheet are monthly budgeted amounts for the main categories (you calculated these in Chapter 3). It is helpful for trustees and staff to see expenses, and the budget all in one place.

Sample Expense Tracking Spreadsheet:
(blank template with instructions at www.replicatemaher.wix.com/tools)

Note that some hypothetical data has been included for illustration only. Data and totals, including monthly budget box in bottom left, match Chapter 3 examples.

YOUR NGO - Monthly Expenses - YEAR 20xx

Category		Jan	Feb	March	April	May	June	July	Aug	Sept	Oct	Nov	Dec	ANNUAL
	Staff	2	2	2	2	2	2	3	3	3	3	3	3	
	Women	5	8	12	10	10	11	15	14					
	Children	10	15	20	18	18	18	22	21					
HOUSING	House Rent	7,000	7,000	7,000	7,000	7,000	7,000	7,000	7,000	7,000	7,000	7,000	7,000	84,000
	Electricity	4,000	4,500	3,500	3,000	4,000	3,000	4,000	4,000	4,200	4,800	4,500	4,500	48,000
	Telephone													0
	Gas													0
	Water bill													0
	House goods	50	150	350	250	300	100	125	175	300	200	150	250	2,400
														0
	subtotal	11,000	11,500	10,500	10,000	11,000	10,000	11,000	11,000	11,200	11,800	11,500	11,500	132,000
FOOD	Groceries													0
	Vegetables													0
	Milk													0
														0
	subtotal	0	0	0	0	0	0	0	0	0	0	0	0	0
CHILDREN	Admission fees													0
DIRECT	School fees													0
	Special fees													0
	Exam fee													0
	Books, supplies													0
	Uniforms													0
	Clothing													
	Annual Medical													0
	Extra curricular													
														0
	subtotal	0	0	0	0	0	0	0	0	0	0	0	0	0
OTHER	Medical - other													0
	Misc Expense													0
	Travelling													0
														0
	subtotal	0	0	0	0	0	0	0	0	0	0	0	0	0
STAFF	Housemother 1	2,500	2,500	2,500	2,500	2,500	2,500	2,500	2,500	2,500	2,500	2,500	2,500	30,000
	Housemother 2	2,500	2,500	2,500	2,500	2,500	2,500	2,500	2,500	2,500	2,500	2,500	2,500	30,000
	SW/part time	200	0	300	0	0	200	0	300	0	0	200	0	1,200
														0
	subtotal	5,200	5,000	5,300	5,000	5,000	5,200	5,000	5,300	5,000	5,000	5,200	5,000	61,200
	TOTAL	16,200	16,500	15,800	15,000	16,000	15,200	16,000	16,300	16,200	16,800	16,700	16,500	193,200

Average	Housing	11,200	(Household goods includes bedding, replacement kitchen items, office items. A new stove or computer would be listed separat
Monthly	Food	14,700	
Budgeted	Children direct	2,360	(About half of the annual total of this is payable in June at the start of the school year.)
Amounts	Other	1,800	(Covers misc medicines & medical care, toiletries, & other stock replacements, house repairs PLUS picnics or special events)
	Staff	5,100	**Approx. Budgeted Total per month** 35,160

Examples of paper-based expense tracking

If you choose to (or are required to) use paper registers, then below are descriptions of the registers Maher has developed.

Monthly Expense Register
This records monthly expenditures collected by expense type (vegetables, utilities, school fees, etc.) from the Daily Cash Register.

TIP Make this process as easy for yourself as you can while meeting all the governmental, trustee, and donor requirements; let the complexity grow as you do. Sister Lucy says "if I could manage with so little education [8th standard], anyone with love for the poor will be able to manage."

Monthly Summary Register
This register includes cash at the start of the month, expenditures by category (from the Monthly Expense Register), donations received, and all bank deposit vouchers. At Maher, a copy is kept on site and the original is sent to the main office. As the number of sites grows, it becomes a significant challenge to copy and manage all these paper notebooks. Alternatively, a computer spreadsheet can simply be emailed, and the central

TIP If you computerize your records be sure you back up files, so that you have a separate copy to keep offsite. This will protect your files in the case of theft, fire, or equipment failure.

office can compile the spreadsheets from different sites to create an automatic summary of all the sites.

Ledger Book (one for each year)
This book contains the monthly totals from the Monthly Summary Register. A table of contents lists all expense headings, and on which page they can be found. (For example "Food pp. 7-9" and then, starting on page 7, all the foods bought each month are listed.) This book also records totals of all Indian donations received by donor name, check number, total amount, and receipt number.

TIP Hybrid system: You might use the Monthly Expense Register as a worksheet to prepare the expense data for the spreadsheet. Housemothers can be trained to do this, leaving you to enter the results into the computer.

Capital expense tracking

In a year when the NGO is acquiring and furnishing a new site, there are a lot of capital expenses to track. All of these costs, such as construction costs, purchases of furniture, a computer, and bedding, will have to be tracked in the same manner as other expenses. You can keep a separate Capital Expense Register (on paper or computer) or include these in the daily cash register, simply noting "capital" as the expense type. The daily cash register will show all of your cash flow in one place. Again, save all receipts.

Reporting: What Reports to Generate

In the same way that NGO planning included both a narrative and budgets, you will be expected to provide both narrative reports and quantitative reports. Reports should always refer back to plans and promises made. Different audiences might require different reports.

- The trustees' job is to oversee operations, to assure that goals and objectives are achieved and resources are used wisely. They require both narrative and financial reports.

- Donors want to know that their donations were well spent, and they will want results reported in terms of the mission they hold dear: how many residents there are, how many

people have been helped, and stories of how your NGO made a difference in individual lives. They will appreciate photos too.

- Governments require primarily financial information.

Narrative reports

Narrative reports generally refer to the start-up or annual plan, where you described what you would accomplish during the year in terms of the NGO's mission and objectives.

Reporting on your start-up plan (or an annual plan) is fairly simple if you have kept your plan current (noting accomplishments and making updates as needed). At the end of the planning and reporting period, summarize what you have accomplished with respect to each goal, noting what has been completed early and what is still incomplete. Be sure to explain why a plan item was not completed on time. If possible, include photos of the new building, residents, etc. This is a chance to celebrate all that your NGO has accomplished! Such reports will serve both trustees and donors, although you may wish to customize the final reports, providing more detail to trustees and more photos to donors.

Financial reports

Financial reports refer back to the capital and operating budgets you created in Chapter 3. Governments have very specific reporting requirements regarding content, formats, and schedule. In most countries, the NGO must file an audited annual operating report, whether or not the NGO is required to pay taxes. There may be other reporting requirements from other government agencies. Be sure to learn right away what is required, so that you track the correct information in the correct manner. The tracking systems above should provide all the needed data or require only minimal adaptation to meet local reporting requirements.

Operating reports

Operating reports, like your operating budget, reflect the performance of daily operations of the NGO. If you follow all the steps above in tracking your income and expenses, you are well prepared to create all reports easily and accurately. If you have been using computer spreadsheets, your financial reports will be ready to print, because all of the required information is built into them.

You will need to report both income and expenses of the NGO. Annual reports are required by law, but trustees or donors may request interim reports as well (every three or six months). The reports below are annual, but the process is the same for any period of time. In a nutshell, you will put together totals from the expense tracking spreadsheet total and the donor tracking spreadsheet (plus government subsidies or other income if applicable) for the year to compare income to outgo. Here you can see at a glance whether the NGO had a net loss or gain during the year. You can

do a similar check at any point during the year. Additionally it is helpful to include how many clients were served each month to demonstrate cost per person served.

Reporting income

- Annual summaries of donated cash and capital goods received, subtotaled by source (or at least by cash domestic, cash foreign, and goods in kind). Note that this information is found on the donor tracking spreadsheet and should match any donation registers you use. Generally, small items like clothing, toys, toiletries, and other items that get used up fairly quickly and used items (such as a used computer) do not need to be tracked as income. However, a major capital donation such as a car or land will need to have its value assessed and added to the NGO's list of assets.[13]

- Schedule of government subsidies if the NGO receives these for the support of any residents.

- Any other income of the NGO.

Reporting expenses
- Monthly and annual summaries of expenditures by category (at least housing, food, children direct, staff, and other).

---

[13] Assets are the capital goods the NGO owns: land, buildings, equipment, cash on hand, etc. See Balance Sheet section later in this chapter.

- If the NGO is making monthly payments on a bank loan for land and/or housing, you will need to report on the loan status each year, showing payments made, any penalties, and the new outstanding balance. A summary of this information will also be found on the Balance Sheet.

Sample of an Annual Operating Report
(based on earlier example of 12 children and 2 staff in a rented home)

NGO Name
Annual Operating Report for the
Year Ending December 31, 20xx

Revenues and Gains	Amounts in Rs.
Public contributions	4,11,320
Gifts in kind	16,000
Government payments	0
Total Revenues, Gains, Other Support	4,27,320
Program Expenses	
Housing	1,34,000
Children direct	2,04,720
Staff	61,200
Other	21,600
Total Program Expenses	4,21,920
Net gain/loss	5,400

Analysis and variances

Review the summary numbers and compare these to plans and projections.

- Compare donations received to donations planned, from the fundraising plan. This is an opportunity for staff and trustees to review how well the fundraising plan worked to generate the resources needed to run the NGO.

TIP Remember that, when you prepared your budgets, you listed assumptions you used to create your projections, such as how many children you would have each month, or what it would cost per person for food. When creating a start-up budget these assumptions are difficult to get right. Some variations will simply be due to inaccurate assumptions. You can correct this on your next budget.

- Compare the actual results to the budget. For example, did you spend more or less in each expense category than you predicted at the start of the year? Be sure you can explain the differences. For example, if food costs were 20% more than you budgeted, is this due to 20% more residents? Weather-induced price increases in food? Waste of food? Understanding these variations will help you improve your operations and plan better for future years.

Other useful expense analysis includes calculating and reporting per child costs for food, schooling, clothing, and medical care. These are useful numbers for reporting to donors, for comparison with other NGOs, and for future projections. If you know what these costs are per child, you can make accurate projections of resource needs if the NGO adds 5 children or 15 children. You will use calculations like this to create the next year's budget later in this chapter.

Capital Reports

Capital reports will refer back to your capital budget. Your first capital budget reflected what you expected to spend to acquire, build or renovate, and furnish the NGO's new site.

For your capital report, you can copy your capital budget and change the last column to "actual cost." In your analysis, note *any* deviation from the budget and include the reason.

TIP Donors sometimes like per child information to help decide how much to give. They might, for example, like to give enough to support one child for a year. Therefore you might calculate and quote the "cost per child" by taking the total annual budget and dividing it by the number of children in residence. If the number of children has varied over the year, you can do a similar calculation for each month and then average those. This factual data will help build trust with NGO donors.

2 residents of Prem Sagar home in Pune

Hypothetical Capital Report (Start-up for 12 children plus 2 staff) This will be relatively easy to complete. You prepared a full capital budget in Chapter 3. Simply replace the last column (was US$) with "actual cost" and enter in exactly what was actually spent for each of the categories. Be sure to explain any differences between what you planned to spend and what was actually spent.

Item	Quantity	Cost (Rs.)	Actual cost (Rs.)
Land acquisition costs	3000 sq. ft.	10,00,000 38,782	10,00,000 38,782
Building construction	1535 sq. ft.	(Rate: Rs. 1500 per sq. ft.) 23,02,500	23,02,500
Engineering and design fees	2.5%	57,563	57,563
Other	• electrical installation • bore well	15,000 60,000	15,000 60,000
Furnishings and goods required to begin operations	• Furniture and bedding • Kitchen equipment and dishes • Office equipment and furnishings	28,200 60,000 42,000 1,30,200	28,200 62,000* 42,000 1,32,200
TOTAL		36,04,045	36,06,045

*Variance: kitchen supplies cost Rs. 2000 more than budgeted.

Other government-required reports

The government requires additional financial reports (and possibly foreign investors or corporate donors as well). A chartered accountant will prepare these based on the financial data you provide. The Annual Operating Report and Capital Report as outlined above will generally be sufficient, with copies of either your spreadsheets or registers as backup information. This same firm will prepare the NGO's final audited statement and any other government financial filings. Examples are listed below. Samples of some of these can be found on the book's website.

Balance Sheet
A financial "snap shot" the NGO at a point in time. Includes: summary of all NGO assets (land, equipment, cash) and liabilities (debt).

Statement of Activities

This report summarizes income, expenses, and changes in net assets for the year.

Audit

At least once a year, the NGO's financial records must be audited by a chartered accountant. Exactly how often will be specified in the NGO Society or Trust formation documents. This audit can be scheduled by the NGO, generally following annual tax reporting. The same accounting firm can provide both services.

WARNING In India, the Child Welfare Committee can also audit NGO records at any time without any warning. They may check in great detail. For example, if they notice that you moved the NGO bank account from one bank to another, they may ask to see the minutes of the trustee meeting that authorized this move.

Part Two: Creating an Annual Plan and Budget

- creating an annual plan

- creating annual budgets (capital and operating)

Once the NGO has a site and a building and has been operational for a year, you will need to prepare a new plan and a new budget for the following year. The next year's plan is generally written and agreed to before the next year begins.

Planning, budgeting, and reporting activities will become key parts of ongoing operations. Every time you do this it will be easier.

Generally by about ten months into a given year, if you have been tracking NGO performance against plans and budgets, you will be able to estimate how close your projections were. At this point, you can begin preparing the next year's plan and budget.

Writing an Annual Plan

Now that the NGO is fully operational, the annual plan can focus on developing care and services for residents. Use the same planning form and the same process as for the start-up plan. Only the content will be different. Trustees should be involved in the process of assessing where the NGO is now and what its priorities for the next year should be.

To begin, assess where the NGO is now, what goals may be as yet incomplete from the current year, and where you would like the NGO to be at the end of the next year. Decide what new goals should be accomplished, and list new activities to be included. These are generally activities beyond the daily ongoing operations of feeding and housing residents. Projects might include developing staff skills, starting a dance program for the children, fundraising for a computer lab for the residents, or starting some local self-help groups. Whatever is on your list, be clear about what outcomes you, the trustees, and the donors expect to see by the end of the year. Outcomes should be measurable. As an example, write a goal starting six self-help groups in the local community. Then list the activities involved, estimate the timeline, note who is responsible, and list the resources needed. Add a fifth column to track completed activities. Trustees should approve the plan before the start of the next year.

List each goal on a separate page. Use the following five columns.

Activities: list the major activities needed to meet this goal.

Timeline: estimate the dates you will start and finish each activity.

Who is responsible: state the person overseeing the activity's primary work.

Resources needed: for each activity, give a brief description of what will be needed. Include the dollar amount and the funding source.

Accomplishments: this column will be filled in once work on the plan begins.

> **TIP** To help think of activities, it may be helpful to work backward from the goal. What has to happen in order to accomplish it? In what order?

Enter progress on each goal throughout the year. For the self-help group example, write the date and indicate a new group formed, and that discussions are starting for two more.

Monitoring your plan

Check your progress on this plan quarterly, and adjust the plan as needed. Be sure to begin work on the following year's annual plan at least a month or two before this one expires. If you miss major deadlines, be sure to state why, and use this information to improve next year's plan.

Creating an Annual Budget

Just as for the NGO's start-up year, you will create both a capital budget and an operating budget.

Capital budget

The capital budget will follow from the NGO's annual plan. Do any of the plan items require acquisition of a new building, a new computer, a car, or a motorbike? Remember that items like replacement bedding, dishes, and clothing, are not capital expenses.) Do you foresee needing to add an addition to the NGO's building to separate girls and boys? It is good to plan ahead! This budget will have the same format as the start-up capital budget.

Operating budget

Once you have at least a partial year's worth of financial data and experience, budgeting for the following year will be easier. You now know what food costs and school fees are. If you completed the start-up operating budget worksheet in Chapter 3 and you have used the similar expense tracking spreadsheet to record monthly expenses, you will have all you need to easily complete next year's budget for the NGO. The steps will be similar. Again, either print a blank budget spreadsheet to use as a worksheet or fill out the worksheet directly on the computer, building your budget month by month. (Instructions are online for using template and adding a tab for the new year.)

Below is a step-by-step guide for developing an annual operating budget. You will repeat these same steps every year.

Step 1: Review the NGO's new annual plan
Do any of the goals or activities have any resource needs that the NGO will need to hire or purchase? For example, the NGO may have a goal of hiring a part-time social worker halfway through the year, or beginning a program of music lessons on Sundays, requiring a teacher.

Step 2: Estimate client numbers
Make an "educated guess" about how many new residents you expect during the course of the year, and how many may leave. This should allow you to project approximately how many people the NGO will have to care for each month. This will help you accurately project the direct expenses such as food and school fees.

Step 3: Review previous year's monthly expenses
Review the expenses on the previous year's financial operating report and note any changes for the coming year. Add these changes to your list of budget assumptions.

Step 4: Build an operating budget
Begin to build a budget month by month, based on your assumptions and past experience. Fill in as much as you can, estimating costs and entering new expenditures, as projected in the NGO's annual plan.

You now have a monthly projected budget and totals for an annual budget. This will tell you how much in money and goods you need to ask for from supporters, as well as when you will need the funds.

You should keep this budget and review it each month. If there is a drought and food prices rise dramatically, you will be able to anticipate a need for extra food or money donations before you actually run out. If you plan for 10 residents and suddenly have 14, you can quickly estimate the NGO's additional needs.

Summary

Remember that all the work described in the last three chapters, including planning, fundraising and reporting, is part of how you make your dream manifest and fulfill your vision. If you do not have resources or properly manage those resources, you cannot do what your heart calls you to do. After the first year or two it will get much easier! And if this part of the work is not your strength, be sure to find someone with these skills who shares your vision.

Altar with circle of religions and holy books of different faiths.

All work develops in phases. If you look only at the immediate consequences instead of the goal, you are likely to get emotionally entangled and burn out or lose hope. You may even get so personally involved that you begin resorting to wrong means just to get things done the way you think they should be. In the long run, this can only weaken your work and turn results against you.

–Eknath Easwaren commentary on Bhagavad Gita

6 | Creating the Essence of Mother's Home

"I alone cannot change the world, but I can cast a stone across the waters to create many ripples."
—Mother Teresa

Now it is clear what services your NGO will offer to which groups of people, a geographical area and a site have been secured, a start-up plan of goals and activities has been made, and some committed people are ready to help. You are ready to set up the first home. It is assumed that you will be starting small with one building, office space included, and a small group of either women with children, or children only. You will most likely also live here, directing the work, helping and serving the residents, doing village and local outreach, and more. It is time to put your ideals into practice!

The overarching principle of Maher's homes is that each woman and child feels as if he or she is living in a family home. This is true whether it is a single home for 15 to 25 children or a larger facility for many women and children in

smaller units, and whether the children will be with Maher a few months or the rest of their school life. *Maher* means "mother's home" and so implies all of the qualities and experiences that one would expect to experience in a loving and safe family home. Everyone eats the same foods, from the same dishes, and everyone helps in all household duties, regardless of caste or other status. Everyone looks after and helps each other. Guests are welcomed warmly. Ideally you, perhaps along with some of your trustees and major supporters, might go to experience "mother's home" firsthand as guests at Maher.

While running a home includes hiring and development of staff as well as the actual day-to-day work with your residents (women and/or children) these topics are covered in depth in the next three chapters.

The focus of the current chapter is:

- Creating the feel of mother's home, from physical space, to the structure of days, to rules and celebrations

- Administration required to keep everything and everyone running smoothly

- Community outreach

Creating Mother's Home

These homes are heart-centered, and this is reflected in every aspect, from setup to decoration and in every detail of daily life. In each home the space feels welcoming, comforting, and cheery and is able to handle the energy of a lot of active children. Ideally it will have

plenty of fresh air and be kept clean and neat. In short, it feels like the refuge a mother's home should be. Daily schedules are organized with the best interests of the particular residents present. All residents feel cared for in body, mind, and spirit.

Physical Space of a Single Home

Most projects will begin with a single unit, or with two buildings so boys can live separately. Each home is designed for 15 to 25 residents with two or more housemothers and possibly a social worker. While the exact layout of each home will be different based on the building design, there are many common features. The following discussion also provides useful guidance to an architect designing a completely new space. Local regulations also affect design. The overall feel of the house is warm, inviting, often noisy (what house full of

CASE At Maher, children still get to be children!

Within the wide guardrails of Maher, the children enjoy a lot of freedom. They can ask for their favorite foods from their housemothers, squabble with them, hide during chores time, read storybooks during study time, and smile apologetically when caught. They will climb trees at school, fall down and skin their knees, make a mess of their clothes (and themselves), sulk over trivial matters, and refuse to eat their food. The housemothers and others usually do not interfere with this growing up process. And the children will compensate for all their misdemeanors with a mischievous twinkle and a tight hug. Whatever they may lack by way of facilities, one thing that they never lack at Maher is love.

15 or more children would not be?), cheerful, neat, and respectful.

Every home has similar room requirements. Below are the types of rooms and spaces each home will have, with a bit about how each is set up and used.

Large multi-purpose room

Every home has a large open space for gathering all the residents (and even a few guests) together. This room often also serves as a space for sleeping and for meals, with both taking place on the floor. This space becomes the "heart" of the home, since it is often the only place large enough for everyone to gather. It should be open so that some daylight and a fresh breeze can come in. The walls should be painted a cheerful yet soothing color, and the space should always be neat and clean. If the house has a DVD player or a TV it will be here, for occasional Sunday or holiday use. The walls can be decorated with colorful posters that might include a listing of children's birthdays, a photo collage of all the house members, house rules, etc. (See box inset for more ideas). The room is often also used for group exercise, meetings, study and homework time, and dance and other classes. You may display photos of respected role models such as Mother Theresa, Gandhi, Nehru, and Savritri Phule (who started the first girls' school in Maharashtra).

Multi-purpose room in Prem Sagar (note altar)

Multi-purpose room in Bakori (note world religion image)

Multi-purpose room in Vatsalydam (note wall paintings)

Sleeping space

When the space is used for sleeping, residents roll out bedrolls at night and sleep on the floor. Every morning all residents roll up their bedrolls and put them into a large sack stitched for this purpose for daytime storage. At least

TIP Make colorful wall charts and hangings

- Birthdays

- Children's New Year's goals

- Team standings in sports (house teams)

- Daily chores checklist

- Core values

- Health and hygiene tips

- A copy of Maher's "Twelve Religions" batik

- Charts with school lessons (such as names of animals in English, or the English alphabet)

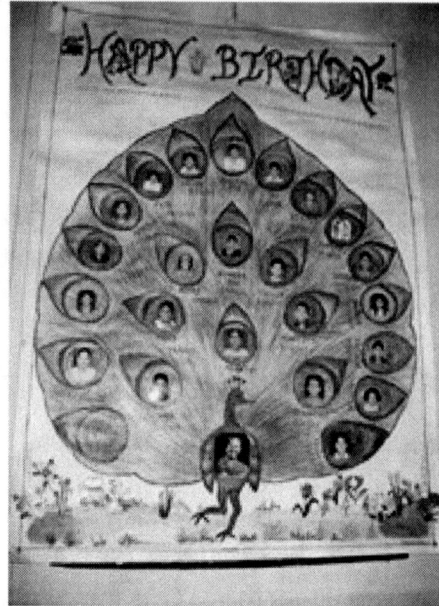

Wall chart: Children's photos and birthdays

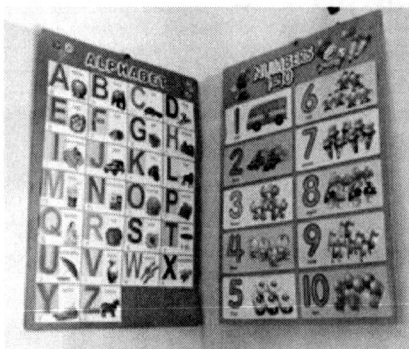

Wall chart: English lessons

one of the housemothers will also sleep in this room with the children, either also on a bedroll on the floor or on a cot on one side of the room.

In an alternative setup, Kerala has two bedrooms, each with eight or ten bunk beds where all the boys sleep. There are tables on the covered veranda for eating, homework, and other gatherings. In Kerala it is never too cold to eat outside.

When there is a separate space or buildings for boys, generally only sleeping and living space and bathing and toilet rooms are needed. The open sleeping space can be used as well for studies, exercise, etc. Depending on size and local regulations, kitchen space and meals may be shared. But even if they must eat separately, the office and guest rooms and some of the storage space need not be duplicated.

Beds and Maintenance

Every resident, adult or child, has a cotton floor mattress with a carpet or woven mat beneath. The mattress is covered with a hand-sewn cotton cover to protect it, which can be removed for washing. This bedroll also includes a bed sheet, a light blanket, and a warmer wool blanket, as appropriate for the climate.

Bedrolls and cupboards: each child has a shelf

At least two times a year the mattresses are put in the sun to dry out, especially after the rainy season. The same setup is generally used on cots or bunk beds if these are provided. In India, standard thicker mattresses are impractical, given their expense and how quickly they become moldy or sour in damp weather. Most of India's poor and middle classes sleep on similar cotton mattresses, if not directly on dirt floors.

Checklist for bedding:

- Pad or carpet under mattress
- Mattress; cotton mattresses should have a thin removable cover
- Bed sheet
- Light blanket plus wool blanket
- Pillow and pillow case

Bedrolls and girls' trunks: Ratnagiri

Storage spaces

Generally, cupboards or shelving along the wall have a shelf or storage bin for each child, where they keep personal items such as clothes, toothbrush, and the like. There is usually a separate space for book bags and school materials to be stored. Everything is always picked up and neat. There are also storage spaces for household items, such as replacement dishes or donated clothing that has not yet been distributed. It is helpful to have a supply of items such as toiletries, bedding, brooms, undergarments, and school supplies, so that each time some small item is needed staff does not have to go out and buy it.

Girl rolling up her bedroll after inspection

Kitchen and food storage

Each home has a kitchen with at least a stove, refrigerator, sink with running water (ideally purified water), and storage shelves for stainless steel eating dishes (plates, cups, bowls, forks, knives, and spoons), and also cooking and serving dishes (pots, pans, large bowls, *chapati* [flat Indian bread] warmer, large serving spoons, etc.). Other kitchen equipment often includes an electric mixer, cutting boards, knives of different sizes, peelers, and other specialty equipment relative to regional foods. For example, in Kerala an *idli* maker will be on hand. (An *idli* is a rice pancake that is a common food in Kerala.) Each kitchen also has storage space for about one week's worth of fresh food, bins for flour, rice, and dal, and a supply of dried spices. Kitchens are kept clean at all times and food is used before it spoils, minimizing waste, flies, and the spread of disease. Compost consisting of vegetable trimmings and other food waste is kept outside and covered. There may also be an additional outdoor cooking place (such as one large burner with a fuel cylinder) and dishwashing area.

Kitchen: Ratnagiri

Staff, guest, and infirmary rooms

Housemothers sometimes have their own small room. If a social worker is in residence, she will have a small bedroom, and ideally there is a guest room for visitors. The guest room may double as an infirmary where an ill resident can be cared for.

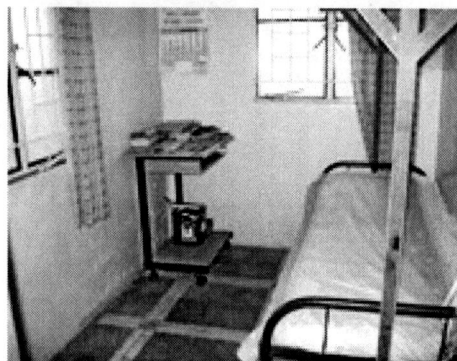
Typical social worker room

Office space

The office should be a room large enough for two or three desks, a phone, one or two computers, a printer (or, ideally a printer/copier), a storage battery for power failures, storage, and locking record cabinets. An Internet connection is required as well. The office should have extra chairs and space for several people to meet. It must have a door that can be closed and locked. This is not only to protect the computer and other electronics, but also to protect the privacy of the residents and their files. When new residents first arrive and are being interviewed, when counseling is needed, or when other requirements for privacy arise, this is the room that will be used. When guests come, including potential donors and government officials, it is helpful to have a quiet place to meet, with minimal interruptions and distractions. Ideally, the older children will learn to use computers for their schoolwork, so a computer for their use is advised. (It is suggested that this is not the same computer with all the NGO data and records.)

Physical Space of a Larger Facility With Multiple Homes

Each home is designed to stand alone, even when it is part of a larger complex such as at Vadhu Badruk. Bakori (see Chapter 1) is an example of a site with two separate homes within a single building, with shared garden, office, social worker and guestrooms, and play space. Each home has its own living area, kitchen area, storage areas, and washing area. All homes are generally designed for an average of 20 children with space for 2 housemothers, with the same characteristics as the single home described above. At Vadhu Badruk, a larger facility with nine homes, there is, in addition, a large outside space for celebrations and gatherings, as well as rooms for guests and a full infirmary. Here there are also common rooms for music, computers, and classes, as well as a common administrative office. (Refer to photo in Chapter 1)

CASE This is no ordinary institution

At Maher, the first sounds of the morning are not wake-up bells. The housemothers, and sometimes the older children too, go around to each child, gently nudging them to tell them it is time to wake up. Or perhaps a housemother will play some music, such as interfaith prayer songs. The morning schedule on school days includes prayers and meditation, yoga or other exercise, morning hygiene, breakfast, some chores (for example, washing or sweeping), and homework. Often, with mixed ages, children attend different schools with different start times for the housemothers to manage. The housemothers often walk the younger children to school. Sometimes the children come home for lunch and then hurry back to school. After school is snack time and more time for homework, chores, and play. Sometimes there are also extra classes on computers, dance, English, or tae kwon do, for example. Every child, beginning by about age 6, is given a little light housework, such as sweeping, cleaning, cutting vegetables, or making chapatis, to help him or her learn the skills and values of running a healthy happy home. Prayer precedes dinner, and everyone eats together.

When there are multiple homes, they are ideally close enough to each other that all can join together for community events, such as dance classes, birthdays, and holidays.

Schedules Contribute to Creating the Right Atmosphere

Daily Routine

Maher has learned that keeping to a very structured time schedule supports women and children who have lived through trauma or on the streets. Keeping busy helps to keep the mind from dwelling on painful memories, anger, or loss, so that children and women can more easily move on. The strictly scheduled time (even playtime is scheduled) also helps them learn about time management and discipline. This is standard at every Maher facility.

> **TIP** Just like a mother's home, Maher's doors are open 24/7, there is always room for one more, and guests are always welcome.

Sample schedule: Monday through Saturday

Time	Activity
5:00 a.m.	Wake up
5:15-5:30	Meditation and prayer
5:30 -7:00	Yoga, tae kwon do, etc. and study
7:00 -8:00	Bathing, clothes washing, chores
8:00	Breakfast
8:30 – 9:30	Homework and then off to school
4:00 – 5:00 p.m.	Return from school, snack
5:00 – 8:00	Chores, homework, classes, play
8:00 – 8:15	Prayer and meditation
8:15	Supper
8:45 – 10:00	Study, newspapers, games
10:00	Sleep

Note: this sample schedule applies to children. If you also have women in your home, they will generally follow the same schedule before and after school, helping with the care of the children as needed. See Chapter 8 for a discussion of activities for resident women during the day.

School in India is six days a week, Monday through Saturday, although Saturday school is only a half day, so the children come home about 1 p.m. Generally children walk to school, although housemothers may walk the younger children to school in the morning. Sometimes transportation is arranged. For example, SOFKIN (in the city) hires a van and a driver who drives the children to and from school each day. Some schools send the children home each day for lunch. Ultimately the timetable depends on the timing of the schools the children attend.

Sundays

Sundays the children are allowed to sleep an extra hour, but the day is still structured with things like homework, washing clothes, and studies in the arts such as music and dance. Sometimes community groups visit. If there are no visitors, the social workers organize games according to the age level of the children. There are different games each Sunday. Scores are kept, and the groups compete against each other. Boys and girls are together up to the 6th standard; thereafter they are separated for these activities. Sometimes there is an outing to somewhere entertaining and educational outside Maher. Once a month, there might be a DVD movie shown. Many of the houses have TV and can watch news or movies on Sunday afternoons.

Special daily activities

Meditation is a powerful tool for these women and children. It helps to balance the mind and calm the systems, so that they may heal from past trauma and the individual is better able to meet daily challenges. It is also a way to communicate privately with the Divine if one chooses. Whole community meditations are simple, essentially silence, and many gatherings begin this way.

Yoga and tae kwon do are taught to the children as well as many of the women and are included in daily routines as ways of harmonizing body, mind, and spirit.

> **TIP** Weekly home meetings are a good time to lead discussions on values. In preparation for a major holiday that will be celebrated, such as Divali, staff might ask the residents to call out what they think the underlying meaning of this holiday might be, and how these relate to the core values of the organization. Help them to talk about this in interfaith terms, such as celebrating the Illumining Light in each of our hearts, and perhaps discussing where there is darkness in their hearts and how each might release this.

Sample schedule for staff

The days are long and full for staff, and built around the children's school schedule.

Time	Activity
4:45 a.m.	Wake up
5:00 – 8:30/9:30	Supervise children's morning bathing, eating, dressing, chores, and homework, lead/send to exercise, lead prayers and meditation, walk younger children to school.
9:00 – 4:00 p.m.	Complete chores, bathing, clothes washing, cooking, administrative tasks, and errands; meetings with guests, officials, or other staff; taking classes
4:00 – 10:00 p.m.	Prepare snacks and supper; supervise play, homework, etc., for children

Meetings and gatherings

In a home with 10 to 20 children plus staff and any mothers, there is always a lot going on. Even in the early days of Maher, Sister Lucy met with the other women, and then later when there was staff, with them too, in order to hear what might have happened that day when she was out. Meetings are a way to let others know about something that happened, or about new rules to follow, etc. One of the children may have had something difficult happen at school, for example, and all the staff need to know. Sometimes the only time to meet is late in the evening when the children are in bed. The whole house (all children and adults) needs to gather regularly too, to resolve issues and to support each other, or even just to celebrate and enjoy each other's company. Based on experience, Maher now schedules regular meetings for these different purposes to keep the home running smoothly.

Housemeeting: all staff and residents

Weekly and monthly meetings
The chart below lists weekly and monthly meetings that are held at Maher homes. Note that the weekly home meetings are also an opportunity to talk about values, ethics, and interfaith spirituality. This will help the residents learn to interact as loving family members and prepare them to be good citizens and future leaders of the new India.

Meeting Name	Frequency	Who Attends	Purpose/what is covered
Staff meetings	Weekly	All staff	• Review each resident • How things are and any issues in the home • Upcoming events and plans
Home meetings	Weekly	All residents and staff	• How things are and any issues in the home • Upcoming events and plans, projects, etc. • Discussions/*satsang*[14] (for example, values or interfaith spirituality)
Small groups	Weekly	Different groups, such as teen girls or other child subgroups, meet with staff	• Progress reports • Issues or questions that arise • "Time with mother"
Women's meeting	Daily	Short-stay women plus housemothers with staff supervision and support	• Group meditation time • Issue resolution • Women's development
Parents' visiting day	Monthly	Parents of resident children, child, plus one staff member, usually	• Review each child resident's wellbeing, schoolwork, extracurricular activities, etc. • Time for parents and children to be together and share

---

[14] *Satsang* is an Indian tradition of keeping company with wise souls with the purpose of discerning truth. This is done through listening to or reading scriptures, reflecting on, discussing and assimilating meaning, and bringing that meaning into one's daily life.

Meals

The government child welfare office often proscribes menus. Three meals a day are required (one may be served at school). In India, a vegetarian diet is not required but is acceptable as long as milk is included daily. All the meals must include cooked grains and legumes or protein (soy protein is acceptable). Vegetables must be served daily and fruit two to three times per week. Staff must keep a record of every meal and every snack every day. Small samples of each meal must be set aside each day in case an inspector stops by. Check local regulations.

Meals at Maher are simple and nutritious. Generally a warm breakfast is served. Lunch is sometimes eaten at school, but if not the children come home to Maher for lunch. Then Maher provides an afternoon snack and a warm dinner. Meals are primarily vegetarian, with *chapatis,* (flat Indian bread, usually wheat) rice, and *dal* (beans) as staples, plus vegetables or potatoes daily. This varies by region, local food habits, and seasonal availability. Warm milk is served daily or at least most days of the week. Dried soy proteins are sometimes used as well. Fruit and eggs are available at least a few days a week. Most of the children have not eaten many vegetables or fruits before Maher, so these foods need to be introduced creatively and tastily so that the children learn to enjoy balanced diets. Occasionally chicken may be served as a treat.

TIP Just as in real families, the children see and smell the food being lovingly prepared by the housemothers. Slowly they learn to help, from chopping vegetables, to stirring a large pot, to making chapatis. And they also learn to clean up (both boys and girls). Children are encouraged to try everything served and to eat a balanced diet, even when some foods are not their favorite. As in any family, children will have favorite foods, and the housemother might cook a favorite on that child's birthday.

The teenage girls often help with meal preparation, learning to cook from their "mothers" just as if they were at home, including the art of *chapati*-making. When guests come, all residents help prepare extra food or chai (Indian tea), and welcome any guests. In most Maher homes, meals are eaten sitting on the floor, children, staff, and guests eating together. Older children help serve. There is always enough to eat and children can have additional servings if they are still hungry, although they are taught not to waste food. After eating, everyone scrapes any food still on their plate into the compost bucket and washes their own dishes.

Everyone says a short interfaith prayer together before meals. Here is an example, loosely translated: "Oh lord. Thank you for this food. Bless all the people here, our children and families. Guide us, give us success in our work here." Some homes sing their meal prayer.

Housemother and girls making chapatis

Mealtime

Purchasing Food and Basic Household Stocks

Planning ahead and keeping appropriate quantities of all food and supplies on hand is a challenge. There must be a balance between having some extras to meet arising needs and having items go to waste or spoil. Household items, such as cleaning supplies, toiletries, bedding, clothing, and personal care items, are also bought (or collected) in quantities so there are always extra in storage to provide to a new arrival or to replace something used up.

Shopping for food and household items

On market day, one week's worth of fresh vegetables is purchased, rather than making daily trips. Dry goods are purchased in large quantities and often delivered.

Basic food that should be stocked by all homes

(Note that this list will need to be adapted according to local foods and diets.)

Rice
Wheat
Jowari (Indian grain, high protein)
Flattened rice (*Poha*)
Dal (beans)
Jaggery (form of sugar cane)
Cooking oil
Vegetables
Fruits
Biscuits and snacks
Eggs
Milk
Tea powder
Salt
Sugar
Spices

Clothing and personal items for residents

Donations of clothing, ideally clean and in good repair, are solicited, and a supply is kept on hand. These must be sorted as they arrive. Unfortunately many donated items are either too stained or worn or are otherwise inappropriate. Useful items should be sorted and stored by size. Preferably these are stored as full suits of clothing (that is, a top and a bottom) but this is not always possible for children's play clothes. As a child needs a new or replacement set, there is a ready supply. Younger children often wear western pants and tops, as these are frequently donated. As the girls enter their teen years, they may be given cloth to have a full *salwar kameez* suit (traditional Indian long tunic top and pants) stitched new for them at the local tailor.

> **TIP** It is important to be frugal with resources and to repair and reuse items whenever possible. One girl's book bag had a broken zipper, so staff took it to a tailor to replace the zipper. Other girls' bags were threadbare. Using a heavy cotton nightie that had been donated but was much too big, staff cut pieces and relined and reinforced the bags. The older girls sewed the patches by hand. The bags will last another few months this way.

Clothing checklist for children (minimum)

3 school uniforms

3 sets daily wear/play clothes

1-2 new suits for special occasions

1 pair socks

1 petticoat, 2 slips (girls)

2 undergarments (knickers)

School supplies checklist for children

Backpack or book bag

Pencil case and pencils

Chalkboard and chalk (younger children)

Paper notebooks, pens (older children)

Schoolbooks (the children often cover these in newspaper to protect them)

Other items school requires

Clothing checklist for women

Married women in India traditionally wear a sari, but the choice is left to them. Saris, sari slips, and blouses, as well as *salwar kameez*, are kept on hand for new arrivals.

Toiletries

Hair oil

Bath soap and shampoo

Toothbrush

Toothpaste

Comb

Menstrual pads

Clothes washing powder

Health and Wellness

Just like in any family, physical and mental health of members is monitored on an ongoing basis. Medical exams are given within one to two days of arrival for all women and children, according to government requirement. Children then have annual medical checkups, generally just before the start of the new school year. Careful records are kept of all injuries, illnesses, medications, and treatments. Girls' menstrual records are kept as well. Regular checkups for all residents include general health, dental, eye, and ear care.

Immunizations (vaccines) required for children are:

- Measles
- Mumps
- Rubella
- Hepatitis-B
- Polio
- Diphtheria
- Tetanus
- Whooping Cough (Pertussis)
- Typhoid

Maher's main site is large enough to warrant a full-time nurse, who oversees the health of the nearly 300 people who live at Vadhu Badruk. She also supports the other sites in the greater Pune area. For smaller sites, it is important to build relationships with local clinics, hospitals, and doctors for immunizations, checkups, and medical issues that

TIP Sometimes, instead of taking each resident individually for a checkup, medical people can come to the NGO site to give all the needed checkups. For example, a team of eye doctors may come on a Saturday afternoon to give all the children vision tests and general eye exams.

require more than basic motherly first aid. Schedule regular health, dental, eye, and ear checkups for residents.

Ayurvedic practices are the first line of health care. Accordingly, dietary, hygiene, nutritional, and exercise guidelines are followed, and emotional and social wellbeing are attended to. Ayurvedic practices are followed and herbal remedies are included with first aid supplies. Housemothers must know the basics, such as:

- Drink warm water every morning to encourage a "clean stomach" (to support good digestion); at SOFKIN, cumin seeds are soaked for one hour in warm water for the same purpose

- How to clean, treat, and bandage wounds and sores

- For fevers, use cool water and cloth to wipe and cool the body, and possibly give paracitamol

- For coughs, prepare turmeric in warm milk

- For skin issues give *neem*[15] paste or bath

- For head lice, take preventative action to keep the house very clean and use Ayurvedic medicine in hair oil to control the lice (children are exposed at school)

- Daily multivitamins and vitamins C and B complex if there are general health issues; if children are healthy vitamins are not needed

Many residents arrive with conditions that are the result of poor hygiene or psychological or emotional problems. First aid kits are in every home, and the housemothers are trained in basic first aid.

- Sample first aid kit includes iodine, cotton, boric powder, Betadine, sulfur powder, bandages, antibiotic salve, neem paste, paracitamol, loose motion syrup, cough syrup, worm medicine, anti-nausea (for vomiting) medicine, and antacids for digestion.

- Basic first aid training includes at least: loose motion, fevers, coughs, minor accidents and falls, skin problems (such as scabies), and lice.

---

[15] Neem is a plant whose leaves are useful for alleviating a variety of skin disorders, including itching and blemishes.

Home Rules and Behavior Guidelines

Almost all of the following rules and behaviors have their foundations in the core values.

Unconditional love for all, demonstrated by:

- Every resident is seen and valued as an individual; no bullying, making fun of, shunning, name calling, etc.

- Everyone looks out for and helps one another, as family members

- Discipline is learning-focused, rather than punishment-focused

- Understand each other's mistakes, do not hold anger or hurt in the heart

- Nonviolent problem solving

- No partiality to any caste, religion, language, or gender

- All eat the same food, together, from the same dishes

- Speak the commonly shared language

- Share and participate equally and respectfully in all holidays, respecting observances of different religions (for example, headdress for Muslim women are allowed)

- All prayers are interfaith

Cleanliness and good hygiene are followed and reinforced at all times:

• Clothes clean and neat

• Bathe and brush teeth daily

• Wash hands before eating

• Follow good toilet habits

• Keep hair neat and wash daily (unless too cold in winter), also oil daily if choose

• Cut fingernails and toenails regularly

• Wash dishes well, store in correct place

• Homes kept neat (cupboards tidy, clothes folded, books and toys put away) and clean (sweeping, washing floors, washing food), etc.

Everyone behaves as a good citizen:

• No lying, stealing, cheating, or harming of others

• Honesty expected and rewarded

• On-time arrival at school, meals, programs, daily meditation, etc.

• All students do their best at school

• Competition is to inspire best in each other, gracefully acknowledging winners

• Resident privacy respected; individual records and history kept confidential

Respect for nature:

• Resources, such as food, water, and energy, are not wasted

• Manmade materials such as plastic, aluminum, books, and clothes are used sparingly and recycled when no longer usable

• Plants are well cared for

Other:

• No tobacco, alcohol, or drugs

• Limited mobile phone usage

These home rules and guidelines may be more challenging for some residents than for others. It can be difficult to convince children to follow these good habits when they have lived on the street or in the slums for long. The older the children are when they arrive, the more accustomed they are to doing what they want whenever they want. And if they had little access to clean water or to toilets, how could they have learned good hygiene? You must be patient with these children (and women too). It is easier to work with village or city children as they have more likely been exposed to more of these good habits at home. Similarly, for the women, how easily they can adapt to these rules depends on where and how they lived before. For example, Sister Lucy has found that prostitutes are less likely to settle and be content at Maher. They come thinking it will be good for their children, but they cannot bear the rules and schedules: they miss their freedom, so they leave.

Conflict Resolution

Conflict resolution is essentially heart-based, and always guided by the core values. If there is a conflict between a child and a housemother, first listen to the housemother and to the child separately to understand the issue and what each side needs. If one is clearly incorrect, instruct them. If you need to correct the housemother, do so only one-to-one, not in front of the child. Teach the child about the housemother role, and that in addition to loving her children, like a mother, it is also the housemother's job to correct the children. Support the housemother's authority. Then, if a meeting is needed, set it up. Pray for five minutes together at the start of the meeting, and then guide them to speak with and listen to each other. Help each to say "sorries" when appropriate, such as for not listening, breaking rules, or losing patience. Make agreements about future

---

CASE When house rules and religious practices or cultural traditions collide: a delicate balance

For daily living at Maher, rules of religious traditions (especially those that are more culturally based) are not enforced. For example, many women ask staff, "If I have my monthly bleeding can I still participate in prayer and meditation?" Many villagers and Hindus believe women are dirty when they are having their monthly bleeding. Therefore, they are not allowed in temples and may not cook food, or sometimes even enter the kitchen. Others go to prayers without regard to these concerns. At Maher, staff teaches the women and girls that they are always pure, and all are encouraged to come to sit together for prayer (and to cook) every day. However, these are deep-seated beliefs, so you will have to be patient.

There are disagreements among staff about what to teach the children. Sister Lucy supports both perspectives. Village life is hard and women need the rest, so let this tradition of not participating in daily prayer continue, respect it. But Maher children may get jobs in the cities, and they may be fired if they do not show up because of having a period. So the children have to know both worlds. She teaches too that their period is a sacred gift from God. How else will they have children? So both ways of being are "right." The children need to learn how to be in the modern world, while still respecting the traditional ways.

interactions and what behaviors are appropriate. Support expressions of love between the housemother and the child.

A similar process is followed in child-to-child or woman-to-woman conflicts. First listen to each individual to see what is going on. Often you can do this with both present, each person knowing she will get her turn to speak. Staff may provide teaching to both at once, helping them to understand what is important. Tell or remind them about NGO values and goals and how these will affect their lives. For example: "This is your sister." Teach them that actions and choices have consequences. Again, help each to say, "I'm sorry" as appropriate. Sit for prayer or meditation together. Eat together. Laugh together. Smaller girls may kiss each other, showing they love each other, just as the housemother loves them.

Special challenges with women and children from trauma

When conflicts arise, remember the experiences these people had before coming to you. Most have survived trauma and are still learning how to live now that they are safe. The shorter the time at Maher and the older the person, the more likely she is still under the effects of her past. Be patient, loving, nonjudgmental, and compassionate, like the most loving mother you can imagine, while still being firm with what is okay and what is not. Work or school studies which require concentration and quiet,

are difficult for these women and children to tolerate. When they sit still, the painful memories and thoughts arise, so they want to play and dance and forget, or even run. Sometimes they act out in anger from the hurt. Meditation, yoga, and tae kwon do help with this, as does a structured routine with activities mixed in with the homework times. Also, programs, such as music, dance, and gardening, help keep the memories, anger, and fear at bay. When these feelings do erupt into conflict, as is inevitable, help them learn to speak about what is bothering them and to resolve issues without violence. This teaches them ways to manage and to grow.

Celebrations

At Maher it seems there is always some event for the residents to look forward to. It could be a birthday (whether of a resident or of a special role model such as Mother Theresa or Gandhi), a national holiday (such as Independence Day), a holiday of one of the many local religions, or Maher Day (Maher's anniversary). These events accomplish multiple goals:

- Respectful and fun celebrations

- Respect for all local religions

- Educational, with an essay contest, or by sharing the underlying interfaith value behind a particular religious holiday

- To teach and demonstrate core values such as interfaith respect, sharing, and good sportsmanship

- Community outreach (guests are often invited)

Special events, celebrations, and holidays observed at Maher

Below is a list of the events the full community of Maher celebrates. This will vary by region and country. Note that friends of Maher may be invited to any of these, as a thank you, and as honored guests. Trustees often come as well. Hindu and Muslim celebration dates are based on a lunar calendar, so the exact date varies each year.

TIP When big celebrations are held, it is hard to supervise all the children. Housemothers need to keep them busy and also to lock up the extra rooms so there is no chance for any children to hide away and do things they are not supposed to do. Any sexual activity among the children would lead to closure of the NGO.

TIP Respect local realities in your planning. For example: the date of Divali varies depending on the Hindu (lunar) calendar. One year, Divali was during the sugar cane harvest and many children had gone home to help with the harvest. Social workers went to visit each of the families and invited them all to Maher for Divali. Whole families were fed, given small gifts, and honored.

A holiday celebration gathering

Date	Event	Type	What happens, who is invited	Sample teaching points
Jan. 26	Republic Day	National	Each home does its own activities, usually involving flag ceremony, speeches, and sweets for the children	
Feb. 2	Maher Day	Maher Anniversary	All homes come together for celebration that includes games, speech competition, and a shared meal; friends of Maher invited	Always do your best, be grateful for what Maher has given, and seek to share with others
Feb. 19	Shivaji Maharaj	Hindu	Each home does its own activities, usually involving speech competitions to commemorate this Hindu king who freed the Marathi people from Mughal rule; school holiday	History, value of religious peaceful coexistence
Mar. 8	International Women's Day	International	Some women, social workers, and village self-help groups go together to big rally in Pune	Exposure to women's issues, including women's rights and ending violence toward women and girls
Mar. - Apr.	Gudi Padwa	Hindu Lunar New Year	Each home begins day with special morning prayers and preparation of traditional foods	Reflect on accomplish-ments and "victories" and goals for the next year
End of school term (Apr.)	Sports Camp	Maher	All homes come together; four days of sports competitions	Pride in doing one's best, good sportsmanship

Date	Event	Type	What happens, who is invited	Sample teaching points
Jul. 23	Savritribai	State	Savritri started education for girls in state of Maharashtra during British rule; often focus on "Each One Teach One" literacy program	Value of education, girls' right to be educated
Aug. 15	Indepen-dence Day	National	Each home does its own activities, usually involving a flag ceremony, speeches, and sweets for the children	Practice writing and public speaking
Aug. 26	Mother Theresa's Birthday	International	Each home does its own activities, beginning with special morning prayers; large photo of Mother Theresa near the altar	Recall Mother Theresa's virtues and qualities; ask how we can demonstrate them
Aug.-Oct.	Eid al-Fitr Eid al-Adha	Muslim	Each home has special morning prayers, prepares traditional sweets; basics of Islam and the holiday explained; Muslim residents may go home to family	Highlight Muslim charitable practices and empathy for the poor; ask how we as well can help others
Aug. - Sept.	Krishna's Birthday	Hindu	Each home does its own activities, begin with special morning prayers; often an earthen pot with curds and prizes is hung up for the children to burst and get treats	Good sportsmanship and teamwork
Sept.	Ganesha Festival	Hindu	Each home does its own activities, beginning with special morning prayers; on day 1 of 10 day festival baby Ganesha is put in a crib in the home; traditional sweets prepared each day	Cultivate qualities of good listening, especially to those weaker; removing obstacles
Oct. 2	Gandhi's Birthday	National	Each home does its own activities, usually speech competitions	Value of truth and nonviolence
Oct. – Nov.	Divali	Hindu	Each home begins five-day holiday with special morning prayers and candle procession; Hindu residents may go home to family	Nurture the light within ourselves and others

Date	Event	Type	What happens, who is invited	Sample teaching points
Nov. 20	International Children's Day	International (also Nehru's Birthday)	Children in Pune area, including kindergartens, slum classes, and local village children, gather for speeches, dance, games and homemade treats	Celebrate the potential in each child, regardless of caste, gender, or religion
Dec. 24/25	Christmas Eve and Day	Christian	Christmas Eve candlelight ceremony, everyone gathers for Christmas Day to share special meal, prayer, performances; gifts for every resident (generally needed items like clothes, soap, towel); school holiday for English-medium children only; all families, past Maher residents, trustees invited	Essence of the Christmas story is love; how this is demonstrated in our lives

CASE Maher Day and awards

Maher Day offers a special opportunity for awards. The purpose of all these awards is to inspire "others to achieve so they too can be honored," says Sister Lucy. You can develop awards and ceremonies appropriate for the NGO, the culture, and the values you wish to promote. All awards are given on stage with a small gift, often presented by a trustee as well as Sister Lucy.

- *Best house award, judged on things like cleaning, studies, gardening, neat cupboards, etc.*
- *Best child award, character evaluated, linked to Maher values, such as not fighting, not being lazy, not back-sassing, showing respect to elders, and helping each other without being told*
- *Best studies award, for any children who won awards at school*
- *Best social worker award*
- *Best housemother award*
- *Best driver or worker award*

Unique qualities of Maher homes, according to the housemothers:

- Maher is a family atmosphere.

- All children are loved, as members of a family.

- Cleanliness is taught and valued.

- The food tastes good and includes vegetables and variety and there is always enough.

- Time management: our time is organized, but playtime is also scheduled.

- Children have music, dance, competitions, trips, and sometimes even movies.

- There are games, outings, and gifts for housemothers (for example, after three years and after five years here there is a celebratory picnic).

- Children may be punished, occasionally even slapped, for wrongdoing, but never beaten.

- The children are never afraid to ask for things, and when they do ask for things such as help with homework, advice, or company, they get it. In fact, social workers and housemothers watch the children to anticipate needs, especially new, traumatized, or shy children.

- Staff takes time for the children and women—they are available 24/7.

- Maher is very welcoming and people are warm and supportive, more so even than other places run by nuns. (It is also partly Sister Lucy's smile.) There is no differentiation between rich and poor; all guests and residents are treated the same.

- Sports camp for all Maher children is unique and wonderful.

- There are naming ceremonies and birthdays for all of the children.

Summary

Creating a heart-centered home is the essence of the Maher model. Design of the space, schedules, meals, rules, and celebrations, are all part of creating a heart-centered home. Ultimately everything is planned for the wellbeing of the women and children who come to Maher for refuge, love, and a new life, rather than for staff convenience or even cost effectiveness. Further discussion of heart-centered operations, family life, and discipline can be found in Chapter 10, "The Art and Genius of Maher."

Office Administration and Recordkeeping

The NGO will need to maintain an office. In addition to setting up the physical space, what should you be thinking about?

The office will often be the first room that newcomers see, whether they are prospective clients or donors, government officials, or neighbors. Think about what message you want to convey: a warm welcome, cleanliness, orderly records and information, and easy access to information about the NGO, at the least. Be sure this room is easily accessible to the road and bright and inviting. Staff or someone should be nearby at all times in case visitors should arrive. Brochures describing the vision, mission, and values of the NGO, as well as current goals and accomplishments, should be on display and available to hand out. Artwork created by residents might decorate the walls, as well as newspaper articles about the NGO, photos, and awards. You might also post a list of current donations needed, especially items for the women or children. Licenses for operation should be posted as well.

Administration involves a great deal of recordkeeping and reporting, as well as monitoring overall operations.

Recordkeeping

The need for financial recordkeeping was addressed earlier. Detailed and accurate recordkeeping in every realm of your work is mandatory, both to meet government requirements and to satisfy donors and others regarding proper stewardship of NGO clients and resources. Various government offices (such as child welfare authorities) require a great deal of documentation regarding people and resources to assure that residents under care are well treated and that NGO staff are neither pocketing resources meant for the needy nor abusing people under their care. Running a good NGO includes the paperwork necessary to provide evidence of happy children and other clients.

CASE Government inspectors are wary for good reason!

There is a story of an NGO that had records of several hundred children, with, in reality, only fifty residents. On inspection day, after bribery of local officials for advance notice of the inspection, staff paid over a hundred slum children Rs. 50 each to come for the day and say they lived there, attended school, and ate well. There are many stories like this, and probably not only in India.

Recordkeeping has been a huge challenge for Maher. At Maher, the current system is primarily paper based, which is labor intensive and makes it difficult to access, summarize, or analyze data consistently. However, many government offices still require handwritten registers that they can check during unannounced visits, so paper books are here for the foreseeable future. Check your local area to see what is required.

In order to help standardize recordkeeping so that information is gathered in a consistent manner, templates have been developed for some of the primary records listed in the table below. The templates are designed to be easily convertible to computerized versions; even at Maher some records are now being computerized. Staff will eventually have to learn how to use the computer systems. For foreign and corporate donors, computerized records and reporting in certain formats will be very helpful. Maher is being gently pushed to improve their recordkeeping

in order to satisfy the requests of some of these larger donors. This has become necessary as Maher grows exponentially rather than gradually.

Sister Lucy greeting children of Ratnagiri

List of recordkeeping performed at Maher

List A: Client related

Record name	Who fills it out	How often	Required by government?	Purpose, content summary
Admission register for children	Social worker	Arrival	Yes[16]	Demographics and final disposition (see Chapter 9)
Admission register for women	Social worker	Arrival	Yes	Demographics and final disposition (see Chapter 8)
Admission file	Social worker	Arrival	Yes	All admission paperwork;(for Women see Chapter 8; for Children see Chapter 9)
Residential certificate		Arrival	Yes	Proof child lived at home address listed; part of admission file
CWC permission form	CWC	Arrival, then renewed as required by CWC	Yes	Permission to keep child for specified time period; part of admission file
Medical file for each woman and each child	Social worker	At arrival, updated for every illness, injury, checkup, medication, or treatment	Yes	Initial medical checkup plus all later medical treatments and checkups
Girls' menstrual register	Housemother	Monthly	Yes	Every period start and stop date
Medicine distribution register	Social worker	As medications distributed	Yes	Prescription medicines from doctor, each dose recorded with date
Children's attendance register	Housemother	Daily	Yes	"P" for every day present

[16] If "Yes," unless otherwise noted, the government office requiring the records is the Welfare Office, or its subsidiary office, the Child Welfare Committee (CWC). The Welfare office licenses Women's homes, and the CWC oversees all child welfare issues and NGOs who work with children. Every country will have similar government entities.

Record name	Who fills it out	How often	Required by government?	Purpose /content
Women's attendance register	Social worker	Daily	Yes	"P" for every day present, note if women leave even for part of one day
Observation register	Housemother	Updated as needed; monthly short summary for each child	Yes	Notations of behaviors, such as not eating or sleeping, or fighting; included in case file
School summary report register	Housemother	Every two months	Yes	Grades for each class every two months, summarized yearly; included in case file
Home visit reports	Social worker	Updated with every home visit or contact	Yes	Full record of observations of home and family, actions taken, recommendations, etc.; used in making decisions about returning children home and for women's reconciliations
Parent, grandparent, or guardian meeting register	Staff	Each meeting	Yes	Date, time, relative's name, relationship to child, child's name, signatures of social worker and relative
Savings register for residents' personal accounts	Director	As deposits or withdrawals made	No	Keep track of bank accounts that Maher maintains for women and children

List B: Home related

Record name	Who fills it out	How often	Required by government?	Purpose/content
Guest register	Staff	Any overnight guests	Yes	Date, name, address, purpose of visit, departure date; passport and visa numbers for foreigners
Welcome register	Staff	Any non-Maher person who comes, including electrician, dance teacher, etc.	Yes	Date, name, address, purpose, remarks
Government official visits register	Staff	Any time government official comes	Yes	Date, name/role, observations about NGO
Staff attendance record	Staff	Daily	Yes (Labor Commissioner Office)	"P" for each day present
Phone usage register	Staff	As needed	No	Phone calls children make – so know to whom, for their safety
Incoming letter register	Staff	As letters received by children	Yes	Date, from whom, contact information – for children's safety
Letters sent register	Staff	As letters sent by or on behalf of children	Yes	
Postage register	Staff	As needed	Yes	Must match letters sent
Menu register	Housemother-cook	Daily	Yes	All meals and snacks served
Dietary register	Housemother-cook	Every meal	Yes	Daily foods for each meal, time served, quantity per person (differs above and below 12 years old)
Milk register	Housemother-cook	Daily	Yes	Date, quantity bought, from whom, price
Vegetable register (includes rice, *dal*, wheat, etc.)	Housemother-cook	All food purchases	No	Date, item, amount purchased, price

Record name	Who fills it out	How often	Required by government?	Purpose/ content
Grinding register	Housemother-cook	As needed	No	How much wheat ground each date
Stock list: general supplies	Housemother	At start, plus any purchases noted	Yes	Cleaning supplies, etc.
Stock list: equipment	Housemother	At start, plus any purchases or losses noted	Yes	All equipment, pots and pans, furnishings, office supplies, etc.
Educational materials, bedding, clothing, and toiletries stock register	Staff	As purchase supplies, reconcile monthly with distributions	Yes	All goods bought, date, and price
Toiletries, bedding, clothes, and educational materials distribution register	Staff	As needed	Yes	Each child has own page(s); items given, date, signature of child (toiletries, school supplies, bedding, clothing, etc.); must match education materials stock register
Library stock register	Staff	As needed	No	All books and materials in library
Library book check-out register	Staff	As needed	No	Books taken out by which child and date taken and returned
Toys register	Staff	As needed	No, but CWC often asks	What toys are on site, and which given to children
Gas cylinder register	Staff	As needed	No	Expenditures, date, and price
Vehicle maintenance register	Staff	As needed	No	Expenditures, date, and price

Programs and meeting records

Record name	Who fills it out	How often	Required by government?	Purpose / content summary
Programs for children	Director	As needed	No	Program name, date, purpose/objective
Programs for women	Director	As needed	No	Program name, date, purpose/objective
Outreach programs	Director	As needed	No	Program name, date, purpose/objective, location, how many attended
Programs attended by staff at other organizations	Director	As needed	No	Program name, date, purpose/objective, location, who attended
Staff meetings register	Director	As needed	No	Date, main agenda items
Trustee meetings file	Director	As needed	Yes	Copies of approved minutes, including all decisions made

Some of these registers may only ever be looked at in the case of an inspection. Others contain critical information that will be used to develop reports useful for tracking and analyzing NGO performance. Others are useful for reference when summarizing NGO activities and outcomes. Additional registers collecting financial information such as donations and expenditures were discussed in Chapter 5.

Some registers carefully control stock to guard against theft. Sister Lucy has said that for many stealing has become a habit of survival and if it is too easy, they will be tempted. Keeping extra stock locked away with all the registers helps people make good choices and learn new habits.

Maintaining all these records is a tremendous amount of work. Find out which of these local government bodies require and which are required for financial and other reports to the government and to trustees. Finally, remember that these registers help provide the transparency that is a core value at Maher. It is easy to see how the money is spent, down to every rupee.

Examples of how some of the above records are used for reporting

Narrative reports for trustees and donors:

- Annual summary of information on women, including how many were admitted, left to work, returned home, are working at Maher, have completed training, sheltered in Maher, (re)married, and died (from Women's Admission Register)

- Services for women (list of offerings and programs)

- Annual summary of information on children, including how many were admitted, returned home, sheltered at Maher, in school, younger than school age, left for other institutions, received training (from Children's Admission Register)

- Services for children (list of offerings and programs)

- Services and outreach (services and outreach offered to which groups other than residents)

- Trainings and workshops attended by staff (date, place, training, objectives, who attended)

- Awards won by staff, by residents, and by groups (such as Best House or a sports team)

Standard Site Inspection

The government is allowed to perform surprise inspections of any facility it licenses. Doing your own periodic spot inspections is a good way to protect the NGO from being shut down after a failed inspection. It also helps assure that staff is operating the NGO as required; your standards may be higher than the government. This is especially important if the founder is not living and working on site daily. The Maher director inspects every site once or twice each year.

While this author had no access to government inspectors, Maher's internal inspections can be a good model for preparing for a governmental inspection. The inspection is very detailed. The

---

CASE Inspection benefits

At one site, two 7-year-old girls from the same class had Jesus storybooks in their book bag. Their schoolteacher had given the books to them. Maher staff removed these and made a note to talk to the teacher immediately. If the children's Hindu parents had seen these, they would assume Maher was trying to convert their children. They would possibly remove the children and even file complaints against Maher.

director checks to be sure all is as it should be, and notes areas where staff must improve. This is also a good chance to note what needs the site has for goods, stocks, etc.

Sample inspection summary

- All registers and record books checked for accuracy and if up-to-date, with complete information (including case and medical files)

- Money recorded in all registers and bank account balances

- Children's clothes, bedroll, and schoolbook bags individually examined for contents, cleanliness, repairs, etc.

- Food storeroom examined for cleanliness; food supply checked for quantity and quality; meals and menus reviewed for nutrition, waste, etc.

- Back stock of donated clothing, school supplies, and other items checked for organization and sufficiency to meet needs of current residents and anticipated new arrivals

- Building assessed for condition and cleanliness and properly functioning lights and plumbing

- School-age children meet with director one at a time; director asks how they are feeling, whether they are happy here, how their family is, whether there are any troubles here or at home or anything they would like to tell us; children below 1st standard are assumed to be okay

- All children as a group meet with director, without staff, in case they need to say something about a staff person

- Director meets one-to-one with every staff person

- All staff as a group meet with director

- Whole community together meets with director; director asks children questions and listens closely to the children; reviews staff roles so that children have clear understanding; may assign some roles to the older children

Community Outreach

Having good relationships with the community is a key factor to NGO success in many ways.

Who is "the community?"
Community can be interpreted broadly and may include the geographical village or area where facilities are located as well as parents and relatives of residents, local businesses and service clubs (such as Rotary), local leadership and law enforcement, trustees, donors (Indian and foreign), and any other supporters of the NGO.

What are the benefits?
Good neighbor relations will help ease community problem solving that may be

needed, make children feel safer, and make expanding NGO operations easier. Also, families with troubles will come to you for help instead of falling into violence. When children cannot be cared for and educated at home, they will be brought to you instead of ending up in the fields or on the streets.

When emergencies happen, such as a lease being denied, someone needing expensive medical treatment, or the need for new bedding for a new group of children, you have friends you can call who will jump to action. As an example, Weikfield Company is a loyal friend of Maher. Sister Lucy tells me that she can call and ask for 100 umbrellas for the children at the start of the rainy season, and the umbrellas will arrive that afternoon. They will send bags of rice as needed, or custard powder. (Custard

TIP India has recently begun a corporate social responsibility program requiring all companies over a certain size to spend a percentage of their profits on charitable projects. Many other countries may have similar programs. This can be a great source of funds and support. Companies may not know how to select NGOs doing real and beneficial work. You have all the data to prove your results. Go make contacts and ask for support under this program.

powder is a product Weikfield manufactures and is a favorite dessert of the children.) The owners and leaders of companies like Weikfield in turn appreciate the work Maher is doing and the opportunity to give back to their community. They also benefit by having a source of dependable workers.

Summary of benefits:

- Good relations mean that when issues arise it is much easier to discuss problems and come to a resolution.

- Being known and respected in the community leads to referrals of potential residents, potential brides or grooms, and potential jobs for clients and their families.

- Women and families may seek assistance or mediation before the problems are so severe that a woman and her children must flee.

- When emergencies arise, there are supporters at hand to call on for assistance.

- Achieving the NGO's overarching purpose requires reaching many more people than the residents. With good community relations, more will listen and learn. Slowly attitudes, behaviors, and beliefs will change too.

There are many ways to develop positive relations with neighbors as well as with the community or village around a home. However, it takes planned and focused work. To this end, guests are encouraged and welcomed in many ways, and many programs for community benefit are offered.

Outreach Methods

Holidays (any of the special occasions listed earlier) and sponsoring

TIP Each Maher children's home also functions as a crisis and referral center for women in that village (and neighboring villages). When Maher starts a children's home in a village, the news is spread that women are welcome to come there when they are in trouble in any way. Sister Lucy will often get a call from a village-based home with news that there is a woman who showed up during the night needing help. Maher will help, generally sending a vehicle to pick up the woman and bring her to Maher's main site. In this way, the housemothers out in the villages act as social workers. They are trained in crisis management (through a course offered in Pune). If your NGO is offering only children's homes, you may want to have contacts with alternative places where you can refer such women until your operation expands.

competitions for local children in sports or essay writing can be wonderful opportunities to invite local families for a fun, festive, and even educational introduction to your NGO.

Short, one- to two-hour awareness programs are excellent ways to begin connecting with people. Food and tea is served and a topic, such as hygiene, AIDS awareness, or alcoholism, is discussed. Sometimes villagers are told they will get a free wool blanket if they come to listen to an awareness talk. Be sure to bring extra blankets so that no one goes home without one. (Additional information on this and other programs can be found in the final chapter, the Appendix, and on the website).

Other examples of Maher outreach programs

The Kerala Project holds "study circles" every second Saturday and invites village children to come together with Maher children. There are talks on different topics, such as the environment, alcohol, health, or interfaith spirituality. There are often guest speakers. They also hold competitions for singing, and the Maher children compete against the non-Maher children. Food is served. Village children are also invited to festivals such as Gandhi's Birthday, Kerala Day, New Year's Day, and Christmas. Sister Lucy offers a further reason why these other children are important to include too. "Our children feel they receive so much and they like the opportunity to give. It makes them so happy."

Maher offers classes in the villages and slums. These include afterschool tutoring and classes in adult literacy, classical Indian dance, and skills such as tailoring, and kindergarten teaching. Maher residents teach these classes, or sometimes Maher hires a local teacher. Recently, as Maher's first children are attending college and university, they wish to give back, so many of them now teach classes in dance, tae kwon do, etc. to village children or other local groups.

Maher also offers to have the children come to perform dance or music at events of friendly local corporations.

Be creative. Listen to local needs. Experiment. There are endless ways of developing productive relationships with your community.

Village Politics

In India, if you are thinking of working in one or more villages then you absolutely must build relationships with and gain the trust and respect of village leaders. They, more than any central government body, will determine what kind of access the NGO will have to the village and how successful you will be. Often the central governmental bodies do not go out to the villages, or if they do it is rare. Therefore, in reality, the village leaders rule. Every village is different, based on the personality and traditions of that particular village. You cannot simply arrive and tell them what is good for them, their families, or their neighbors. If the NGO arrives with a lot of gifts, money, and programs, they may smile and nod, but life will quickly go back to traditional ways as soon as you are gone. If you move in, they will be politely, even warmly, welcoming, but they will not come to you with their troubles or their needs, let alone their children.

Maher has learned to start small and slowly, by listening first and seeking to understand. Staff is respectful of village elders and leaders and follows their advice about what the village needs, even when staff does not agree. Once there is a relationship, Maher can begin to suggest changes and new ideas. This

---

CASE Wise recognition of village politics

While this author was visiting Maher, there was a new "head man" elected in Vadhu village. Maher held a special ceremony to welcome him and his aides. The staff and children greeted these men as honored guests. The children performed a short dance in their honor, and food and tea were served. This is a good practice for Maher, because the relationship will start off well and not wait until problems arise.

is the essence of "we see how it is," a core Maher value. Soon the leaders will see the NGO as a partner in their village. Together you can do most anything!

Guests

According to Indian tradition, guests are warmly welcomed, respected, and always offered at least Indian tea. When honored guests arrive, Maher usually organizes a greeting from the children, during which they sing welcome songs and offer _aarti_ (bathing in light). A flower _mala_ (a necklace of either fresh flowers or flowers constructed out of scraps of colorful materials) is often given as well. Then the younger children rush to hug the guest. Sister Lucy or a senior staff person always makes time to talk to them, learn why they have come, show them around if they like, and serve in whatever way possible. Any guest, even a first-time guest, is a possible lifelong friend and supporter of Maher's mission.

Local people who wish to help support the NGO are encouraged to come on Sundays, as the children are not in school. They sometimes come to play games with the children, or they may hire a bus and take the children on an outing. Some even come to celebrate their birthday at Maher, bringing cake, sweets, or food for all, and the Maher children sing to them. Often these guests fall in love with Maher and become faithful supporters, providing donations of money or goods, time, talents, and love. Be creative in providing opportunities for guests to

come and experience first-hand what you are doing.

Foreign tourists also come to support Maher and sometimes to volunteer. If arranged ahead of time, they may stay from a week to several months. Some come to play with the children and help with other daily tasks that arise: painting walls, repairing donated clothing, or chopping vegetables. Others who come for longer stays might teach an English class for the older children or a dance therapy class for the women, or help in the office with recordkeeping. There is now a steady stream of European social work students coming to Maher for their internship, staying from three to six months. (See Appendix for guidelines regarding visits from foreign guests).

TIP Community volunteer groups can help supplement staff on Sundays. Church groups, women's groups, and local service clubs such as Rotary can be invited to volunteer to come and lead activities for the children, such as teaching them dance or crafts or arranging cricket matches. Plan ahead with these groups to be sure that activities respect your interfaith and other values. Groups may also take the children on educational outings, or even to the beach (always with staff supervision). These events benefit both the givers and the receivers.

7 | *Staff: the Heart of Maher*

We are sent into life for one task: to enrich the lives of others. ....
Generous work brings the fruits of giving: loyal friends, security,
faith in human goodness, and the increasing capacity to give more.
—Eknath Easwaran

Maher began with Sister Lucy's vision and determination, and her commitment is still a driving force. However, Maher's growth could not be sustained without its amazing staff. One unique factor of Maher's staff is that many women who work there first come to Maher seeking refuge. Some choose to work with Maher for a limited period of time, while their children are young or while they save money and decide what to do next. Others decide to remain at Maher, as housemothers and social workers, forever. Other staff come to Maher as professionals. For most Maher staff members, their work is more than a job: it is their passion and they share in

Maher's mission and vision. Most staff members live full-time on-site at Maher.

In previous chapters you have seen references to four primary roles: director, housemother, housemother-cook, and social worker. Even in the beginning stages of the NGO, the work of all of these roles must be done. However, if a single individual is founding the NGO, the founder may initially fill all of these roles, as Sister Lucy did in the beginning of Maher.

Depending on your skills and strengths, you will add staff in roles that

155

complement (are different from) your own skills. For example, if you have a social worker background, you might hire or train a housemother-cook to see to all the food purchasing and preparation. If you have raised children and feel most comfortable in their daily care and development, then you might hire a social worker to help with family reconciliations and the behavioral challenges common with children who have not known a safe, loving home or attended school before. Whether your residents are children only or women with children will influence your choices regarding staff as well. It is important to create a well-rounded team by choosing employees who have backgrounds in complementary areas.

As the NGO grows, you and the staff will decide how best to share the workload. This chapter summarizes the essential daily operating tasks of an NGO, and then provides basic summaries and formal job descriptions for each of the four main roles. Please note there is room for flexibility around how the tasks are divided between the roles. Below is an overview of the chapter contents:

- Summaries of essential tasks and roles

- Hiring

  o Sources for candidates for each role

  o Key selection criteria (general and role-specific)

  o Interviewing, background checks, and selection (general)

  o Employment contract, salaries, and benefits

- Performance Management, Training, and Development (general and role specific)

- Key challenges for each role

- Evaluations

- Staffing levels and combinations of roles for smaller homes

- Staff meetings

Essential Roles and Tasks

When the NGO first begins operations, one or two people will likely fill the four main roles. Therefore the first focus is on what work must be done for daily operations. As the NGO grows, adding residents and programs, increased specialization toward the more formally defined roles will occur naturally. In the meantime, it may be necessary to contract part-time outside specialists such as a bookkeeper or a social worker.

Essential Daily Tasks

The following summary lists the minimum daily and weekly tasks that staff must do to run the home, both inside and outside. This chart focuses on children; if your organization also takes in women, you will need to add activities related to their specific needs (see Chapter 8). If you as founder are initially responsible for all the tasks below, keep in mind that these are in addition to other tasks covered in the previous chapters, such as annual planning, fundraising, and reporting.

Sister Lucy and a social worker engaging children in fun

CASE Evolution of staff roles

In Maher's early days, Sister Lucy performed all of these tasks. As women staying at Maher became emotionally stable, they naturally began helping with the daily tasks and Sister Lucy began training them in caring for the home and the children and in preparing meals. Soon she hired the first staff member, a professional social worker. In addition to bringing her valuable social work expertise, she also helped with household tasks and in training the women in the daily care of home and children. She and Sister Lucy soon realized that this model of training the women clients to help worked well. Maher began to offer these women employment as the first housemothers. This had the additional benefit of allowing the women to stay beyond the three-month short-stay limit set by the government for women's shelters. Next, a man arrived at Maher's door seeking refuge and employment. Sister Lucy hired him to help with maintaining the building and completing odd jobs. In this way Maher's initial staff was formed according to both need and opportunity.

Outside work (external focus)	Inside work (internal focus)
Interview, select, and admit new residents (via police, other institutions, referrals, or arrivals at the door)	
Purchase necessary supplies such as groceries, household goods, and clothing	Direct daily schedule for house and for school attendance
Arrange and pay for electricity, phones, etc.	Clean house and kitchen
Purchase and replace gas cylinders	Prepare baths for children
Meet with parents and guardians	Organize menu planning; prepare all meals and snacks
Make school visits (each school about once per month)	Help children with studies; track book bags, homework
Arrange outside counseling, doctor, or hospital visits as needed	Purchase, track, and repair clothing (and wash clothes for younger children)
Make home visits and provide family mediation and intervention where needed	Monitor children's physical, mental, and emotional health and wellbeing, treating and counseling as needed
Plan and lead outings for children	Lead exercise, yoga, and meditation
Keep records of all purchases, meetings, and outside activities (in handwritten notebooks and on computer)	Teach children hygiene, basic cooking, and other living skills; teach all Maher songs and rituals
Conduct outreach (village elders, police, local businesses, community groups, local functions) and welcome guests to Maher	Guide and correct children's behavior according to learning goals, Maher rules, and core values
Conduct banking and post office activities	Mediate in conflicts
Provide moral support to friends of Maher and neighbors, such as visiting families if someone is sick or has died	Plan special events and festivals
As time allows, engage in community projects, such as slum programs, village self-help groups, hygiene and sewing classes, etc.	Maintain garden, yard, building, plumbing, bio-gas, etc.
	Keep records of all daily activities, attendance, menus, case files, etc.

Essential Roles Summarized

The overarching focus of all the roles is to carry out the NGO mission: to attend to its residents' physical health, emotional wellbeing, creativity, and learning. Remember, in the start-up phases of operation one or two people may need to perform the functions of *all* of these jobs. Complete job descriptions are included at the end of this chapter as well as on the website for ease of adaptation to specific circumstances.

Executive director

Objective: to lead and oversee the NGO, helping to create a loving family home for all residents. The director is responsible for successfully executing the NGO vision, mission, and values. In addition to ensuring that all daily tasks are being completed efficiently, the executive director manages the administration of the NGO, making the most effective use of its resources.

Summary of duties

- Report to trustees (including reports on admissions, staff, finances, growth, and programs)

- Direct and oversee daily operations and staff (household and administrative)

- Plan and lead all planning and finance-related operations (annual plans and budgets, fundraising, reports, and analysis)

- Determine NGO priorities and direct energies and resources accordingly

- Serve as a resource for problem-solving on an interpersonal level as well as in the community and for the NGO

- Model good habits of hygiene, diet, holistic self-care, communication, kindness, and core values

Special considerations

In most cases, the NGO founder will be the executive director overseeing start-up and all preparatory activities, right up to and including welcoming the first residents and providing the support and care needed. This requires an ability to balance both the strategic long-term management and the day-to-day operational needs of the NGO. If a group of people is founding the NGO, then select the person who is most qualified. If there is no one who has the skills and the interest in the strategic functions, an executive director will, sooner or later, need to be hired.

Housemother and housemother-cook

(These roles are listed together since they are closely related.)

Objective: to create a loving, secure, stable family home. The housemother lovingly cares for all children physically, mentally, emotionally, socially, and spiritually.

Summary of duties

- Provide children with loving guidance and care

- Supervise children's health; hygiene; emotional, social, and spiritual development; education; and other activities

- Prepare well-balanced meals consisting of nutritious, tasty food, according to good habits of diet and hygiene, within the budget provided (when there is a housemother-cook, this will be her primary duty)

- Plan menus; purchase and maintain all foodstuffs

- Model and teach good habits of hygiene, diet, self-care, and all core values, especially love, respect, interfaith principles, and caste-free living

- Remain approachable to children so that they feel comfortable sharing problems and questions

- Maintain recordkeeping of associated responsibilities

Special considerations

The two housemother roles form the heart of each home, providing structure, care, guidance, security, and unconditional love. Generally two or three housemothers divide these two roles. One is the housemother-cook and is responsible for all the meals and snacks, shopping, the kitchen, and

related recordkeeping. The other(s) share primary responsibility for the children's other needs, such as helping them with hygiene, completing schoolwork, following daily routines and rules, and all the other tasks any mother does for her family.

> **TIP** While this manual will continue to use the term housemother, it may be essential to hire a housefather if your home will be for all boys. If so, the qualities, skills, and training mirror those for a housemother. If the NGO has both boys and girls, it is beneficial for the children (especially the boys) to have either a housefather or a male social worker as a positive male role model. You could also manage this with the participation of trustees or volunteers.

New housemothers often fill the cooking role, gradually adding menu planning, shopping, and recordkeeping, while being trained in childcare. The more experienced housemother will handle menus, shopping, and recordkeeping at the beginning. They gradually train the newer woman, giving her more tasks and responsibilities as she demonstrates ability. In practice, the housemother and housemother-cook share some duties, helping one another as needed and creating a system that works well for them.

In larger operations, some of the developmental work with children (and women) may be done by a resident social worker, and there might be office and administrative support.

Sometimes, as in the Kerala home, a professional cook may fill the housemother-cook role. This person will have experience in meal planning, provisioning, and cooking, and will handle all the related shopping and recordkeeping. The cook interacts with the children and models good values and habits, including Maher core values. In this case the role is not a stepping-stone to becoming a housemother with more child-care duties.

Social worker

Objective: to support maintenance of a loving, supportive, stable, and safe family environment, whether at Maher or in reconciled families. The social worker facilitates the care, education, and development of all Maher residents, as well as raising awareness in local communities and conducting community outreach.

Summary of duties

- Assess physical, mental, emotional, and spiritual wellbeing of residents and staff; counsel, mediate, problem-solve, and support as needed for residents to thrive

- Reunite families when safely possible, through provision of services and support, following up until families are stable

- Learn, model, and teach good habits of hygiene, self-care, and values, such as love, respect, interfaith principles, and caste-free living

- Maintain recordkeeping of associated responsibilities

Special considerations

This role is often filled by a person holding a master's degree in social work (MSW) who is then trained in the NGO's specific style and operations. Sister Lucy has found that the "Maher way" (living on site and being available 24/7, for example, and disciplining with the goal of learning rather than punishment) is very different from what an MSW will have encountered in his or her training and previous work experience. A para-social worker may also be able to fill this role. A para-social worker has a certificate of completion of study, similar to a college-level vocational program. These people, while lacking some of the formal education, may possess valuable life experience and knowledge of their communities. Typically, a para-social worker earns about half what an MSW earns, although this depends on years of experience.

161

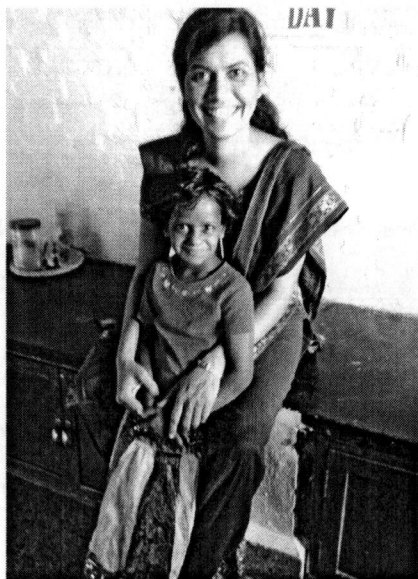

Social worker with recently admitted girl

Job Descriptions

While the summaries above provide an overview of major jobs, more complete job descriptions are recommended. A job description is useful in four primary ways.

- Helps in recruiting the most suitable candidate for the expected job work and can also be used to advertise the job

- Provides a clear record of tasks to enable the organization to provide better orientation for newly hired staff

- Clearly outlines the role and responsibilities of each staff member and how the person is contributing to the overall vision of the work

- Supports monitoring and evaluating the performance of the staff

When you are hiring people from outside the NGO, you need to set very clear expectations of what you want them to do. It is in everyone's best interest if each staffer knows exactly what is expected of her or him, even before agreeing to the job. It is a great waste of time and energy to hire someone, invest in on-the-job training, and then learn that the person either cannot or refuses to perform some of the job functions.

You should adapt these job descriptions to reflect what people are actually expected to do given the specific needs of the NGO at any particular stage.

For simplicity, a separate housemother-cook job description is not included. Often all the housemothers will share all the roles to start, so you can provide all with the same job description, with notations to recognize specific responsibilities of individuals. As new staff are added—perhaps a new housemother-cook who is being trained, or a full-time professional cook—you will create the job descriptions based on the housemother one. Copies of all are included on the book's website. Note that there is some overlap in housemother and social worker job descriptions (such as keeping case files up to date). Who ultimately is responsible for what depends primarily on whether you have rescued women as your housemothers (they will likely do less) or whether you have full MSW

162

social workers (they will do more). You will need to specify who is responsible for these tasks in your own versions of the job descriptions.

Hiring New Staff

- Sources for candidates for each role

- Key selection criteria (general and role-specific)

- Interviewing, background checks, and selection (general)

Sources

Sources for director candidates

- Other institutions or NGOs

- Local businesses

- Internal promotion (training a housemother or social worker to become first an assistant director, then director)

The founder should be prepared to perform all of the duties of the director, at least at the beginning. You will be wise to seek the skills and experience you are lacking in people you consider for trustees, or when hiring other staff. This may be the last role you hire someone else to fill!

Sources for housemother and housemother-cook candidates

If you begin as Sister Lucy did by taking in women and children, you have the best source for future housemothers: the women themselves. And their work as housemothers will in turn be a central part of their own healing and development.

If you begin a project focused solely on children, however, you must rely on outside sources for candidates. These include:

- Mothers in the local area who are widows or whose husbands have left

- Wife and husband pairs who have experience working with children from other institutions

- Social workers and para-social workers—perhaps someone seeking their first job out of school and willing to start in a combined role

- Maher-trained housemothers who may be willing to relocate to other parts of India permanently, or perhaps just for 6 to 12 months to help get you started and to train other local women, as SOFKIN did

Sources for social worker candidates

- Local universities
- Other NGOs
- Internal promotion

A master of social work (MSW) is an internationally recognized professional degree granted by universities, generally requiring completion of both bachelor's and master's degrees. Check local universities and search on the Internet for social work degree programs in your area, and ask to include your NGO information in the school's job placement process. Also, your NGO, with its unique values-based orientation and commitment to helping children thrive instead of only survive, may look particularly attractive to social workers at other NGOs who really want to make a difference in the world. Consider hiring a para-social worker trained at Maher or in your local area. Finally, once your NGO has been operating for several years and has seasoned housemothers, some may wish to receive training to become para-social workers, trained and certified by Maher or another local source.

Key Search and Selection Criteria

In order to promote the vision and values your NGO holds, certain qualities are critical for any person you hire, no matter the role. Many of these values cannot be instilled if the seeds at least are not innate to the person. Skills can be learned; values must ultimately be felt and lived. Over time you will certainly be able to develop new sensitivities in others, and even help people develop better character, but in hiring staff you should select people already possessing at least the basics in this regard. During the interview

process, look for demonstrations of these qualities in your interactions with them and in their interactions with residents. You can see evidence of these values in their past experiences as well, and when talking to their references.

TIP Finding candidates who already hold the Maher core values will be next to impossible, unless they come from Maher. Therefore these values will have to be developed. Be sure to choose people who are at least inspired by them and happy to work and live that way. At first you will likely be the one preparing these new housemothers, whether they are residents you are helping or they are hired from outside. It is essential that whoever is training them has a strong understanding of and belief in the core values, including all their related values, in order to keep the "Maher way" alive. Because many of these values run counter to the culture of village life, the staff will need patience, guidance, and support as new people adapt.

Basic selection qualities required for all roles

- Love and compassion for all children

- Honesty, integrity, and a positive attitude

- Good personal hygiene (evidenced in body and hair care, smelling and appearing clean, good food manners, and proper use of toilet)

- Clothing and footwear appropriate for job, neat and clean, and respectful of local standards

- Compassionate toward all people equally, regardless of religion, caste, gender, or ethnicity

- Daily prayer, contemplative, or meditation practice

- Willing to actively embrace all of the NGO's vision and values, especially interfaith and caste-free values, such as maintaining and respecting the artifacts and significant practices of the major religious traditions

- Ability to quickly and skillfully make a natural empathetic human connection, building trust and understanding

- Ability to maintain calm steadiness when confronted with challenging or surprising people and situations

TIP Ideally a candidate will have work experience. For example, the housefather in Kerala was hired from the local community. He had worked with aged people at a center where he did jobs like trimming hair, turning clients in bed, and taking clients to the hospital; as food and grains manager at a meditation center; and with service activities when in school. Even if a candidate has not worked outside the home, he or she may have similar work experience and a good work ethic. Sister Lucy has even questioned family or neighbors to learn more information about applicants.

- Ability to discipline and guide children without use of force, hitting, or yelling

- Creative problem-solver

- Ability to read and write at least the local language and Hindi

- Willingness to learn and apply new skills and ways of doing things

- No tobacco or alcohol usage (unless off-duty and off-site)

Additional selection criteria for director role

- Management experience, either managing people or managing a service-oriented program

- Computer skills (for recordkeeping, financial reporting, and letter writing)

- Math skills (addition, subtraction, multiplication, division, fractions, percentages) to manage money, maintain bank records, and do financial reporting

- Professional demeanor; able to build effective working relationships with government officials, trustees, donors, and guests

- Leadership skills, including ability to inspire and guide others to follow (not authoritarian), ability to delegate appropriately, ability to develop others and inspire them to do their best

- Basic spoken English to welcome foreign guests

Additional selection criteria for both housemother roles

When hiring people from outside Maher

- Experience raising children (at least their own)

- Basic math such as addition, subtraction, and multiplication (for example, for adjusting recipes)

- Basic knowledge of first aid (such as attending to cuts, sore throats, and other normal childhood issues) and understanding when to consult a doctor

- Basic life skills such as the ability to use a mobile phone; buy a railway ticket; post a letter; select, bargain for, and purchase basic household items such as food and clothing

- Ability to speak to new people, both men and women, and to groups and authorities (for example, on behalf of Maher or a resident)

- Ability to replicate regional and local cultural and social traditions, such as the Indian traditions of *aarti* and *rangoli* ("painting" on the ground with colored rice flour)

Additional criteria for hiring a professional cook

Sometimes, as at Maher's Kerala site where the number of children grew fairly quickly to more than 30, it makes sense to hire a professional cook instead of sharing that role among housemothers. Candidates for a professional cook position are expected to have the basic housemother criteria, plus experience in healthy menu planning, food procurement and preparation (especially vegetables and the local style of cooking), cooking for groups, and recordkeeping. Ideally they will have prior work experience managing a kitchen and preparing food for large numbers of people.

Criteria for selecting from among rescued women

Rescued women who have potential to be housemothers or housemother-cooks are assessed through direct observation by staff before being given a formal housemother role. All have lived at Maher as residents, participating in daily life and celebrations, and have already begun to learn the Maher way and values, effective parenting skills, meditation, and more. All women— whether or not they choose to stay as official housemothers—begin slowly

learning the basics of food preparation, hygiene, and childcare almost as soon as they arrive. Therefore the staff has ample opportunity to observe whether a resident woman has the qualities required to be a housemother. Then she can be trained as needed on the job.

It is important that a woman has an interest in taking on this role; no one is coerced. She begins by assisting the existing staff with children and projects as requested, demonstrating interest and ability for the role. As she develops more and more skills and a readiness for the role, she may eventually be given a formal housemother or housemother-cook position if she desires to stay at Maher.

TIP To help judge these abilities, watch applicants for a job interact with residents, staff, and yourself when they come for an interview. Test their computer skills by asking them to review some part of your computerized records, and ask them questions that require them to navigate the spreadsheet. More information on interviewing and assessment is given below.

Apti Krupa House staff: social worker and her husband (at left), their child (held by housemothercook), and two housemothers

> ## CASE Social workers do more than traditional social work
>
> *Madhuri is one of Maher's best social workers. She holds degrees in social work as well as psychology. Her primary position is counseling children, but she handles related jobs such as searching for a child who has run away in the night or picking up children from the street, soothing their fears, and welcoming them to Maher. She is always willing to help with the hands-on work, such as bathing children. She has both the training to see to complex social work and a good work ethic, willing to help out wherever it is needed (even helping to hand-decorate holiday cards to mail to friends of Maher).*

Additional criteria for social worker role

- Master's degree in social work (or para-social worker certification)

- Willingness to live on-site and be on call 24/7

- Ability to mediate disagreements between peers and among family members

- Professional and confident demeanor; ability to build effective working relationships with school officials, village and government offices, guests, and challenging people (whether upset, afraid, angry or even abusive)

- Math skills (addition, subtraction, multiplication, division, fractions, percentages) to manage money and all types of reporting

- Basic computer knowledge; ability to use both word processing (for letters or case files) and spreadsheets (such as for admissions data)

Interviewing, Assessment, and Selection for Staff Roles

Selecting staff is a critical process and needs to be handled with care. Staff will be working with vulnerable women and children, so it is very important to make decisions only after gathering a lot of information about the character of the applicants. The following section will guide you in this process. Be sure to check all applicants' references to confirm details about their backgrounds and their integrity, and observe them closely to assess key selection qualities.

Job application

You might use a formal application form that everyone will complete before the interview. This can be fairly simple with basics such as name, address, contact information, list of schooling completed, and a history of previous employment. A

168

sample application is included at the end of this chapter, plus a downloadable copy is on the website.

Interviewing Applicants

Prepare your interview questions ahead of time for each position you are filling. Ask all the applicants the same core questions so you have a basis for comparison. (See next section for developing interview questions.)

It is important to take notes during each part of the interview process, including the very beginning. Note whether the candidate arrived on time, how he is dressed and groomed, and how he interacts with staff and residents while waiting to speak to you. You can learn a lot before you even start the interview.

TIP Have candidates complete the job application in writing at your site, so you can assess their ability to both read and write.

Upon the applicant's arrival, greet her and take a minute or two to get to know her. This will help put her at ease. You might ask what interests her about this particular job and why she believes she would be successful. Then move on to your prepared list of questions. Remember to take notes during the whole process indicating how strong a

match she is according to your list of knowledge, skill, and attitudes. It will be helpful too to note examples from her answers so you can more easily recall what was said in each interview.

Once you have heard his answers and if it seems he has the necessary qualifications for the job, tell him more about the NGO. Be sure he knows the basic requirements, such as living on-site. Go over "a day in the life" of a housemother or social worker, including a typical daily schedule and list of duties. Clearly indicate that there is little personal time (for example, one afternoon off per week). Social workers and housemothers must be available around the clock to tend to the needs of children. This flexibility must be something he can imagine embracing as part of the job. Let him know what holiday or vacation time is allowed.

Provide the applicant with a printed copy of the NGO's vision, mission, and core values. Describe these values and how they affect daily operations and practices. Some of the most important aspects to cover are interfaith and caste-free values, unconditional love, respect for all, and nonviolent communication. Explain that she will be working and living with people from different castes and religions and that she will be expected to treat everyone equally and to show all coworkers and residents respect and love. Also tell her the position includes leading community celebrations in observance of major holidays from several different religious traditions. All employees' participation in these festivities is necessary to convey respect and appreciation for the religious beliefs of the residents. An applicant who resists any of these aspects will likely not be a good choice to hire.

There are difficult aspects of this work, and it is important the applicants understand this. Working with troubled children can be challenging, and it can also be highly rewarding to see them flourish when loved and supported by the Maher family. Especially for social workers, the Maher way will be very different from their training and previous work experience. You want to find social workers who are excited about your way of working. You will be offering them a chance to help make a real difference in people's lives, and they must really want that. They must be agreeable to the long hours and the deep commitment required, if they will be a lasting employee. Assure the applicants that you and other staff members will offer support and guidance on the job. Finally, see if they have any further questions for you.

TIP Watch each candidate in action: give her a tour of your NGO, meeting residents and staff. Watch how comfortably she interacts, and notice how the children respond to her. Afterward you might ask her to tell you what she noticed that was interesting or unique.

Developing interview questions

Be sure to hire people who both really want to work with you and have the qualities you desire. It is sad but true that many people will say anything they think you want to hear in order to get a job.

In order to assess what applicants will bring to the job and how successful they are likely to be if hired, you must accurately determine what knowledge and skills they have that are relevant to the job. You also want to get a sense of their general mentality and temperament to determine what kind of attitude they will bring to the community.

You need to be able to assess *competencies*. Competencies include *skills,* a set of learned activities (for example, how to wash a dish); *knowledge*, or information (such as understanding why something is important, what its purpose is, what "clean" means); and *attitudes* (for example, caring about doing the right thing beyond merely complying with a rule, and commitment to doing a task well and thoroughly).

Knowledge is often the easiest to assess: social workers will have degrees and certificates, and a director should have some sort of university degree, perhaps in business. Other knowledge, such as what good nutrition is, you can ask about directly and evaluate the response given. Skills and attitudes are somewhat harder to assess. It is easy for someone to say he is skilled with a computer, for example, and then you may learn once he is hired that he is far less capable than he claimed to be. Attitudes are even more challenging to assess. A thorough interview using competency-based questions can help to reveal applicants' skills, knowledge, and attitudes, particularly their true attitudes as demonstrated through actual past behaviors.

Competency-based questions allow applicants to demonstrate knowledge, skills, and attitudes that are relevant to the position you are looking to fill. The best predictor of future performance is past performance, so ask for specific examples of duties performed and how someone dealt with challenging situations in the past. Avoid asking about hypothetical future situations. Avoid asking questions that can be answered with "yes" or "no." For example, when interviewing for a housemother, do not ask, "What are your thoughts about raising children? How might you handle an angry child?" Instead say, "Tell me about your experience raising children—how many, what ages? Tell me about one challenging situation that stands out. What happened, what did you and others do? What did you learn?" These kinds of questions are much more difficult to make up answers to on the spot. Listen carefully for details and consistency. Ask follow-up questions to be sure you are clear about their answer.

Prepare questions ahead that are specific to the requirements of each position for which you are hiring. Each role will require unique knowledge, skills, and attitudes, identified in the job descriptions at the end of this chapter. These can serve as a base for the creation of questions. Knowledge can be assessed through reviewing education and work experience, posing simple tests (samples below), observing skills, and asking direct questions. Note that competencies can be usefully thought of in categories, such as leadership, decision-making, and child development. Following is a series of questions you may find helpful in assessing skills and attitudes. Choose several that relate most directly to the job you are seeking to fill, and adapt them as needed to your specific situation.

TIP To get more information about knowledge or attitude, you can ask "why?" as a follow-up to many of the interview questions.

Competency-based interview questions (Following each question in parentheses is a tip suggesting what to listen for in the answers given.)

Interpersonal relationships and respect

- Tell of a time when you had to quickly build trust and understanding with a child (or an adult) you just met. (skills to build relationships)

- Describe a situation when you had to help and work with someone from a lower caste or a different religion. What was the situation? What was your role? What did you do? How did you feel about it? (ability to work within NGO values)

- How have you handled interactions with a person in a case when you could not agree upon certain issues? (ability to be creative, to compromise)

Guiding, developing, and disciplining children and clients

- Tell me about a time when a child you were responsible for misbehaved. What was the situation? How did you handle it? How did it turn out? (discipline)

- Tell me about a time when you had to guide or mentor someone. What was the topic, and how did you explain, correct, and develop the person's capacity? How did it turn out? (mentoring, developing)

Initiative and ability to solve problems

- Tell me about a time you used your initiative to solve a difficult problem in the workplace [or in school or at home, if they have not worked elsewhere]. (taking initiative, ability to solve problems creatively)

- Give an example of a case in which you anticipated problems and were able to go in a new direction, and still complete your project on time. (ability to think ahead, plan, take initiative)

- Tell me about a time when you were asked to solve a difficult problem (at work, at home) without being told all the details of the problem. (independent thinking, data gathering, ability to solve problems)

- Describe a situation in which you had to take actions that were beyond your responsibilities, in order to solve a client's problem. (initiative, judgment)

Handling difficult people and situations

- Tell me about the most difficult situation you have ever had to handle. (ability to handle challenges well)

- Tell me about a person with whom you found it difficult to work, the reasons why, and how you handled one situation with this person. (ability to work with difficult people)

- Describe a demanding situation in which you managed to remain calm and composed. What helped you to be able to do this? (ability to control emotions, think under pressure)

Leadership

- Give an example of a situation in which you demonstrated leadership skills. (ability to direct, guide, take charge, or lead; self-confidence)

- Give an example of a time when you were faced with an unexpected situation and how you used leadership skills in coming up with a creative solution. (ability to take initiative; self-confidence; creative problem-solving)

Mediation and influence

- Tell me about a situation in which you had to help two people who were facing a conflict (related to differing opinions, approaches, or priorities) come to a compromise. (ability to mediate, such as during reconciliations or among residents)

- How do you get others who do not wholly agree with you to listen to, and accept, your ideas? Give an example that demonstrates your approach. (ability to inspire or influence)

- Give an example describing when you had to explain a complex issue to someone. (clarity of thought and speech, ability to break something down into parts)

Personal learning and development

- Describe a recent learning experience. What did you take away from that experience? (ability to reflect and learn)

- Give an example of risk that you had to take. Why did you decide to take the risk? How did it turn out? What did you learn? (risk taking, ability to reflect and learn)

- Tell me about a time when a team member or your boss criticized your work. How did you respond? (ability to take developmental criticism and learn)

- Tell me about an important professional or personal achievement of yours—how did it happen? (drive, strength to succeed)

Assessment of interviewed candidates

In order to make a final hiring decision, do a careful analysis of each person's qualifications, including background checks and listening to your intuition.

How to assess the interviews:

- Were the answers to your questions concise, clear, and to the point? Could you follow clearly what the problem or issue was, and then what the person did and said, and how others may have contributed?

- Did the candidate wander away from the point while answering these questions, or did you get confused listening? Rambling or being confusing often indicates someone is avoiding the question, or even possibly inventing an answer.

- Did the person try to place blame on anybody else, or seem to complain a lot?

- Did the applicant demonstrate an ability to learn from situations, particularly those that did not go well, and to apply that to future success? (Sometimes being able to learn from failure is a better indicator of success than doing it right the first time.)

- Did the candidate offer real examples in response to your questions, or hypothetical ones? (Be sure to clarify this during the interview, asking for specifics such as time, place, and who else was present.)

- Review the notes you made during the interview, and rate the person on each requirement for the job.

Background checks

Checking references can also help with assessing applicants' competencies. If you are hiring people whom you do not know and with whom you have not worked personally, you need to be very thorough in verifying that what they tell you is true (unless they were trained at Maher). This step is essential anywhere in the world. If he claims a degree, you need proof he graduated. If he claims past work experience, check his references. Ideally, speak with his supervisor to verify how long he actually worked for the company or institution as well as what duties he performed. Was the quality of his work acceptable? Was he reliable, on time, honest, and creative in meeting challenges? How did he get along with other workers and clients? Why did he leave?

By this point in the process it will often be clear who the best candidate is. If you are fortunate to have several apparently equally well qualified applicants, then settle inside and listen to your heart about who will be the best fit for the NGO.

Wages, Benefits, and Employment Contracts

Once you make your choice whom to hire, you will need to discuss salary, starting date, and relevant details.

Salaries and benefits

Check in your area for similar jobs at foreign-run and local NGOs as well as at local government institutions. If relevant (for example, for the director job), you might also check for salaries in the private business sector. The closer you can pay to what other similar jobs are paying, the easier it will be to get qualified people. And remember, if staff will be living with you, providing a home and food should be noted as part of their overall compensation. Of course, there is the trade-off with longer working hours. To estimate comparable value, find out what a typical cost would be to rent housing and pay living expenses in the area.

Sample salaries at Maher, for comparison

Social Workers
Salaries for those with master's degrees in social work (MSW) begin at Rs. 7000 per month and go up from there, depending on years of experience and skills. They receive an annual increase of 12%, assuming they are performing their duties satisfactorily. Most of the social workers live on-site, so their food and room are included as additional benefits. If they are married, their spouse and children also live on-site,

with housing and meals covered. If staff live outside Maher, they receive the same salary, but then must pay for their own housing and food. This arrangement seems to compensate the ones who live on-site who work longer hours, since they are on call 24/7. Maher carries an accident policy that covers non-routine medical care. Cell phones are provided if duties require staff to travel, such as going to meetings or transporting clients.

Para-social workers' salaries are much less (about half), as they have much less education and training. Some para-social workers may eventually go to school for an MSW. A full-time para-social worker might start at Rs. 4000 per month, and might eventually earn as high as Rs.10,000 depending on the type of work and years of experience.

Housemothers
Housemothers' salaries begin at Rs. 2000 per month plus most of their living expenses. Including the approximate value of the food, clothing, housing, and medical care they receive as staff, this may become equivalent to more than Rs. 5000 per month. Maher additionally often pays all or part of their children's school fees. Cell phones are provided as well.

These salaries are deposited directly into each woman's bank account, and most housemothers are able to save nearly 100% of their salaries to help them start a new life after Maher. Bank accounts have both the woman's name and the director's name and require both signatures for withdrawal. This protects

TIP Raises should not be guaranteed but should be based on job performance. If an employee meets all expectations, then the standard raise is given. If he or she exceeds performance on a number of criteria, then perhaps a bit extra is given. By the same logic, if someone is not meeting expectations, then a raise may be postponed or not given at all, until the issue is resolved. There should always be clear and consistent communication between the management (director) and the employee as to why he or she is getting (or not getting) a raise and what he or she can do to improve the situation.

the money from being taken by husbands or in-laws.

When hiring local women from outside the NGO, you will have to assess several factors to come to a fair starting pay: their experience, their relative skills, how much responsibility they can take on right away, and the local job market. For example, a new housemother might start at Rs. 1500 with the promise of Rs. 500 increase after a six-month trial period. If another woman can step right in and take responsibility with little or no training, she might start at Rs. 2500 per month.

All employees' salaries increase annually, assuming satisfactory job performance. As skills improve and as they are able to take on more work, pay is increased by about 12% per year. As the women come to earn higher salaries, they might also be asked to cover half or even all of their children's school fees. Some of the senior housemothers who have been at Maher a long time earn Rs. 4000 per month (plus their living expenses are still covered).

Salary payments to children in higher education
Once children reach age 18, they can no longer be cared for as children by Maher. So in order to support their ability to continue their education, Maher employs them part-time. Their pay varies and hours are arranged to accommodate their studies. For example, one young man works six hours a day and earns Rs. 5000 per month plus food and lodging. He works in the office, acts as photographer at all events, and manages Maher's photo library and imagery needs (website, newsletter, and more). Another young man works three hours per day and earns Rs. 3000 per month plus food and lodging. He works in the office and is skilled with computers and software. Both support other projects and needs as requested.

Sample vacation and personal time at Maher for comparison

Social workers (who work seven days a week generally) get twenty personal days, six sick days, and four holidays of their choosing off per year. After seven years of service there is an additional bonus for all staff: Sister Lucy takes them with her to Kerala to see that part of India, stay with her family, visit the Kerala project, and play. Maher pays all expenses.

Housemothers and housemother-cooks work seven days a week. Each woman gets a few hours a week off to attend to personal business. If there is a family issue requiring attention that calls her away from Maher, generally a way is found to accommodate this. One month per year housemothers may go on holiday when the children are on summer break from school. Sometimes an orphan child or two will travel with the housemother to her family to experience family life (more in Chapter 9 on children).

Pension

(Note: Maher was only able to offer this benefit after 14 years of operation.)
All full-time staff are now eligible for the Provident Fund, which is a government pension fund. Staff make monthly deposits and Maher matches these amounts. In this way, employees are eligible for a government pension and insurance. An insurance representative comes to set this up and earns a percentage for each person who signs up. Employees must have three years of service with Maher to be eligible to withdraw funds as a loan against the pension. Maher's participation in this fund is a great advantage for staff, as they will have a government pension when they retire or in the event of an injury that prevents them from working.

For Maher, however, it means that the NGO is subject to additional government rules and oversight. If your NGO is considering such a program, be sure to learn all of the rules and requirements that will apply.

Rules for all employees

- No tobacco or alcohol use is allowed on-site.

- Mobile phone use is limited, to ensure that they are not disturbing others and not neglecting the children.

- No visitors of the opposite gender are permitted, except for spouses or direct family such as a parent, brother, or sister.

- No bad or offensive words are used; polite, respectful treatment of all is expected.

- Punctuality is required, for all functions, meetings, and other events.

- Housemothers and housemother-cooks are equal; no one is superior. Even though the housemother-cook may be newer and receiving guidance from a more experienced housemother, her voice still matters as an equal member of the community.

- Children must be treated equally; staff should have no favorites, assigning jobs equally and fairly to all, paying equal attention to all.

Employment contract

Once you come to agreement with a new employee, draft a formal letter of employment (appointment letter) stating all the details regarding the job you are offering, including the expectations of time commitment, work, leisure time, and benefits. The applicant will sign it and a copy is retained on file. This serves as an employment contract. A sample Maher contract is included at the end of this chapter and on the website to modify and use. For NGOs in other countries, you may wish to have a lawyer review and adapt this employment contract as needed for additional legal protection.

Performance Management, Training, and Development

Performance management is just what it sounds like: managing the work results achieved by each staff person. Begin by establishing clear expectations for what each employee is responsible for doing, according to what standards (using personalized job descriptions plus the NGO's vision, mission, and values statements as the base). Then provide both support (such as mentoring and training) and feedback (is the employee meeting your expectations, and if not, then where are the gaps?). Finally, reward success—and, just as importantly, do *not* reward failure. That is, do not give the annual raise to someone who does not meet expectations.

Training and development are two related but distinct functions. Training refers to the learning and application of specific knowledge and skills to correctly and efficiently complete *current* job tasks. Development focuses on growing someone's potential for the *future*, to take on more complex work and roles within the NGO and sometimes even beyond. Training might be learning to complete and crosscheck all of the different recordkeeping functions of the particular job. Once this is accomplished, further training might cover the use of computer-based spreadsheets to track expenses or admissions. Development may include areas such as confidence building, honing negotiating skills, and learning to work effectively with diverse groups of people, including government ministers and business executives. It might also involve preparation to take on new job responsibilities, such as adding responsibility for self-help groups to a housemother job, or even training to become a para-social worker. Begin with a focus on training so that the person is competent in his or her current role. Once someone is competent, then consider both training, to boost efficiency and skill at the current role, and development, for future personal or professional goals. For an NGO in its early years, the focus will be on training to build a depth of experience for each of the basic job functions. Most of this will be on-the-job training, with you or another mentor.

If the NGO takes in adults as clients and develops them into staff, then you will have two types of staff: professional staff (people hired by the NGO to do a particular job) and client staff. This section on performance management focuses on professional staff. These people are assumed to have all the basic life skills plus basic job skills, and should be able to perform the full job within a few months of hiring. Client staff will require emotional and spiritual healing as well as basic life skills, in addition to job skills. The two types of staff will have different needs. Both groups however must learn to live and work in accord with the NGO's vision, mission, and values. For client staff, refer to Chapter 8 for case management plans instead of using the performance management process discussed here. At some point, when housemothers have acquired the background life skills, confidence, and experience, they can be graduated from client staff to professional staff.

TIP Even though someone hired as a social worker or housemother may have training and experience disciplining children, doing this in accord with Maher's values usually requires new knowledge, skills, and attitudes. Also, women in particular may need support in developing self-confidence and self-esteem, given the local cultural history of devaluing women.

Five Stages of Performance Management

Performance management refers to a continuous cycle of five stages:

1. Set clear job and performance expectations.

2. Assess competencies.

3. Develop an annual plan to support successful performance and development for future professional goals.

4. Carry out training and development, and monitor progress.

5. Evaluate performance and reward success.

Each year this cycle repeats. Successful performance often leads to added responsibilities, new goals, new training and development needs, and so on. While it may look complex, the cycle actually reflects a natural thought process for developing staff to their fullest potential for the NGO and also for effectively focusing your time and money spent training people. As you work through each stage, keep written notes at every step.

Stage 1: Set clear job and performance expectations

For each employee, customize the job description to match your expectations of the person for the upcoming year. For example, if a social worker is hired to fill the roles of both housemother and social worker, then summarize this combined role. Make sure that each job description also contains a sentence about "additional duties as requested." Provide written copies of the job description and the NGO's vision, mission, and values at time of hire, so that the staff member understands that all these duties must be completed in a way that is consistent with the NGO's values.

Stage 2: Assess competencies

Stage 2 includes three steps.

Step 1: Assessment
Assess each employee's competencies (knowledge, skills, and attitude) as required by her job in the context of your NGO's vision, mission, and core values. Identify gaps between what she is required to do and what she is able to do. If she is a new hire, then you know this information from your selection process, such as the interview or references you checked. Once she has worked for the NGO for a year, you will have your own observations. Be sure to discuss your assessment with her so you both agree. It is very difficult to get someone to learn something that she believes she already knows, or something for which she cannot see the relationship to her job. Written notes of strengths, weaknesses, and missing competencies can be included in her plan.

Step 2: Identify additional personal and professional goals
For a staff person who has worked for the NGO successfully for a couple of

years, consider with him future personal and professional goals. For example, a social worker might really like to work in the villages running self-help groups or leading local projects to improve village life. Linking a person's training and development to his personal dreams will build commitment. Again, keep written notes summarizing what you discuss with each staff member.

Step 3: Identify and prioritize gaps
Together identify gaps in his knowledge, application of skills, and attitude. Do this first in relation to the current job description, and second in relation to the employee's personal and professional goals. Prioritize the most important of these to address in the current time frame.

Stage 3: Develop an annual plan for each employee

Stage 3 has 2 steps.

Step 1: Performance plan
A simple performance plan will consist of having the employee complete her job according to the expectations set in stage one, with two to three top-priority goals highlighted. These goals will reflect any gaps identified above. An example of a gap-based goal is for a new social worker to become comfortable in her role, and to learn how to adapt her methods to align with NGO core values. For a housemother who is already capable in the basics of her job, her goal might be to develop a new yoga program for the children, or perhaps to improve her mentoring of children's

schoolwork so that their grades go up. If there are no gaps for the employee, then goals might reflect NGO needs. For instance, someone may take on a project for the year of computerizing all or some of the record books to reduce the amount of time spent on this task, and work with government officials to be sure what she creates is acceptable. All such goals take place within the context of fulfilling current job descriptions. Additionally, if it is appropriate, you might agree to one or two personal development goals for the year.

It is important that these areas of focus have measurable outcomes so that achievement, or lack of, can be assessed during the year. It is a good idea to have a limit of two to three specific high-priority outcomes per staff person. More will be too much to focus on.

Step 2: Training and development plan
Next you are ready to create the training and development plan for your staff. Each staff member may copy the agreed-on list of goals, beginning with the higher-priority ones, into her training and development plan. Next you will discuss what kinds of activities and resources will be most useful to support this employee, as well as when and how this will happen.

Every person's plan will be unique to his or her specific situation. The example below shows a sample format for a performance, training, and development plan for an imaginary social worker who was recently hired. Note that just one or two activities are listed as examples. You will need to be more complete.

Sample performance, training, and development plan

Annual Plan for Social Worker Lila Shah
Performance plan
Perform all of the duties of a social worker, and any other duties as specifically requested by founder.

Professional goals for current year:
1. Become comfortable in new life and work at Maher and consistently behave in accordance with the Maher core values and ways of working.
2. Develop mediation and problem-solving skills to successfully reunite families.
3. Accurately complete all recordkeeping functions for this role, on paper and in the computer.

Personal goal for the current year:
1. Begin a personal daily practice of meditation to help in managing stress.

Training and development plan

Needs	Resources	Target timeline	Accomplishments
Professional Goal #1			
Learn all 7 Maher core values and actively explore each in daily work at Maher	Study in handbook, discuss at staff meetings	Over next 6 months	
Create values wall chart and discuss with residents	Coaching from staff	Month 2 & ongoing	
Professional Goal #2			
Observe founder as she works with families	Coaching from staff	Immediately	
Take the lead on mediating a case, with founder mentoring	Coaching from staff	After 5-6 cases	
Professional Goal #3			
Keep all assigned record books current and correct	Coaching by staff	By end of month 2	
Personal Goal #1			
Begin daily meditation practice	Initial guidance by staff, then 3-day Vipassana course	Go for course within next 6 months	
Developmental Goal #1*			
Begin one village self-help group	Talk to villagers, learn what needs are	At end of year, and only if current job is not compromised	

*Because this example is for a new employee, it is not likely she will have a developmental goal; this one is included merely as illustration.

Stage 4: Carry out training and development, monitor progress

Especially as the NGO is starting, most training will happen informally on the job by means of coaching and modeling by the founder and other well-trained staff. The advantage to creating a plan is to make sure that the coaching happens and is not forgotten during the busy days, or is suddenly remembered only when there is a problem. A new employee may not even know that how she does things is not correct according to Maher ways until she makes a mistake, unless you have this planning conversation at the beginning.

As issues arise in the course of daily business, do not just fix it yourself and let it go. Take the time to talk to the employee about what is going on, and guide her to think through options, their consequences, and what would be the best choice in the situation. If the moment has passed and a mistake was made, make the time to go back over what happened and guide her to think through other options or learn a new skill, as needed, so next time will be different. Do this as soon as possible while the situation is still fresh in everyone's minds. Also look to the core values, both to help everyone understand how the problem came about and also to see what actions might be appropriate to take. Remember, many of these values are different from people's social and cultural upbringing and even from their professional training. It will be a slow

process as people shift in their behavior, let alone in their thinking. (For more about applying the core values, see Chapter 10, "The Art and Genius of Maher.")

> **TIP** Some ideas for developmental projects for staff wanting to expand their jobs:
>
> - Teach hygiene classes in area villages.
>
> - Start and lead a local self-help group (such as for women, for men, or for teen girls).
>
> - Teach classes such as adult literacy, sewing, or non-violent communication.
>
> - Run a slum kindergarten school. (One housemother might prepare a breakfast that Maher delivers, another might teach the small children in the morning, and a third could lead an after-school class or make supper.)

TIP Stages 3 and 4 can be done over several weeks, with employees digesting their discussions with you and thinking about the next step. You might ask an employee to reflect for a week and list the gaps he thinks he has in knowledge, skills, and attitudes. Then he can come back and discuss this with you. Once you both agree to the assessment, develop and prioritize goals for the coming year. While you may need to coach him at first, the process will help him develop accurate self-reflection. Also he will become an active, committed partner in his own learning and development.

Informal learning at staff meetings, lunches, or outings

When there are several staff members, you can meet with them as a group while the children are at school. At this time you can do informal teaching and practice, such as role-playing, to help develop core skills.

Examples of job-related topics in which all staff need continual development:

Working with children:

- How to handle challenging children (especially new arrivals who might be scared, angry, fighting, hurting inside, silent, or having bad dreams)

- Nonviolent problem-solving and communication

- When to call a social worker or counselor for additional support

- Games to play with children of different genders and ages (generally with a learning goal such as good sportsmanship)

Developing good peer relationships:

- Managing peer relationships with women, men, and authorities (such as a boss or a school principal)

- Maintaining respectful relationships with other staff that set an example for the children, based on communication and understanding

- Understanding each other's mistakes and moving on (do not keep these in the heart)

Creating other learning opportunities for staff: be creative!

- "Field trips" such as going to the village market and teaching staff how to select and bargain for quality and price

- "Borrowing" a social worker from another NGO, if you do not have your own on staff, to speak about helping children recovering from trauma

- Exposure visits to other NGOs with staff and even trustees, followed by a discussion of differences and similarities to your NGO

- Inviting a trustee with valuable skills, such as a doctor who can teach basic first aid, to offer a training session for staff

- Guest lecture by an official from the CWC addressing ways of streamlining the process of admitting children (This could have an added benefit of strengthening the NGO's relationship with this critical government office.)

- Calling on other community resources to share useful expertise (for example, staff at a local clinic could speak about first aid, nutrition, or AIDS)

More examples of topics:

- Nutritional guidelines, menu planning, food combining
- Gardening and caring for plants (also teaches reliability and dependability)
- Women's rights and basic legal issues
- Legal guidelines relevant to your operations
- What to do when someone dies
- Report writing
- How-to sessions: school bag checking; handling problem children; using a computer and smart phone for common basic tasks; assessing, choosing, and caring for various dress fabrics; and more
- Games and tips to draw out traumatized children
- Hygiene and the value of cleanliness (body, clothes, food, house, dishes, yard)
- Banking and money management
- Developing confidence, for example to speak to men, groups, or public officials with confidence
- Self-esteem
- Designing "street plays" as a tool for village awareness meetings

Stage 5: Evaluate performance and reward success

The "Accomplishments" column of the training and development plan should be updated regularly. Plans and progress should be reviewed two to four times per year at least. This way each employee will know if she is on track for achievement of her plan. And if she is not on track, then she should be in discussion with you about how to correct the situation.

- Did each person meet the expectations in each part of his or her annual plan?

- Did he fail expectations anywhere?

- Did he exceed expectations anywhere?

Performance shortcomings should be discussed immediately as they occur. If significant problems arise, write a note for the employee's file specifying the issue and how it will be addressed. Also include what consequences will happen if the issues are not fixed, such as no raise, or even being fired.

Some of the expectations of housemothers will differ depending on whether they are rescued women who are learning both a job and life skills for living independently, or local women who are seeking employment and who likely have a more professional demeanor. For example, a woman who has had to survive on the streets may have developed bad habits, and it will

> **TIP** What helps someone become a good housemother? Interviews with Maher housemothers suggest that training sessions in the following areas particularly helped:
>
> - How to handle the children, especially challenging situations (role-playing exercises especially helped)
>
> - Nonviolent communication training
>
> - Naturopathic training—basic first aid for normal childhood illnesses and injuries
>
> - Health and nutrition training
>
> - Laughing session
>
> - Exercise, yoga, Vipassana meditation
>
> - Talks by Sister Lucy and the social workers
>
> - Exposure visits (to other institutions for comparison)
>
> - Celebrations, each with due respect to that tradition, including decorations, special foods, meaning, and more

take a while for her to learn new behaviors, so she is given more leeway than would be given to professional staff.

Completing an agreed-upon performance plan such as the example

TIP Compassion is the key at Maher. If a woman has an issue with another housemother, then this is written up. The woman might even be transferred to a different location, and she must acknowledge in writing that she will do her best here, and that it is her "last chance." But Maher does not enforce this "last chance" too seriously because, as Sister Lucy says, "we know their backgrounds: we are flexible and compassionate. No one rule fits everyone. We see how it is and adapt to each woman's needs."

above is directly related to wage increases at the end of the year. If the plan is completed satisfactorily, then the raise is given. If the individual failed to complete one or more of the goals, then the raise may be canceled or delayed. Every employee should be aware of this practice.

Be sure to recognize and reward when goals are exceeded, such as when a staff person goes beyond what is normally expected or takes initiative leading to good results. There are many ways besides salary to reward people, such as public recognition and thanks for a job well done, or sending them to a developmental learning opportunity off-site.

Acclimating New Staff Hired from Outside

Even with good selection and a thorough discussion of core values and expectations, new employees will still need to "see how it is" at Maher. Patient guidance, ongoing training, and support will be needed.

- Before the job formally begins, have the new person simply live in the community for one to three weeks to "see how it is." This is the best way to learn the NGO values and way of life, including child-care guidance and corrections, caste-free behavior, prayer and meditation, and to get accustomed to the schedule and feel of daily life.

- If an experienced housemother is already present, have the new hire "shadow" her, following her everywhere as she performs her duties. Social workers might shadow the founder when she welcomes and admits new residents, goes on home visits, deals with government workers, or observes teachers.

- Begin assigning the more standardized tasks first, each with clear instructions and supervision to be sure they are successful. Patiently and respectfully guide the new employee when she is unsure or makes errors.

- Assess ability, and as the employee gains confidence and competence, gradually add more responsibility, more challenging work, or more children. This helps assure success, instead of possibly overwhelming her.

Key Challenges for Each Role

Based on Maher's years of experience, below are some key challenges likely to be encountered in each role. While specific suggestions for dealing with many of these will be offered in the next two chapters, it is helpful to be aware of these for the housemother and social worker roles as you plan your training and development strategy.

Key Challenges for Housemother Roles

These issues were suggested by a group of seasoned housemothers in conversation with the author:

- How to handle the toughest children (such as those who have never been to school and do not want to go, or who hurt themselves or others)

- How to get children who have suffered trauma to open up, to share what is in their heads and hearts

- How to prepare food and treats in the right quantities for so many children

- Handling a home with a large number of children, each of whom is

unique, with different backgrounds, natures, and habits

- How to respond to sexual problems of children (for example, seeking sex prior to marriage)

- Dealing with children coming with so much anger from their previous situations; these are even difficult for Sister Lucy

Key Challenges for Social Worker Role

It is useful to understand the context wherein essentially all Indian social workers are trained. Most of those with an MSW will have worked or interned only at government facilities. The job was 9 to 5, and often the women clients, and therefore their children too, were not residential. They had very large caseloads, leaving little time per client. Often the social worker would see someone once or twice and then never again. They would not know the results of their work. Or if they worked in, for example, a government orphanage, the primary goal was merely to contain children (that is, feed, clothe, and see them through the 8th, or sometimes the 10th, standard). Here too the caseloads were too large for social workers to really develop relationships with the children. Relying on authority, rules, and punishment were the primary forms of managing all people and all situations.

CASE Maher's first social worker

Marla, an MSW, was hired early in Maher's history when there were fewer than 10 women and 15 to 18 children. Since there were no housemothers yet, she simply did whatever needed doing. She and everyone else got up at 6 a.m., washed up, brushed teeth, did prayers, tended to gardening or other work, then had breakfast and helped the children do homework before they went to school. When the children came home from school, there was playtime, homework, prayers, supper, and sleep. In between she organized the women who were able to help cook and clean, and helped them stay occupied.

Marla quickly saw that Maher was a family. Through living with the women and children, she got to know them and learned what was in their hearts as they opened up. Counseling happened when it was needed, sitting when there was time.

Marla spoke to this author about her work at Maher, and it is clear she still feels part of the family: "Their problem is our problem—and so we get emotionally involved. This is so different from working in the city as a social worker where you would have a one-hour meeting with a client and offer solutions and help, but would never see how it goes. Here if a child cries in the night, we get up and hold them. It's special here—we are all family. It's really okay to become attached to the children and women as family."

Even at that early stage, Marla was going out and doing village awareness sessions and learning about life in the villages for women and their families. She started self-help groups, women's support groups, and groups with teens, boys and girls separately. She asked about their lives and studies, what problems they had and what help was needed. All the time she was building trusting relationships, and, of course, helping spread the word about Maher.

Marla says the support of Sister Lucy was very important. Because she was able to talk to her, learn from her, and receive encouragement, she got stronger. She also benefited from a one-week Vipassana course where she learned not to cry about problems, but just to do what needed to be done. Marla worked because, as she said: "I love Sister Lucy, the women, and the children." Even many years after marrying and moving to Mumbai, she comes to visit, bringing her husband and daughter.

The work at Maher is therefore challenging to these social workers in some essential ways.

- Maher is relationship-based, so staff must develop a relationship with each resident. (Even with more than 700 residents at more than 20 locations, Sister Lucy knows all the children and women at all the homes, their names, their situations, and their challenges! And, of course, she remains in contact with many of the "graduates" as well.)

New arrival: young woman found on the streets and brought to Maher by staff

- The social worker is residential, living with the clients—and just as in any family, everyone at Maher helps with what needs to be done. So a social worker will definitely be asked to do things not generally part of a social worker's job. This will be especially true in a newer or smaller organization where there are less distinct boundaries between roles.

- The whole concept of Maher is foreign to most: raising children in an institution as if it were a home and a family. It may take some time for the social worker to grow used to the practice of guiding each child and woman individually, allowing them to make and learn from their own mistakes, lovingly correcting and steering them toward better choices, instead of simply punishing or expelling those who break the rules.

- Social workers must embrace the goal of developing clients into all they can be, "India's future," rather than simply helping them to stay alive.

- For all staff, Maher values take some getting used to. Even now Sister Lucy has a male social worker who has been at Maher for many years, a good one in most ways, who still cannot accept women colleagues as equals.

- This is a first job for many social workers, so they also need to also learn work ethic.

- Maher is in many ways a lifestyle rather than simply a job.

Staffing Levels and Combinations of Roles for Smaller Homes

Staffing levels depend on several factors:

- Number, age, and gender of children

- Depth of experience of the housemothers

- Whether there are other women residents or teenagers to help with childcare and cooking

- Whether a home is "stand alone" or part of a network of several homes in one area, where a central office and staff does part of the administrative work

In cases where there are only one or two homes and the staff do both the daily administrative work and the externally focused work, the ratio is 2 housemothers to 12 to 15 children. Where a home is part of a larger network of homes with administrative and other support, the ratio is closer to 2 housemothers for up to 25 children, supported by a social worker in residence or on contract, plus some administrative support. In most cases, some of the older children need to help with the younger ones. If many of the

children are younger, or all are new arrivals, then a third housemother is required. The project director, if not living on-site, visits regularly and assists in staff and client development and in problem solving.

Samples of Staff-to-Residents Ratios

Staffing is handled differently at each of these sites; it tends to develop organically based both on the needs of the site (see factors above) and who shows up—whether in response to a hiring notice or seeking refuge. In the examples following, the director role is filled by Sister Lucy for Maher or Chaya at SOFKIN, with the exception of the Kerala project.

> **TIP** In India it is generally not safe for a woman to go out at night alone, for example to take a sick child to the hospital. At Maher at each site they try to have either a man on staff, or at least an older teenage boy among the residents for this reason.

191

Name and stage of organization	# women	# children	Housemother / housemother-cook	Social worker	Office work
Maher at start	7–8	+/- 15	Sister Lucy	0	Sister Lucy
Maher at 1 year	15+	40+	Sister Lucy with help from 1 social worker and from rescued women	1	Sister Lucy
Prem Sagar 2013 (Maher, Pune home)	0	25	2	1 (shared)	Pune office
Ratnagiri 2013 (single home)	0	26	3	2	Social workers & Pune office
Kerala Project 2012*	0	44	2 (+ their wives)	1	Mostly local staff
SOFKIN at start	0	8	2	0	Chaya (US-based)
SOFKIN 2013	0	22	3	0	Chaya + part-time accounting help

*Kerala Project is unique in that it has no governing trustees. There is a full-time director who oversees and manages the project and reports to Sister Lucy. He is responsible for much of the administrative work and arranges the significant outreach work, including a program on alcoholism. The housefather, a social worker, and a professional cook do the recordkeeping for their specific roles, plus the daily errands such as banking, shopping, and school visits, as well as supporting the outreach programs. Wives of two of the staff also work full-time, assisting their husbands. The wife of the housefather is a nurse—an extra bonus. This is a great illustration of staff roles evolving in part based on who is hired!

Staff Meetings

Staff meetings should be held regularly. In the early days when it is just the founder plus one or two others, the meetings may be more informal, perhaps in the evening after the children have gone to bed. But as your organization grows, formal staff meetings will become vital time for the full group to come together (likely while the children are at school), discuss challenges, review priorities, problem-solve, and plan for upcoming programs and celebrations. It is also a great opportunity to slow down and appreciate the wonderful hardworking staff, publicly noting accomplishments and successes of each staff person. This both rewards good work and reinforces the kinds of outcomes you value.

Housemother Meetings

Maher gathers all the Pune area housemothers monthly. Since all of these are women who originally came to Maher seeking refuge, these women are continually learning not only job-related information and skills, but also life skills.

A typical agenda includes:

- Welcome, formally acknowledging and thanking all for their work

- Recognition of accomplishments of the team and of individuals

- Reports on status of NGO (facts and figures, status of outstanding issues, updating team on recent events)

- Problem solving, either by reviewing a recent challenge and what went wrong, or by sorting out a current unresolved challenge together (referring to core values)

- Game that is fun yet raises awareness on some relevant topic (breaks up the seriousness of the meeting, gets people moving and interacting with each other)

- Planning for upcoming programs and celebrations

- Values review, focusing on one specific core value, with discussion of what it means in daily life and how it might lead to different choices from those that staff might have learned elsewhere

- Training in some topic, such as Vipassana meditation

Many sample training topics for staff meetings were listed earlier in this chapter.

Closing Notes

All of the steps and processes in this book may be too much for your NGO as it is just being born. And certainly some will need to be adapted to fit local laws, circumstances, or practices. Some you may decide to skip, and a couple years later realize they would be useful. No problem—just add back in what you skipped! In a small operation, some steps you will do more in your head, and only formalize these as you grow.

Think of these guidelines as a recipe—and, like any cook, ultimately you use what you have at hand, substituting as needed. Even a recipe prepared with exactly the same ingredients but by two different people will taste slightly different.

Client Testimonial

What is so different here is that the staff are educated. They know life in cities, in villages, and even in tribal areas. They sit with us and seek to understand us and then guide us, as mothers, and as women. Only when the problem or issue is clear, then they offer help. Even small things like sitting properly when eating, these add up to big things, and so we learn how to be. And whenever we need them, staff are there.

Group of Maher staff and women residents

Forms and Templates for Staffing Chapter

Job Descriptions

JOB DESCRIPTION Executive Director

Objective of Role
To lead and oversee the NGO, helping to create a loving family home for all residents. The director reports to the trustees and is responsible for successfully executing the NGO vision, mission, and values. In addition to ensuring that all daily tasks are being completed efficiently, the executive director manages the administration of the NGO, making the most effective use of its resources.

Special Qualifications

- Past success managing people or managing a service-oriented program; able to work strategically (set and achieve strategic objectives, and manage a budget) as well as operationally (daily tasks with clients and staff)

- Marketing, public relations, and fundraising experience with the ability to engage a wide range of stakeholders and cultures

- Professional demeanor; able to build effective working relationships with government officials, trustees, donors, and guests

- Leadership skills, including the ability to inspire and guide other to follow (not authoritarian), ability to delegate appropriately, ability to develop and inspire others to do their best

- Computer skills (for record keeping, financial reporting, and letter writing)

- Math skills (addition, subtraction, multiplication, division, fractions, percentages) to manage money, maintain bank records, and do financial reporting

- Basic spoken English to welcome foreign guests;

- Compassion, idealism, integrity, positive attitude, mission-driven, and self-directed

---

Duties and responsibilities

Leadership and Management:

- Ensure ongoing programmatic excellence in accord with vision, mission, and values, rigorous program evaluation, and consistent quality of finance and administration, fundraising, communications, and systems; carry out periodic site inspections

- Model core values in all decisions, actions, and interactions; model good habits of hygiene, diet, holistic self-care, communication, and kindness

- Lead planning process annually with trustees, recommend timelines and resources needed to achieve the strategic goals, report on progress monthly, explain any deviations from plans

- Hire, lead, coach, develop, and retain NGO's high-performance staff; delegate appropriately, both as a tool to help staff develop, and in order to stay focused on strategic needs of the NGO

- Establish and nurture effective partnerships with local institutions, police and village leadership, and with government officials; assure NGO compliance with governmental obligations

- Actively engage and energize NGO volunteers, trustees, event committees, alumni, partnering organizations, and donors

- Remain firmly optimistic: when setbacks occur, find and follow an alternate path to meeting goals; keep the organization focused on what can be done

Fundraising and Communications:

- Develop and carry out annual fundraising plans to support existing program operations and expansion, while simultaneously retiring debt

- Deepen and refine all aspects of communications—from web presence to external relations with stakeholders—with the goal of creating ever stronger identity of excellence for NGO name

- Develop and maintain relationships with continually growing communities of public, private, and corporate donors and supporters

Reporting:
- Ensure effective systems to track progress, and regularly evaluate program components, measure successes and failures

- Report as required to trustees, government bodies, and stakeholders completely, accurately, and on time

JOB DESCRIPTION Housemother*

Objective of Role

Objective: to create a loving, secure, stable family home. The housemother lovingly cares for all children physically, mentally, emotionally, socially, and spiritually.

Special Qualifications

- Experience raising children (at least their own)

- Daily prayer and meditation practice

- Basic math such as addition, subtraction, and multiplication (for adjusting recipes)

- Basic knowledge of first aid (such as attending to cuts, sore throats, normal childhood issues) and when to consult a doctor

- Basic life skills such as the ability to use a mobile phone; buy a railway ticket; post a letter; select, bargain for, and purchase basic household items such as food and clothing

- Ability to speak to new people, both men and women, and to groups and authorities (for example, on behalf of NGO or a resident)

- Ability to replicate regional and local cultural and social traditions, such as the Indian traditions of *aarti* and *rangoli*

Duties

General care and house atmosphere:

- Maintain a happy environment in house, express love, care, and understanding toward women, children and each other

- Love all the children as if they are your own. Seek to understand each one as a unique

- Be a good model for children in all your behaviors, relationships, clothing, etc.

- Remain approachable to residents so that they feel comfortable sharing problems and questions

- See that things given to children are used properly, and kept in a good condition

* If role is a housemother-cook, then delete non-assigned tasks, to focus on the meal preparation section of the job. As she gains competency, gradually add the remaining parts of the housemother job description.

- Follow all the rules and regulations, and guide children to do so as well (such as being on time)

- Maintain confidentiality of children's family background, mother, and father

- Monitor and limit children's reading, TV, and DVD habits to assure that content is age-appropriate, without sex, violence, bad language, etc.

Daily and hygiene:

- Develop and follow daily schedule, filling time with studies and activities so residents do not have time to brood over troubles, or get into mischief

- Wake up the children in the morning and help the small children to freshen up

- Lead exercise daily

- Teach children good hygiene habits:
  - Supervise daily bathing and good toilet habits, including washing hands after using toilet
  - Check if children's teeth, hair, and nails are clean, with no head lice (See that children brush teeth twice a day.)

- Maintain clean and neat clothes, uniforms, shoes, and socks: do this for the younger children, then let them watch and help, and eventually teach them how to do for themselves (by age 11 boys and girls are generally washing their own clothes)

- Monitor children's physical (rashes, fevers, sores, etc.), mental, and emotional wellbeing (if not sleeping, or withdrawn, or angry, etc.) and provide care or seek assistance as needed

- Schedule regular medical, dental, and eye care annually; monitor and provide needed immunizations.

- Monitor children's attendance; always know where each child is: who went to school, who came home, who is attending what class or program, when, etc.

Meals and food:

- Develop menus based on healthy food according to required standards; encourage children to eat a balanced diet

- Cook food that is tasty and appealing and serve on time

- Teach and supervise proper eating manners and cleanup

- Plan amounts to cook so that each child has enough to eat and so that no food is wasted; (teach children to eat what they take and not waste food)

- If there is food left over, cover and store properly in refrigerator; use or compost by the end of the next day

- Observe safety and cleanliness when food is cooked and eaten

- Select and bargain for fresh good quality foods at reasonable prices

- Boil water to drink each morning (may add cumin seeds to help clean stomach)

- Serve neem leaf water once a week (to promote general good health)

Children's education:

- Supervise on-time completion of all school studies and homework

- Check whether the school bags and their contents are neat, clean, and in good repair; repair or replace as needed

- Visit the children's schools to check their progress at least once a term

- Guide children to participate in physical fitness, dance, singing, games, drawing, etc.

- Recognize and reward achievements

Children's spiritual and socio-emotional development:

- Model and teach NGO values and moral behavior

- Lead and teach meditation with children, and also interfaith prayer and songs for meals, to welcome guests, on holidays, etc.

- Teach residents how to prepare and perform relevant cultural and social rituals and holidays

- Teach underlying universal meanings and values in the major religious and national holidays

- Do not yell or hit children; use of force is discouraged

- Model and help children learn nonviolent problem solving and communication, and to build healthy relationships to adults and to other children.

- Grow residents' confidence in themselves, help them develop interests and talents, reward achievements, and help them prepare for a future beyond your NGO.
- Model and teach good manners, such as please and thank you, good morning, good evening, and treating adults respectfully

- Encourage children to interact with all the children, not only their one or two best friends

- Monitor children's interactions and emotional states, be sure all children are included and treated respectfully; when there are issues, seek to learn what is really going on, support to resolve issues, or seek social worker assistance

- Help all women and children to become happy and helpful members of NGO family and in their communities

Care and cleanliness of home and yard:

- Decorate home creatively: such as cheerful colors, wall charts, and art

- Keep floors and rooms picked up, swept, and clean; wash floors after each meal

- Check children's bed linen, wash weekly, and repair or replace as needed

- Monitor and maintain all household supplies

- Keep office materials and all storage areas all neat and orderly

- Empty trash daily

- Keep yard picked up and neat, and no open trash; if there are gardens, compost, biogas or vermiculture pits, keep these properly maintained

- Periodically empty and clean out refrigerator

- Do not hang clothes to dry in front of house

- Teach children all of these good practices; have them help as part of their daily chores

Recordkeeping:

- Maintain children's case file weekly, and in between as needed when events or issues occur

- Maintain all registers as assigned

JOB DESCRIPTION Social Worker

Objective and Summary of Role

Objective: to support maintenance of a loving, supportive, stable, and safe family environment, whether at NGO or in reconciled families. The social worker facilitates the care, education, and development of all NGO residents, as well as raising awareness in local communities and conducting community outreach.

Special Qualifications

- Master's degree in social work (or para-social worker certification)

- Willingness to live on-site and be on call 24/7

- Ability to mediate disagreements between peers, and among family members

- Professional and confident demeanor; ability to build effective working relationships with school officials, village and government offices, guests, and challenging people (whether upset, afraid, angry or even abusive, etc.)

- Math skills (addition, subtraction, multiplication, division, fractions, percentages) to manage money, and all types of reporting

- Basic computer knowledge; ability to use both word processing (for letters or case files) and spreadsheets (such as for admissions data)

Duties and responsibilities

Admission and assessment of all clients:

- Assess incoming clients and provide initial needs of clothing, food, water, and shelter as immediate support, and begin to develop trust in NGO

- Complete all formal admission paperwork and recordkeeping

- Help new arrivals settle at NGO, care for children as needed

- Advocate for them until they are able to do this for themselves

- Assist guardian or family members as needed, to complete admission process for children

- Gather complete data about each clients' home situation, history, and recent experiences

- Work with clients to relieve effects of trauma they have experienced

Case management for women:

- Help women to settle and acclimate to life at NGO

- Arrange additional medical, counseling, and legal support as needed

- Develop and complete action plans as applicable to the situation including:

  o Identify each woman's goals for herself, her children, and her family
  o Identify, mediate, and resolve conflicts and issues with families, either in support of reconciliation or on children's behalf
  o Work toward reconciliation where appropriate
  o Guide and teach basic life skills and values
  o Recognize and reward accomplishments
  o Help her plan for self-sufficient, safe, healthy, happy life after NGO
  o Arrange training as needed, job placement, and/or remarriage

Case management for children

- Help children to settle and acclimate to life at NGO; until settled, stay in close contact, continually observing and consulting housemothers

- Arrange additional medical, counseling, and legal support as needed

- Track their health and immunizations throughout their stay at NGO

- Develop and complete action plans as applicable to the situation including:

  o Identify goals with each child, revising these as they age and develop
  o Enroll children in school, tutoring as needed, overseeing their progress through completion of highest level of education they choose
  o Monitor and assess progress, taking remedial action as needed
  o Attend parents meetings at child's school, sometimes with parents or housemothers
  o Guide and teach basic life skills such and values
  o Identify and help develop talents, interests, and abilities of each child (including academics, sports, arts, etc.)
  o Recognize and reward accomplishments
  o Help them plan for self-sufficient, safe, healthy, happy life after NGO

- Monitor children's behaviors to be sure they are following all NGO rules and values

- Teach awareness and proper, safe behaviors regarding sexuality and AIDS

- Assure children's safety prior to returning them home after reconciliation or for school holidays, including periodic home visits

- For children with no family to visit, arrange opportunities that meet NGO standards so each child experiences life in a loving family home

- If relatives or guardians come seeking the children, make sure their motives are for the child's best interests and that the children will be safe, well cared for, and educated; home visits may be required

- Arrange training as needed, job placement, and/or marriage

Follow up

- After women and children "graduate" from NGO, check in with them periodically to see they how they are doing; provide additional support and guidance as needed to help them succeed

Build effective working relationships with:

- Clients and residents

- Staff

- Government officials, school officials and teachers, police, other institutions, local employers who may hire graduates, etc.

Daily life:

- Oversee housemothers' in daily home life (timetable, child-rearing, cleanliness, meals, attitudes, etc.); support them as needed

- Hold regular meetings, with staff and children, individually and as groups

- Mediate conflicts that arise between any residents (staff or children)

- Arrange games, outings, programs, classes, and celebrations involving other staff in the planning; all should have educational benefits such as skill or character development, awareness of life issues impacting them, etc.

- Welcome visitors and provide information about NGO

- Organize and participate in all celebrations and programs, in accordance with NGO core values

- Model and teach all NGO core values

Recordkeeping

- Case files for each client complete and up to date at all times, including plans and progress on developmental goals, education and health records, etc.

- Admissions files, attendance files, and all record keeping is up to date and accurate, both in paper notebooks and in the computer

Other:

- Continue personal and professional development, attending programs and seminars as possible

- Any other tasks as requested to support the smooth operation of NGO or its interests

Sample Job Application

Job Application

1. Position Applied For: _____

2. Government Identity Number: _____

3. Full legal Name: _____

| Last Name | First | Middle |

4. Home Phone: (   )   Business Phone (   ) _____

5. Home Address: _____

_____   **6. E-mail Address:** _____

| City | State | Postal Code |

7. Education:

7a. Highest school grade completed: ☐1 ☐2 ☐3 ☐4 ☐5 ☐6 ☐7 ☐8 ☐9 ☐10 ☐11 ☐12

7b. Do you have a high school equivalency   ☐ Yes   ☐ No

7c. Number of years of post high school   ☐1 ☐2 ☐3 ☐4

8. Name and Location of Educational Institution:	Degree Received	Major / Specialty	Dates Attended
8a.			
8b.			
8c.			

9. If you plan to complete an educational program in the future, then indicate the degree or program to be completed

9a. Completion Date: _____

10. Work Experience: Start with the most recent work experience. Describe all traditional, military and voluntary work experience. Describe your knowledge, skills and abilities that demonstrate your qualifications for the position for which you are applying.

10a. Job Title _____
Employer Name _____
Employer _____   Job Duties:
_____ Phone _____
Supervisor _____
Title _____
Final Salary _____
Dates (Month/Year) _____ To _____   Reason for leaving
Hours/week

10b. Job Title _____
Employer Name _____
Employer _____   Job Duties:
_____ Phone _____
Supervisor _____
Title _____
Final Salary _____
Dates (Month/ Year) _____ To _____   Reason for leaving
Hours / Week

Sample Job Application, cont.

11. **Job Skills:** Use the following space to provide any additional information that you think would be helpful in our evaluation of your job application. This can include specialized training, seminars, workshops, accreditations, special achievements or valuable skills:

12. **Licenses Held:** (including drivers) or certifications to practice a trade or profession.

Type	License Number	Granted by (licensing board)

13. **References:**
List the full name, address, phone number and relationships of up to three persons that you'd like to use as a reference:

Full Name	Address	Phone Number	Relationship

Which **Languages** do you speak, read, write?

Computer Knowledge
List tasks and programs you can perform on a computer:

Prior Convictions:
Have you ever been convicted of any violation of law, including moving traffic violations: ☐ Yes ☐ No
  If yes, then please provide the following:
Describe the Offense :
Statute / Ordinance: Date of Charge: ; Date of Conviction

County, City, and State of Conviction:

Work Start Date: When will you be available to start work?

____ Month ____ Day _____ Year

Job Application Certification:
I hereby certify that all entries on this job application and any attachments are true and complete. I also agree and understand that any falsification this information may result in my forfeiture of employment.

I understand that all information on this job application is subject to verification and I consent to criminal history and background checks. I also agree that you may contact references and educational institutions listed on this application

Dated _____

Job Applicant
Signature _____

Sample Employment Contract Letter

Personal and Confidential

Date:
INSERT NAME:
INSERT FULL ADDRESS

Dear INSERT NAME,

This is in reference to your application dated INSERT DATE and subsequent interview you had with us for an employment in YOUR NGO. We are pleased to offer you a position with us on the following terms and conditions.

1. You will be designated as "INSERT JOB TITLE"
2. You will join us on INSERT DATE.
3. Your compensation package has been detailed in Annexure –A, enclosed
   herewith.

TERMS AND CONDITIONS:

1. We expect you to work with a high standard of initiative, efficiency and economy. You will perform, observe and conform to such duties, directions and instructions assigned or communicated to you by the organization.
2. You will devote your entire time to the work of the organization and will not undertake any direct/indirect business or work, honorary or remunerative, except with the written permission of the management.
3. You will not seek membership to any local or public bodies without first obtaining written permission from the management.
4. You shall neither divulge nor give out to any unauthorized person during the period of your service or even by word of mouth or otherwise, particulars or details of our technical know-how, security arrangements, administrative and / or organizational matters of a confidential / secret nature, which may be your privilege to know by virtue of your being our employee.
5. You shall keep confidential all the information and material provided to you by the organization or by its partners concerning their affairs, in order to enable the organization to perform the service. This also includes information already known to the public which also you will not release, use or disclose except with the prior written permission of the organization. Your obligation to keep such information confidential shall remain even on termination or cancellation of this employment.
6. You will be responsible for the safekeeping and return in good condition and order of all the properties of the organization, which may be in your use, custody, care or charge. For the loss of any property of the organization in your possession, the organization will have a right to assess on its own basis and recover the damages of all such materials from you and take such other action as it deems proper in the event of your failure to account for such material or property to its satisfaction.
7. You shall have no objection to work in shift or staggered duty as and when deemed necessary by the company.
8. Your services are transferable anywhere in India or abroad within YOUR NGO.
9. Employees are required to read and acknowledge the rules and regulations stipulated in the Employee Handbook.
10. If accommodation is provided to you, you will vacate the same peacefully on expiry of the contract of employment, after handing over the premises as stipulated.

CHANGES:
In all those matters not specifically covered by this letter, you will be governed by such rules and practices that will be applicable from time to time.

CONFIRMATION:
You will be on probation for a period of 12 [twelve] months during which period your performance shall be reviewed. In this period, we shall review your performance frequently during the first few months. In the event we find that you are not making good progress, we may release you even before the full term of the training period.
On satisfactory completion of the training period, your services shall be confirmed in writing.

SEPARATION:
Your appointment is terminable, by either side, by giving 15 days notice in writing during the training period and thereafter, on confirmation, 30 days notice in writing.

Return of Organization Property: You shall deliver to the Organization, all organization property whether in electronic format or physical tools, to the Organization representative, by the last day actually worked.

Dispute Resolution: You and the Organization agree that, any dispute will be submitted and resolved as per the relevant laws and jurisdictions prevailing in [Insert NGO Location].

CONFIDENTIALITY:
All employees will have to abide by strict security measures adopted from time to time and maintain a high level of confidentiality of the data they handle in course of their work. Such measures will be adopted as and when required and you shall extend your full support and cooperation in implementing those.

DUTIES AND RESPONSIBILITIES:

INSERT JOB DESCRIPTION HERE

Welcome to the INSERT YOUR NGO family.

Very truly yours,

INSERT YOUR SIGNATURE

TYPE YOUR NAME
Founder Director, YOUR NGO

Terms and conditions accepted:

I hereby attest that the terms and conditions mentioned in the appointment letter have been clearly explained to me in a language I am familiar with.

NEW EMPLOYEE SIGNS HERE

Annexure - A

[Monthly break-up of compensation]   Amount in Rs:

Name: INSERT NAME

Designation: "INSERT JOB TITLE"

INSERT APPROPRIATE NUMBERS FOR JOB

Basic Salary	:	2250
HRA [50% of Basic]	:	1125
Leave Travel Allowance [8.33% of basic salary]	:	187
Conveyance [lump sum]	:	713
Dearness Allowance	:	675
Medical Allowance	:	1250
Food Allowance	:	1300
		=========
Total	:	7500

[Rupees Seven Thousand five hundred only]

NOTES:
Conveyance: The money being paid to the employee against this head will be non-taxable to the extent that the employee furnishes expense bills.

Income Tax and all other mandatory government stipulated funds / taxes will be deducted from the salary / allowances as applicable

8 | Assessment, Healing, and Development of Women

"There is no chance for bettering the welfare of the world unless the condition of women is improved. It is not possible for a bird to fly on one wing."
—Swami Vivekananda

Women in India begin life under the control of a father or a brother and go on under the control of a husband and in-laws, and eventually of their sons. They may not even be allowed to leave the house except to go to the market for food or to work in the fields. Most have no idea how to live independently, let alone support children as well. Previous generations were raised to believe that a husband can do anything he pleases. Even with new laws on the books in India protecting women from physical or mental harm, police tend to consider domestic violence, even murder, a "family problem." Women endure as long as they can, for the sake of the family name, for the children, and because they do not know they have options. Expectations are beginning to change, but this is slow. Recently there are more resources for women, such as

counseling centers and increased government support. And there are places like Maher.

Women come to Maher from all walks of life, not just from the poor. Domestic violence knows no caste or religious boundaries, indeed no national or geographic boundaries. All arrive frightened, traumatized, unsure of their rights, worried about their children, and often with nowhere else to turn. The only difference is that wealthier women and women with more education sometimes have more access to alternatives, perhaps even jobs. But even they are grateful to Maher for shelter and support when they need it.

That said, most of the women are poor, uneducated, and illiterate or semiliterate. Many do not know the very basic life skills such as hygiene, proper diet, nutrition, or food preparation. They have no idea how, or even why, to clean dishes, clothing, or floors, let alone how to manage children, a bank account and money, or many of the other daily life skills others take for granted.

Additionally, most women who arrive at Maher have not learned how to express their feelings constructively, how to stand up for themselves, or how to resolve conflicts nonviolently (with either children or adults). Their husbands and families also have little experience with nonviolent resolution of issues. Some are widows (often considered "bad omens" in the villages), and all are unwelcome in either their husbands' or their relatives' homes. They have become a burden, or simply inconvenient. They may even have tried to commit suicide. They may have learned to survive by fighting, stealing, lying, or running away. It is in this context that either reconciliation with their families must be forged, or a whole new life crafted.

Women at Maher are guided, with compassion and understanding, toward a resolution of the issues that brought them here. They are supported down one of two paths: reconciliation with the family or a new, self-sufficient life, whether at Maher or beyond. Regardless of which path they follow, women healing women is at the core of the process.

Goal for Women: More Than Survival

Maher's goal for women is more than survival. The ultimate goal is to help women:

- Walk together toward wholeness

- Discover their power within and develop self-reliance

- Become loving, supportive mothers and guides for children

- Reenter society well equipped to face the challenges that lie ahead, and even to "give back" to others via:
  o returning to husband or relatives, but to an improved and safe situation for them and for their children, OR

  o eventually becoming economically independent and self-sustaining, OR

  o remarrying, if the woman's husband is dead or a divorce is obtained

TIP Maher believes all of us deserve to thrive, not just survive. To thrive, as defined by author and psychiatrist Daniel Siegel, M.D., is to "enjoy meaningful relationships, be caring and compassionate . . . work hard and be responsible, and feel good about who they are."

Overview of Working with Women: Two Paths

All of the women arriving at Maher will eventually be sorted into two distinct paths:

Path A: Reconciliation with family

Path B: New self-sufficient life at Maher or beyond

It is only when they hear a woman's story, hear her hopes and desires, and "see how it is" that staff can begin to determine which path might be most appropriate.

Women come here on their own, are transferred from other institutions, or are brought by the police. They may be referred by any number of sources, even a rickshaw driver. Many have fled life-threatening situations for themselves and their children. They may arrive alone, or with some or all of their children. Most of the women arrive with some degree of anxiety, whether in fear for their own lives or stressed from whatever trauma led them to leave home. They may even have lived for some amount of time on the streets. Most are desperate. They are rarely able to think clearly, or to consider much beyond survival. They are often weeping, or so defensive and withdrawn that it is hard to get them to talk. Experience has shown that women do not leave home easily: there is a big stigma to leaving one's husband. Therefore, Maher begins with the assumption that the presenting issues are no small matter.

In the first meetings, staff listens respectfully and compassionately to the woman who has taken shelter at Maher, gently probing to learn more. What circumstances led to her arrival at Maher? Is there a husband or other family to return to? Is she hopeful of reconciliation? Does she think her husband and his family would accept her back? If so, would it be back to more of the same, or could there be a fresh beginning? If she desires reconciliation and it is possible to achieve safely, this is always the first option staff work toward. If this is not possible or the woman does not desire it, then they will review legal options for supporting the children or divorce. Finally, a path to self-sufficiency is planned. A brief summary of each path follows.

The Path of Reconciliation

Once the woman has decided that reconciliation is at least possible and desirable, the social worker visits the husband and his family, carefully noting the circumstances. (Sometimes a return to the woman's parents may be arranged as an alternative, but this is up to the woman.) The social worker tries to make the family understand that reconciliation is possible, and that there can always be a change for the better. It is also made clear that abuse and fear tactics, let alone murder, will not be tolerated—and will in fact be prosecuted. After many meetings, discussions, cajoling, and persuasion, a meeting is organized between the family and the woman who has taken shelter at Maher.

213

If the man is too proud to come to Maher, the social worker will arrange meetings at the family's home or a neutral safe place to try to bring peace.

The initial meetings are often highly emotional, with tears, anger, and shouting, but the patience of the staff pays off. The social worker, under the eye of the director, emphasizes shared stakes and interests, as well as analyzing and helping to resolve struggles and repeated arguments. They help a family recall good times and shared hopes and dreams. Staff remain positive, supportive to all, and patient, as they facilitate a family learning to interact with each other in new, constructive, and nonviolent ways. Problems are resolved. Suspicion and anger mellow into tolerance and optimism for the future. This process can sometimes last over several months, with trial homecomings, returns to Maher, and trying again.

The Path to Self-Sufficiency

When reconciliation is not desirable or possible, women are counseled about how they might become self-sufficient and become able to care for and educate their children. A key question is what work they might be able to do or can be trained to do. Many choose to be trained as housemothers at Maher, ultimately helping others as they themselves have been helped. This is a key practice at Maher: women's deepest selves are healed as they help and mentor each other, serving primarily as housemothers and social workers. There is much these women need to learn about themselves, about taking better care of their children, and about building constructive, happy relationships with children, peers, and family. They also need to learn about living independently in the world, managing money, and more. Through all this, Maher helps to heal their hearts and souls through teaching and counseling, but mostly through fully engaging them in life at Maher. Most of Maher's core staff are strong, competent, confident, happy

TIP Alcohol is a factor in many of the families in distress. Rarely does alcohol go away entirely, and these cases require patience as the following typical case demonstrates. The husband is alcoholic, and abusing his wife physically and mentally. The social worker talks to him, telling him that he will lose his wife and children, and reminds him that marriage is one time—he cannot remarry. He listens. Staff know that with help he can reduce his drinking at least, and can go to substance abuse support meetings. But this has to be monitored to see that it lasts. Sometimes the woman goes home and things are okay for a while; then the drinking and violence resume, and she comes back to Maher.

women who once came to Maher lost, hurt, sad, angry, afraid—and worse. Now they are the heart of Maher.

Sister Lucy emphasizes an early lesson she learned that became the basis for Maher: It is not enough to provide a roof over their heads and food in their bellies, she points out; most of these women will survive without you. They need more. These women are suffering from violence, despair, and other troubles. What they most need is your love, attentive care, and education. And not just academics: they need to learn how to take care of themselves and their children; they need to learn new skills of relating to others. They also need values education, spiritual values that work for all regardless of religious beliefs. They need to feel hope and self-confidence.

The women who arrive at your NGO will likely come from similar backgrounds and circumstances. Maher's workflow, services, guidelines, and more are offered so that you have some idea what to expect and can model the practices of your NGO after Maher, of course adapting these to local culture and circumstances.

Process for Working with Women

Every woman who arrives at Maher is unique, but it is both possible and useful to think about guiding each woman through a similar process, following a map that applies to all. Just as in cooking, certain steps come before or after others. It is best, for example, to put fresh whole spices into hot oil or

ghee until they roast and begin to pop, before adding vegetables; this is how the spices flavor the whole dish. Similarly, in working with these women, certain elements must be attended to before others, for the best outcomes. Workflow tools are also useful for training staff, showing them an orderly general flow, and then adding details

> **TIP** A unique feature of Maher is that the first step is not paperwork. The focus is on building trust and beginning to build a relationship. Listen to her story and attempt to reassure by providing for immediate needs (for example food, or safety and protection, or medical care), helping her to stabilize.

and nuances as they mature at Maher. Below are three workflow formats, each showing the same four stages, with progressively more detail.

- First is an **Overview Map** showing the high-level workflow for all women coming into Maher and how they progress through the two paths.

- Second is a **Summary Flowchart** expanded to include duration, roles, and more detail.

- Third is the **Narrative Detail** to add depth to both the map and chart.

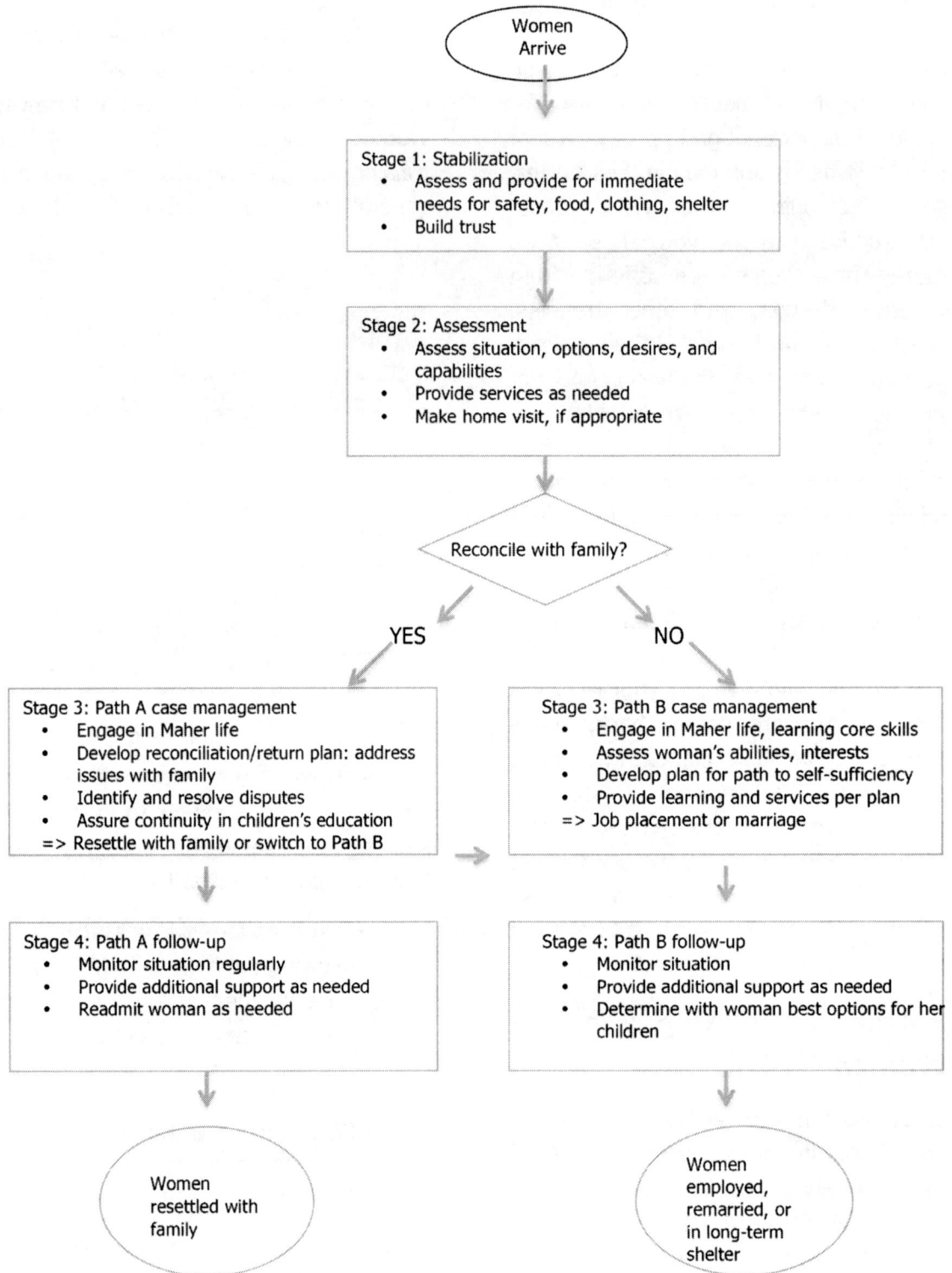

Overview Map

```
                          ┌─────────────┐
                          │   Women     │
                          │   Arrive    │
                          └──────┬──────┘
                                 │
                                 ▼
```

Stage 1: Stabilization
- Assess and provide for immediate needs for safety, food, clothing, shelter
- Build trust

Stage 2: Assessment
- Assess situation, options, desires, and capabilities
- Provide services as needed
- Make home visit, if appropriate

◇ Reconcile with family?

YES   NO

Stage 3: Path A case management
- Engage in Maher life
- Develop reconciliation/return plan: address issues with family
- Identify and resolve disputes
- Assure continuity in children's education
=> Resettle with family or switch to Path B

Stage 3: Path B case management
- Engage in Maher life, learning core skills
- Assess woman's abilities, interests
- Develop plan for path to self-sufficiency
- Provide learning and services per plan
=> Job placement or marriage

Stage 4: Path A follow-up
- Monitor situation regularly
- Provide additional support as needed
- Readmit woman as needed

Stage 4: Path B follow-up
- Monitor situation
- Provide additional support as needed
- Determine with woman best options for her children

Women resettled with family

Women employed, remarried, or in long-term shelter

Summary Flowchart

Stage	Focus & Key Tasks	Special Issues & Concerns	Staff Responsible*
Stage 1: Stabilization 1–2 days	• Assess and provide for immediate needs: safety, food, clothing, shelter, medical care • Medical evaluation for woman and her children • Begin admission form and file, and medical file • Enter into admission register	Safety and physical wellbeing of woman and any children with her Build trust	Social worker primary
Stage 2: Assessment 1–3 weeks	• Determine woman's marital status, situation, wishes, and needs • Assess her future options (reconciliation or self-sufficiency) • Visit home and communicate with family • Provide services as needed • Support her children (see next chapter) • Begin case file	Listen: see how it is; clarify details, inconsistencies, etc. Give household tasks; assess knowledge and abilities; observe relationships with others Assess danger from family; seek to protect woman and children	Social worker for research, relationship, and recordkeeping Housemothers for guidance in hygiene, childcare, and other work
DECISION: Yes/No	**Yes:** Work toward reconciliation => Path A **No:** Return to family is either not possible or not desirable => Path B		Director and social worker agreement
Stage 3 (Path A): Case management toward reconciliation 1–3 months	• Engage in Maher life as long as woman stays at Maher • Develop reconciliation plan: address issues with woman and family • Identify and resolve disputes • Assure continuity in children's education • Even when woman returns home, children may remain at Maher • Update case file, noting plans made, actions taken	Skillful and strategic negotiation and mediation toward reconciliation; creative problem solving Other meetings as required with local authorities, legal assistance, etc. Stage homecoming to determine timing of return for woman, and for children, if different	Social worker leads in counseling, reconciliation process Director supervises and assists as needed

* Staff role differentiation is noted in chart as suggestions, to be customized by each NGO according to its circumstances.

Stage	Focus & Key Tasks	Special Issues & Concerns	Staff Responsible
Stage 3 (Path B) Case management toward self-sufficiency 1-3 months	• Engage in Maher life, learning life skills and core values • Assess woman's interests, abilities, and desires • Develop plan for path to self-sufficiency • Provide learning and services per plan • Update case file, noting plans made, actions taken	Observe interactions with staff, children, and other women Note developmental needs and respond, either through coaching or classes	Social worker leads with input from other staff
DECISION: Ready to leave? Yes / No	Assess readiness: **Path A:** If **YES**, woman returns home If **NO**, either revise plans and try again, or proceed to Path B **Path B:** If **YES**, job placement or (re)marriage If **NO**, assign woman staff role at Maher so she may remain;** continue case management **Both Paths:** Determine best timing for children to leave Maher Client completes feedback form, social worker completes leave form and admission register	Test the waters; be realistic, ease the way as much as possible Identify barriers to a woman's goals; make a plan to overcome them	Director and social worker agreement on decisions Social worker completes forms
Stage 4 (Path A): Follow-up 2 months to 2 years	• Monitor situation regularly • Provide additional support as needed. • Be prepared to readmit woman • Complete readmit form • Update case file	Pay attention to what is said, what is not said, and body language of woman to be sure remaining at home is safe	Social worker makes regular contact
Stage 4 (Path B): Follow-up 2 months to 2 years	• Monitor situation, letting woman know she still has "family" at Maher • Provide additional support as needed • Determine with woman best options for her children • Update case file		Social worker makes regular contact

** The women's license at Maher is for "short-stay women's welfare home;" therefore, according to Welfare office rules, three months is the maximum stay. After that, a woman must either leave or become a staff member, although her children may remain as long as they need to or until age 18 (for this the NGO must also have a children's license and complete the appropriate admissions process). The other option is that if a woman is mentally unstable, for example from birth or due to trauma, then she may be transferred to another Maher facility with a license for long-term care and shelter, or referred to another long-term care institution.

CASE The complexities of assessment of both a mother and her children

A woman arrived at Maher with three children: one about 5 years old, a younger child, and a baby. The oldest girl was completely adorable. She went straight to adults, and everyone cuddled with her. Then Sister Lucy noticed the larger pattern: the girl never approached other children, nor did she play; she only interacted with adults. "She is becoming an adult already," Sister Lucy pointed out. The mother had left this 5-year-old to care for the younger sister and the baby while she worked and looked for food. This girl needed to get her childhood back!

The mother's parents had died when she was small, and a distant relative married her off very young. Her husband was an alcoholic who had died one month before the baby was born. She herself had never known love, and she did not know how to love her baby and her girls. As Sister Lucy explained, first she needed to learn to receive love, and then in turn, she could give it.

Sister Lucy took the mother aside and told her not to use the older girl to care for the baby, but to let the teenage girls of Maher or a housemother help. Sister Lucy then advised the adults not to pick this darling girl up when she came to them, but to smile and send her toward the other children. The girl was confused at first, and kept trying. But within a few days she could be seen up on the climbing bars with another little girl her age!

Narrative Support for Workflow

Copies of all forms and registers mentioned here are included at the end of the chapter and/or on the website.

Stage 1: Stabilization

- Maher's doors are open 24/7. Welcome each woman. Assess her immediate needs, and those of her children if they are with her: is she scared, sick, injured, naked or exposed, hungry? Do something immediately to help and reassure her, such as tend wounds, give chai or food, or replace destroyed clothing, so she can relax a little, and you can begin to gain her trust. Assure her she is safe and that you will not tell an abusive husband where she is. Listen to her stories, letting her tell it her way first; next you can ask questions for more information. Also sense when to stop for that session before she becomes ill at ease with you.

- Begin admission form, gathering items for admission file, and other paperwork. If possible, complete the admission form the first day in case the woman runs in the night, even if you do not get all the details yet.

- Provide for immediate needs: food, clothing, shelter. Reassure her of safety. Show her around a bit. Give her bedding, toiletries, clothing as needed, and show her where she can keep her things and where she,

TIP Sometimes women arrive with nothing more than the clothes on their backs, and sometimes even that is in such poor repair that it cannot be mended. Have a ready supply of donated saris, salwar kameez (Indian tunic and pants), and undergarments at each home, so that suitable clothing can be given to the women who need it on arrival.

and her children if they are with her, will sleep.

- Take a photo of the woman as soon as possible after arrival. Make five passport-size copies.

- If the woman arrives sick or injured, take her to a hospital. If she is injured, also file a police report.

- If she has money or gold jewelry or important papers, lock these away and give her a receipt for them, assuring her she may have these things whenever she wants.

- Arrange for a medical evaluation of the woman and any children. These evaluations are required by the governing agencies within the first two days of arrival. (It is advisable to have a relationship with a local clinic where staff have been prepared ahead of time to work respectfully and gently with these clients.)

- Enter the woman into the admissions register, assigning her a case number.

Stage 2: Assessment

- Assess the situation, and the options, desires, and capabilities of the woman. See how she came to be here, what led up to her arrival, how big and longstanding the problems are. This will include outlining the family constellation: for example, husband, in-laws, and birth family, such as parents and siblings. Also, what is the woman's education and training? Assess her state of mind, see what she wants and needs.

- If she is too traumatized to know what she wants, then give her time and support to settle and see.

- Seek to stabilize the woman emotionally and mentally. Begin to enfold her into Maher daily life, gently, at a pace she can manage.

TIP Acclimation is a slow, gentle process. Sleeping, meals, kitchen work—all are communal at Maher. It is often easy to tell the new arrivals because they have a wide-eyed, startled look as they begin to adjust to Maher. Some are weeping; some look almost frozen. But residents smile at them, care for them, visit with them, sit and chop vegetables with them, and help with their children. The new women begin to learn about Maher and its values. They begin to see a different possibility for their lives, and feel they have a place to belong, even if only for a short time. And slowly, slowly they begin to soften and engage with others, and the healing begins.

CASE Afraid to return

A woman arrived with two of her children, leaving a third child at home, who became sick and missed her mother. However, the woman was afraid to go home by herself. A senior staff member offered to go with her so that the woman could decide whether she wanted to stay there, remain at Maher, or bring the third child back to Maher. A home visit was organized to assess the situation, and the woman was assured she could remain at Maher as long as needed.

- For women barely able to care for themselves, let alone their children, stabilize the mother first, while letting housemothers or a social worker care for her children.

- Give her household tasks to keep her busy, while assessing her knowledge and abilities. Observe how she manages her children and relationships with others.

- Begin to teach the Maher value of interfaith respect, assuring her she is free to keep and practice her faith, and that all come together for prayer and meditation. Encourage her to join the other women and housemothers for their morning prayers, meditation, and house meeting even if she does not want to say anything.

- Observe her closely. Build an empathetic connection and trust, to help the woman feel comfortable to open up. Then learn more about her situation, needs, and wants. Combine the observations of all staff.

- Do home visits to husband, in-laws, and parents, as relevant. If there is any thread of a chance for reconciliation, assess this option. Can the woman and her children return and live safely? Where is best for the children? What are their educational opportunities? Can the mother live on her own? The priority is family unity; if it seems possible to reunite a family, and if the woman wants this, then that becomes the goal.

- Listen both to what is said and to what is *not* said. For example, when a woman is reluctant to go home and also does not want staff to visit her people, yet refuses to say what the situations is about, it is important to learn more. Perhaps she is at fault. (If a woman does not want to tell her husband where she is, that is respected.)

- If applicable, help the woman see how she might have contributed to the problems, via peer and staff input, meditation, and reflection. Sometimes with increased self-awareness and a willingness to change, she is ready to go home without mediation or other assistance.

- Provide other services on an as-needed basis: counseling, medical and psychological assessment including possible medication, childcare if the woman is unable, training in hygiene and childcare, home visits, and legal assistance. If life skills programs happen to be on offer for women residents, she may attend if appropriate to her state of mind and needs.

Note: If a married woman arrives pregnant (whether by her husband or by another man) and seeking an abortion, Maher will provide shelter, but does not encourage abortion. Maher works with the woman to realistically assess her behavior and her options, and to choose either to reconcile with her husband or to leave and become independent, neither condoning adultery nor forcing a woman back to her husband. Sometimes she will decide to birth her child and give it up for adoption. Sometimes unmarried women arrive pregnant (perhaps they made a mistake, or perhaps they were raped). In either case, they usually cannot return home with a child. Here too Maher will provide counseling and shelter. Sometimes, if she is young and can give birth without a caesarean, the woman can give up the baby for adoption and go home again. She can later be married by keeping it a secret that she had a baby.

Mother and Child

TIP The deciding factor in whether a woman returns home is the woman's wishes. If she is unclear what she wants or if the situation is unclear, Maher helps her to try to return, to test things. If the situation feels too unstable, then she is supported to stay at Maher.

Decision point: Reconciliation or independence?

- Assess whether or not family reconciliation is both possible and desirable.

- If YES, then proceed to Stage 3 for Path A. If NO, proceed to Stage 3 for Path B.

CASE Some mothers need to learn how to be mothers

A woman came with a severely malnourished child. He was two years old but was so tiny and weak that he looked to be no more than a few weeks old. When she arrived, she did not even know how to hold the child and properly support his head (like a baby, he was too weak to hold it up himself). Maher immediately took the child to a doctor. With good food and vitamins, he can begin to grow. The woman has seven children; four are at other institutions. For now the mother will stay at Maher and learn how to clean, feed, clothe, and care for her child properly.

CASE The value of compassion and nonjudgment

One day shortly after her arrival, a woman hit her child. One of the housemothers intervened. A social worker, responding with compassion and nonjudgment, used this as an opening to learn more about the woman. She learned that the woman had been orphaned at age 10, put in a government home, and treated badly. An auntie came and married the woman to her drunken son. He then died. She was left with two children and no way to care for them. In despair, she sometimes hit her children. Just before coming to Maher, she'd thrown her daughter from a third-floor roof, and then jumped herself. Miraculously, neither was hurt. Then they came to Maher, and she now loves the Maher way. Sister Lucy advises compassion for these women who have lived traumatic lives: they have a lot to learn, and will sometimes make mistakes, such as hitting a child. Loving correction is the key.

Stage 3 and Stage 4: Case management and follow-up

At this point, Path A and Path B diverge significantly. Information is given below first for Path A for both stages, then for Path B.

For Stage 3 (either path) you can make a plan for each woman and child who comes seeking refuge and help, just as in Chapter 3 you made an annual plan for the NGO listing goals and activities. As before, this case management plan will identify goals and related activities, resources needed, a timeframe, and progress made. Use the headings below as a guide.

Stage 3 (Path A): Case management toward reconciliation

In this case, the goal is to facilitate reconciliation and a return home to family, whether husband, in-laws, or parents. In the first two stages you gathered the necessary information to identify the activities required to begin working toward this goal. Define the steps in order to achieve reconciliation, and estimate a timeframe and resources needed. Be ready to revise this plan as steps are tried, results are achieved, and more information becomes available.

Case Management sample goals and activities: format on the next page follows the NGO planning process from Chapter 3.

Name, admission case number, admission date

Goals and Activities	Resources needed	Timeframe (include dates)	Accomplishments (include notes and dates)
Goal #1 Mental and Emotional...			
Goal #2 Issue Resolution			
Goal #3 etc... (continue with further goals/activities)			

Goal 1: Continue to support the woman's mental and emotional stabilization.
Possible activities:

- Continue giving her household tasks, and develop her skills.

- Coach her in hygiene, childcare, nonviolent communications, and more, as opportunities arise.

Goal 2: Seek resolution to family issues. Efforts are focused on stabilizing the family. Staff are encouraged to be creative in helping families to resolve their outstanding issues.
Possible activities:

- Conduct home visits with the husband and his parents, (or her parents or other family members, if that is a better option for her and her children). Assess the man's character and intentions; assess the safety of the home for the woman and for her children.

- Provide counseling as needed for the woman, her husband, or the family as a group.

- Coach woman and family in nonviolent communication.

- Problem-solve as needed (see box inset).

- Mediate specific disputes (such as dowry, behavioral, financial). Mediate specific agreements such as what behaviors are not appropriate toward the woman and children, or agreements about new behaviors, such as shared management of household money.

- Provide legal aid.

- Coordinate with local authorities (such as police or village leaders) to make sure that everyone knows that violence will not be tolerated.

Note: Coordinate the woman's plan with a plan for her children's continued wellbeing and education, perhaps even with their delayed return home. (Guidance for working with children is offered in the next chapter.)

Path A decision point: Is the woman ready to return home?

- Assess readiness for the woman to return to her family; take her home when she is ready.

- If it has become clear that reconciliation will not be successful, then help the woman to think about other options, moving her onto Path B, and develop a new case management plan for her.

- Send children home only when appropriate for their proper and safe care and education. (This may be at a later date, once the mother's return home has proved successful.)

- Complete leave form. If the woman is leaving for some amount of time, or permanently, then she is leaving on her "own responsibility."

- Ask the woman to provide written feedback about her time at Maher when she leaves. If she is illiterate, ask for her feedback verbally and note it in her file.

Stage 4 (Path A): Follow-up

- Monitor the situation weekly, then monthly, by visiting the home. If the family lives far away, some check-ins will be via phone or letter. Assure that agreements are being kept, violence and drinking are not occurring, and children are attending school regularly. Monitoring may

continue up to two years after a return home.

TIP Creative problem solving

Maher is creative in finding ways to support families to remain together. Many of the issues and the violence have their root in poverty, so if that poverty can be alleviated, often families can cope with the rest. Maher might, for example, provide food assistance while a husband heals from an injury and is out of work, or find him a regular job with a salary that can support the family, or help the woman start a business that can supplement family income. If alcohol is the issue, treatment programs may be required and provided. Also, many of these families live in the open under a tin roof and there is no privacy for the couple, which adds tension to the relationship. Sometimes simply providing a couple a quiet place to talk, while the children are safe and well cared for, can lower tension enough to allow identification and resolution of issues.

- Be prepared to provide more mediation, counseling, or assistance as needed.

- Readmit if the situation deteriorates. (If the woman returns, there is no need for a new admission form, just a short form saying why she has come again and if she wants to work.) She may stay again for a short while, still working toward reconciliation. Or she may choose to stay and work toward self-sufficiency.

Path A final disposition

When she leaves, note final disposition (that is, resettled with husband or other relatives) and date departed in the admission register.

Ratnagiri housemothers with children, both their own and others

TIP When a couple is struggling with poverty, in-law troubles or disputes, alcohol, or abuse, the woman's "time out" while at Maher, especially with the added mediation and services to the family, helps a situation seem resolvable. But when the woman returns with several children, things can get chaotic very quickly and old patterns reemerge. So it can be very helpful to send the woman home first, allowing her and her husband to get things more settled, while the children remain at Maher for another few months, or even through the school year. The fewer times the children's lives are disrupted or they have to switch schools, the better. Parents, of course, are encouraged to visit their children, and children go home for holidays, which is a great test to be sure the family is ready for full reconciliation.

Summary of services for newly arrived and short-stay women

- Provision of food, clothing and shelter

- Counseling or psychotherapy to help women get over the mental and emotional trauma they have suffered; medications when needed

- Medical assistance including checkups and active treatment when required

- Legal assistance to make women aware of their rights and also to help achieve justice for the women and their children

- Guidance and training in basic life skills required of all mothers, such as caring for the home, nutrition and food preparation, supply of provisions, child rearing, and hygiene (see "Sample list of essential life skills" later in this chapter)

- Introduction to Maher values such as unconditional love, respect for all, nonviolent conflict resolution, and gentle child rearing; through living at Maher and joining others for their daily meditation and group meetings, women "see how it is" at Maher and for other women

- Preparation for reunion with family, including:

  o Home visits

  o Family counseling, including alcohol treatment programs

  o Networking within the community (for example, police or neighbors)

  o Mediating disputes, including agreements about appropriate behaviors and the woman's and children's safety and wellbeing, and renegotiation of dowry settlements

  o Keeping some or all of the children at Maher to allow a more gradual transition

  o Helping to relieve poverty issues, such as fixing a roof or providing weekly food assistance

  o Helping the husband or wife to find a job

  o Other creative problem solving assistance as needed

- After reunion, follow-up visits and contact to assure reconciliations are working (up to two years)

Reconciliation often takes longer than the three months allowed by the government for a short-stay home. In such cases, the woman will be assigned to a staff role so she can remain at Maher. If she remains for a longer time, a year or more, her case management may be more of a hybrid between Path A and Path B. Sometimes reconciliation may not seem possible at all; yet over time, situations and desires change. Maher will support reconciliation whenever the woman and her family are ready.

Stage 3 (Path B): Case management toward self-sufficiency

A woman may move right into Path B case management shortly after her arrival if there is no potential for reconciliation with her family or if she has no family to return to. (Or she might shift to this path after trying reconciliation and failing or changing her mind.) This path seeks self-sufficiency and security for the woman and her children through the options of continuing at Maher in a paid staff role, seeking work and a home outside Maher, or remarriage. Which option a woman pursues will depend on her preferences, resources, and skills. Once she stabilizes and her children are

---

CASE Sometimes it takes a long time!

A woman came to Maher because her husband was fooling around with another woman, and was unable or unwilling to care for his family. While he had a good job as a carpenter, he spent the money carelessly and there was never enough to pay the bills. The woman settled at Maher and became a good housemother. After two or three years, the husband came to ask her to come home. He'd realized he had made a mistake and that he loved her and their children.

Sister Lucy told him he could not have her back unless he changed his ways. She asked the woman if she wanted to go back if he changed. There were many meetings with the couple and Sister Lucy. It was agreed that the woman had a right to know and share in decisions about how the money he earned was spent. They would have a common bank account with both signatures required for withdrawing money, and each was accountable to the other about how the money was spent. Finally the woman and children went home. The problems did not come back; he treated her and the children well, and the children remained in school.

settled, she can choose what she wants to do. She may have a dream of completing her education, or opening a tailoring shop, for example. Maher will support these dreams as much as possible, helping her prepare as needed, using the case management process. Sometimes a woman will live and work at Maher for a few years before taking an outside job and living independently. Sometimes she will stay much longer. It is not well accepted in India for women to live independently, especially in the villages.

As noted, a woman may only remain at a Maher short-stay women's home for a maximum of three months. Most women will not even be close to being able to live independently this quickly. Therefore they will continue at Maher, usually working in housemother roles while they continue learning what they need in

order to become self-sufficient and independent. Independence does not always mean work outside Maher. A woman can have a full rewarding future at Maher, from housemother, to taking on projects in slums or in villages, to social worker, and more. First help her discover who she is and all that she is capable of.

In the first two stages, the focus was on gathering the necessary information to identify the activities to begin working toward self-sufficiency. Now you are ready to define the specific steps and requirements to achieve that goal, and to estimate a timeframe and any resources needed. Be ready to revise this plan as steps are tried, results are achieved, and more information becomes available.

CASE No reconciliation—so where to go?

A woman arrived with two children. Her husband was unfaithful and had taken another wife. She had no legal case since they were not married formally and the marriage was not registered. As is common among the poor, to marry, they, they had simply exchanged flower garlands. He had told her this was legal and that she was protected. He abused her. She could not return to her birth family's home either; her brother had married and settled there, and he would not accept her.

Staff members listened, consoled, and counseled her. Once she felt safe and sheltered, and her children were cared for, then she settled. She was able to choose what she wanted to do. She decided she wanted to settle on her own, near her family. Maher helped her find suitable work and a home close to where her brother and parents live. Being near her brother, she could be safer while still living alone with her children.

Case management plan sample goals and activities: same format as previously.

Goal 1: Continue to support the woman's mental and emotional stabilization and acclimation to Maher.
Possible activities:

1. Integrate her fully into Maher daily schedule.

2. Keep her occupied with simple tasks according to her ability, generally beginning with food preparation. Give clear instructions and supervise to be sure she is successful.

3. Guide her in learning the Maher values and way of life, such as interfaith tolerance, loving and respecting all, prayer, and meditation.

Goal 2: Continue to develop life skills.
Possible activities:

1. Teach and mentor her in proper care of children (her own and others) as a loving mother (for example, suggesting alternatives to disciplining children besides yelling or hitting).

2. Take her to establish her own bank account, so her wages can be directly deposited here.

3. Coach her to express her feelings constructively and to build relationships with the other women.

4. Help her learn to quiet her mind and emotions. (A resource might be sending her to a one- or three-day Vipassana meditation course.)

Goal 3: Help her develop a vision for her life, or at least the next steps, whether remaining at Maher or not, and determine future development needs.
Possible activities:

1. Begin to identify skills, interests, and strengths.

2. Assess her ability and gradually add more tasks and more responsibility, still supporting her.

3. Begin discussions of longer-term future, such as dreams, wishes, or fears. If she has outside work interests, assess her readiness for placement outside Maher, or provide training and skills to help her achieve goals.

4. Assign her to a formal housemother-cook role, with regular duties and lots of support.

5. Over time add more responsibility as she demonstrates she can be successful.

6. Assess continually her interest and developmental readiness for the next step of her formal work assignment, outside job placement, or remarriage.

7. Help her make good choices and learn from her mistakes; expect mistakes so she can learn from them.

Once she has mastered most of the life skills and has stabilized in a regular job at Maher, this is a sign she is ready for self-sufficiency, whether working at Maher as permanent staff or moving on to live and work outside Maher.

TIP Some women you rescue may prove to be mentally or emotionally too unstable to take on a housemother role. In such a case you will have to either transfer her to a different NGO with the facilities to provide the needed care, or determine a specific position within her abilities she can perform, assuming you have the resources to support her. One woman arrived at Maher mentally disturbed from trauma. Even with care and healing, her mind will never be what it once was. But she can still work and contribute. Now she monitors the outdoor play area at Vadhu where the gates border a busy road. She helps younger children cross and monitors that no one enters Maher who should not. Even as her son goes off to college, there will be meaning and dignity to her life.

Path B decision point: Is the woman ready to move into self-sufficiency?

The four options include marriage, work inside Maher, work outside Maher, or a move to long-term shelter.

Based on each woman's vision for her life (see Goal 3 above), at some point she will leave Maher's rehabilitation program, even if it is to become a permanent staff member.

- If she desires to marry or remarry, seek an appropriate husband and, pending her approval, arrange marriage.

- If she prefers to remain at Maher and work, assign her a more permanent role. At this point, she will transition from a case management plan to a performance plan like other professional staff. For details, refer back to Chapter 7 on staffing.

- If she has marketable skills and education, and so desires, then seek job placement outside. Follow up to support her transition and mentor her as needed. Her children may remain at Maher for schooling temporarily or for the duration of their education, depending on the mother's ability to support them.

  o Sometimes creative problem solving can help a woman move more quickly to independence, including paying a house deposit for a home in the village she came from (for example, if she is now widowed), if this assistance will help her live on her own and keep her children. Or she may have skills already and be able to work, and just need a bit of help to get started.

- If either trauma or lack of mental capacities prove too great for a woman to take on a full staff role, arrange for more full-time supportive care. In this case, transfer her to a facility for mentally disturbed women, even knowing that one day she may be ready to work again.

- Complete leave form. If she is leaving for some amount of time, or permanently, she is leaving on her "own responsibility."

- Ask each woman to provide written feedback about her time at Maher when she leaves. If she is illiterate, ask for her feedback verbally and note it in her file.

Stage 4 (Path B): Follow-up

- Maintain regular contact with the woman so she knows she still has family at Maher. Invite her to all Maher events and celebrations.

- Provide additional support as needed for her success, perhaps providing money for medical needs or extra expenses.

- Together with the woman, determine the best options for her children, such as how long they will remain at Maher and when they will go to live with her.

Final disposition (Path A and Path B)

Complete admission register by filling in the final disposition for every woman who walks in the door and for whom an admission file is at least begun.

Options include:

- Reconciled with family
- Working outside Maher
- Working inside Maher
- Married/remarried
- Expired
- Shelter at Maher (at either the facility for aged women or the facility for mentally disturbed women)
- Left (destination often unknown)

For some, living in a community of people of different faiths, cultures, languages, food habits, and full schedules is just too much to adjust to. Some women simply leave; this may happen at any time during a woman's stay at Maher. But if she returns, Maher's door is always open.

NOTE: While the mothers are at Maher, their children's schooling is paid for and the children may continue at Maher until their education is complete, whether or not their mother continues to live at Maher, works outside, or remarries. If she or her husband can afford to take on some or even all of the education expenses, they are requested to do so.

More about the "art" of family reconciliations

Maher staff have seen so many family situations and so much of the despair these families suffer as a result of poverty, lack of education, and lack of opportunities, that they have learned to see hope and opportunities that others may not see. They also, of course, see the hard reality of the violence. Many have lived it themselves. They are skilled at assessing people and situations, knowing when to walk away, and seeing when subtle pressures can be applied to make a difference. This combination makes Maher staff uniquely qualified to speak to families about reconciliation.

One of the early steps in assessing whether reconciliation is a reasonable goal is to talk to the man first, without the woman present. Ask him what happened, get him to speak his side of the issues. Assess whether he is a good man and is just angry, or whether he has no good intentions and means only harm. For example, sometimes a man will hit his wife in anger and tell her to go. But when a staffer talks to him, he says did not mean it. He is too proud to fix the situation even though he might wish to. Staff can work with this. They bring the man and woman together and help them sort through their issues. Sometimes just helping them to talk to each other is enough and the woman goes back home. Other times, however, the man is having an affair and does not want the woman back. In such cases Maher will not push reconciliation, as it rarely works out. If the woman really wants to go back even when Maher staff believe the man can do only harm, they will counsel her to stay, but will also let her try again. Sometimes the time apart

---

CASE Staff have lived it!

Anna, a senior Maher staff person, came to Maher with her young son to get away from her alcoholic husband. She worked as a teacher prior to coming to Maher. She became a housemother, then a para-social worker, and later took charge of all the women, both housemothers and short-stay women. Anna also helped train new social workers, oversaw their work, and helped in the more difficult reconciliations. Not too long after she became a housemother, her husband came for her. He too joined Maher's staff, and now takes care of all the site maintenance and helps with whatever is needed. He is a hard worker. He trains the boys in these tasks and is well liked. He still sometimes goes into the village and drinks, although not at Maher and without creating any problems. As Anna explains, people who stop drinking completely often get sick and cannot function.

has changed both the man and wife, and just knowing that the woman has an alternative can make enough difference for both of them to sort out their issues. If it does not work out, she is always welcome to return to Maher.

Sometimes the problem is pressure on the man from his parents. The man loves his wife, but his parents want him to get a new wife to get more money. In these cases Maher can intervene and mute or stop the misbehavior of the in-laws. Threatening legal action (such as preventing the man from remarrying, or court action against any violence) or public shame (the neighbors will all know why the woman is at Maher) can make all the difference. Often villagers do not know that it is actually illegal for a man (or any other family member) to beat his wife. While the courts rarely uphold this law, most do not know that either, so the threat of legal action helps.

CASE Planning and acting strategically

Shweta came to Maher with one child and also six months pregnant. Her common-law husband had abandoned her and gone back to his parents. Shweta was of a lower caste than the man. They were in love and had started living together, then had a child, but were too poor to register the marriage. The in-laws were against the marriage and tried to break it up. They called her a prostitute, but she had done nothing wrong. The in-laws were the trouble. Staff learned that the in-laws had found a woman of the same caste, so they needed to act before this new marriage could happen.

Sister Lucy and the staff strategized how to go to see the man. They talked to him on the phone to learn more about the situation, and found out how to get to where he lived (a long journey). "Do not tell him we plan to visit" Sister Lucy advised the staff, "or he will go hide! Wait several weeks." So after some time, a social worker took Shweta and her child to make a surprise visit to the man and his parents. The social worker had been coached to "be strong" with him, to insist that he tell the family the children were his responsibility, since the woman was an orphan and could not provide for them. Sister Lucy also told him this in a letter she sent with the social worker, and said that he must take good care of them even if he did not want the woman. The family was so scared; they had not expected anyone to stand up for an orphan! So even though the man was at work when Shweta arrived, the in-laws immediately said she and her child could stay. The social worker explained that the woman would call Maher regularly to check in. She instructed the mother-in-law to allow the woman to use the mobile phone and warned them that if there was any trouble, the social worker and Maher would be back.

Maher staff have also learned through experience to think and plan strategically for reconciliations. They can sometimes read a situation and anticipate what reactions and responses are likely. The above case is a good example.

Sometimes the women themselves change. They become stronger and wiser, meeting other women at Maher and learning their stories. They may realize their own situations are not so bad. Or sometimes, through counseling, staff can help the woman see how she contributed to the issues. Meditation and prayer, the examples of nonviolent problem solving, success stories of other women, even the simple guidance in various life skills: all these give the woman skills and hope and strength. Then she is ready to change, and to make her own situation better. One woman who came to Maher saw others suffering more than she was. She decided to go home and deal with her own situation, and is now helping other women in her village!

CASE Sometimes both the man and woman come to Maher

Lily fell in love with a man and they got pregnant. He was a Catholic priest and a school principal. Although he told her to get an abortion, she did not want to, so she had the baby. Yet even then he would not wed her—he would have had to leave both the priesthood and his job. Neither family would accept them. Lily was educated and spoke English well, but still had nowhere to go, so she came to Maher. She settled in, taking on administrative work at Maher, and began learning to control her temper and to meditate. She stayed in contact with her man. After a few months, he came to Maher to visit. He was adoring of his baby, and of Lily. Lily begged him to come to Maher too, and asked Sister Lucy to find him work. But while he too spoke Hindi and some English, he would have to learn Marathi before he could work in the Pune area. He did decide to come to Pune and he and Lily were married. After observing him, Sister Lucy recognized his skills and character. She hired him as the director for the expanding Jharkhand site, where speaking Hindi was acceptable, and so the whole family moved.

Legal options along the way to self-sufficiency

In a majority of cases, women who seek refuge at Maher are illiterate and have no idea of the legal remedies available to them. Maher works with organizations that provide legal aid to women who have experienced cruelty, violence, or other injustices from their in-laws and husbands. Maher at times has had a lawyer on retainer, who is then familiar with Maher, its goals, and its staff.

When reconciliation fails or is not an option, seeking legal assistance—not for retribution but for justice—is another recourse. Maher only approaches the courts when all other options have failed. For example, if a husband has stolen the children and all other efforts have been unsuccessful in regaining them, legal action can ensure that the children receive their rights, even if the mother does not.

With Maher's backing, divorces have been granted, and husbands have been ordered by the court to pay alimony to the wife and, where applicable, child-support. While this does not heal the wounds, it is a major step in restoring the confidence of the woman and reestablishing her faith in society.

Arranging marriages

Some women who come to Maher say they want to marry, but have no family to arrange it. Maher encourages women to marry or remarry so they can have their own homes and families. Whatever the difficulties, if a woman of a suitable age wants help to find a husband, Maher provides that help. Staff will listen to and counsel her, then look for a husband.

Sometimes a man or his family comes to Maher seeking a bride. Sister Lucy may also hear of a family whose son may be looking for a bride and she may approach them. After so many years, she and Maher are well known in the surrounding villages; word has spread and families seeking brides find their way to Maher. These networks develop over time. Likewise, Sister Lucy may also make it known that she is looking for a man of a certain age range. Maher acts in the role of the woman's or girl's parents throughout the negotiations and after the marriage.

Steps to arrange a marriage

- Have each prospective groom fill out a form (included) and supply certain documents (for example, a ration card) to provide relevant information about his background, family status, and financial means.

- Interview him, his family, his relatives, his neighbors, and his coworkers.

  o Will he be a good husband?

  o Will the family support the marriage and take proper care of the wife?

- o "Listen between the lines"— what is perhaps *not* being said?

- Reflect on which girls and women have expressed a desire to marry and whether any would be a good match. Consider age, temperament, caste, and religion when assessing a match. [17] Meet with the selected woman and tell her the man's story and situation, and ask if she is interested.

- If yes, arrange a supervised meeting at Maher. Then, see how it goes!

- Give them both time to think and decide what to do.

- If both are willing, arrange the marriage.

Preparation for the wedding

- Get a written proposal from the man and his family, indicating that they know the woman's history, that they agree to the marriage, and that they will take proper care of the young woman.

- Invite the man's family to Maher to discuss the marriage and customs and to plan the ceremony.

- Arrange wedding clothes for the woman. (Usually the man's family will arrange all of the things for him, and Maher will arrange clothes for the woman, although they may bring a sari for the woman.) If the man's situation allows, ask his family to contribute food for the celebration.

- Prepare and deliver the marriage invitations.

- Provide assistance to the couple when needed, such as helping them furnish a kitchen and a bedroom. (People know that these women have little or no family so they do not expect a dowry, but Maher helps as it is able, to support a successful marriage.)

The marriage celebration

- Call an appropriate religious leader who will perform the ceremony, according to the man's and woman's faith.

- Follow local wedding customs, such as Maher children putting henna on the bride's hands and feet, and each others' hands.

- Maher provides sweets and music, many photos are taken, and everyone enjoys the marriage celebration.

---

[17] This is perhaps the only time Maher takes caste and religion into account. Especially if this is a young couple, it is customary for them to live with his parents. If his parents do not approve of her, then there is little chance for the marriage. For older couples and remarriages, where children will not be raised, matching caste and religion is often much less important.

Marriage Ceremony

After the marriage

- Especially for a young girl in her first marriage, send a girl or a woman of Maher with the couple for a few days, or send Maher staff to visit the family after the marriage.

- Invite the bride back to Maher for a visit not long after the wedding.

- Once it seems things are okay, (three to five days after the wedding), take the husband and wife to court, see that the marriage is registered, and that the marriage certificate is received.

- Welcome the woman and her new husband back to Maher for holidays.

When the first child is born

- Invite the woman to come to Maher for the birth of her baby.

- Arrange a naming ceremony and invite the husband's family.

- Sister Lucy and Maher women do everything the grandmother would do for the child and the mother, such as providing gifts of a cradle, clothing, and other items.

It is not only young women and girls who seek to marry. Women with children sometimes seek to remarry. Maher will arrange these, although this is more difficult. Here, Maher must get firm assurances from the man that he will properly raise her children, even though they have another father. Widows also arrive at Maher with nowhere else to go. In Indian culture, a woman who has been widowed is often shunned by her family and her community, and she is unable to remarry. Sister Lucy can find husbands for them too if they wish. Wedding preparations will not be as complicated, although Maher still hosts a joyous celebration.

CASE Changing culture

In India there has been a centuries-old cultural belief that a widow should die with her husband, or otherwise live life in shame, on the edge of survival, and of course never remarry. Legally this has changed and widows may marry again, but the cultural expectations are deep. When Sister Lucy arranged the first wedding for a widow many years ago, the villagers and even the staff were upset and protested to her. She spoke to the village leader privately and asked him if his daughter had been widowed at age 20 and had raised her children, should her life be over now at age 40? Or if she had been widowed even before having children, would he want her to waste her life, to never have children? Why should she not have a chance again at happiness and a family of her own? Sister Lucy won him over, and slowly the village and staff are changing their beliefs.

CASE Widows remarried

Leena, a 58-year-old widow, came to Maher because she had no place to live. She had been widowed at age 19 and raised a daughter from her marriage on her own. When her daughter married, she left to join her husband's family. Maher staff placed Leena in their home for old women because they did not know what else to do with her. When Sister Lucy met Leena, she asked what she was doing there, as she was still an active, vital woman. Leena replied, "I am a widow. What else can I do?"

**Couple (both widowed)
recently married by Maher.**

An older man from the village had recently lost his wife. He came to Maher asking Sister Lucy to find him a wife. "I can't be alone," he said. Sister Lucy proposed a match with Leena, to which the man readily agreed. When Sister Lucy talked with Leena about this, she was initially shocked, saying, "I was widowed at age 19 and I'm now 58—how can I marry?" However, she gradually warmed to the idea, and Sister Lucy arranged for the couple to meet. They agreed to marry and are now happily living together. (Neighbors say Leena is looking even younger now!)

This author was taken to meet them and also another couple similarly remarried by Maher. Both couples lived very simply yet happily, in homes typical of the poorer city areas in India: small, neat, clean, and closely packed together. The women proudly showed their homes. We were welcomed as honored guests, served tea, and offered special sweets.

Road to Wholeness

Women who remain at Maher for longer than the three months allowed for a short-stay home generally do more than heal physical and emotional wounds: they undergo a transformation. They gain self-respect and self-confidence. They create and live satisfying, self-reliant lives. They laugh, they work hard, they learn to constructively deal with conflicts, they use their creative abilities, and more. They become whole again. They help others to heal and become transformed in turn. How does this happen?

Women Healing Women

Women healing women is at the core of this process of transformation. Women remaining at Maher become staff, almost always beginning as housemother-cook and then a full housemother. These women simultaneously learn and provide motherly love and care in their roles as housemothers responsible for the daily needs and development of other women and children in a safe, structured environment. This is how they learn the full breadth of the life skills, and also vocational skills, they will need to thrive in life beyond Maher. At the same time, this strategy is essential for the operation of Maher, in that all who arrive are nurtured by staff who have walked in their footsteps and who know firsthand at least some of the experiences of the arriving women and children.

While working in these roles, the women learn day to day many of the life skills, child-rearing skills, interpersonal skills, home care skills, and more, that they will need. They learn by doing; they are taught and guided daily by other staff. No class can substitute for this. They also learn Maher's core values, which are a great stabilizing support that can help lead them beyond the narrow confines of women's lives in traditional village life. They learn how to navigate the freedom of making decisions for themselves, of having their own money, of being independent of a father or a husband. And they make mistakes, and are lovingly guided to better choices by Sister Lucy and other staff.

It is one thing to read a list of services Maher offers, and quite another to guide women step by step in this transformation. Maher's secret is that it is not program-based, but relationship-based. First and foremost, Sister Lucy and her staff build loving, empathetic relationships with the women (and men, and children) who come seeking shelter.

Women healing women

Therapeutic Framework

The goal of this volume is not to train you, the founder, or even your staff, as counselors. Nevertheless, it is useful to say a bit about an effective framework for working with people who have experienced some degree of trauma.

The most effective process is "empathetic relationship-based support." Recognize that you are not, no one can be, a truly objective observer: your own heart and emotions will be touched, should be touched, by each arriving client. The ability to hold your heart as wide as possible, without summarily judging anyone involved, will help you develop the most useful place from which to help not only the client but the whole family. One of Sister Lucy's gifts is that she innately sees each person and hears each story in the larger context and culture of village life, of economic and emotional stress, *and* she holds the possibility of redemption for all. Resolutions are sought by working with all the parts of this larger context.

You and your staff must be able to make an empathetic connection quickly with each new arrival. As described earlier, an important first step is to look, listen, and immediately respond to essential needs such as hunger or thirst, or fear, anger, or hurt. You might reassure the woman that no one will be allowed to take her away, or you might provide food or clothing. You may simply be present with her while tears are shed, or listen to the outpouring of a story, likely only disorganized bits of a larger story in

this first telling. Your first task is to begin to form a relationship, to begin to build trust. Problem solving and paperwork come later. This is the heart of Maher's core practice: "to see how it is." People begin to respond to a natural feeling of connection to staff and residents. Once the relationship begins, then you listen, reflect back, and support the client in making sense of her experience. This in turn allows the client to learn and grow. Ultimately you are helping traumatized women to feel they have found a community of belonging. This supports healing because, universally as humans, we are naturally relational beings and we all seek belonging.

Maher's brilliant strategy of women healing women is built on developing such relationships. For example, you do not build self-esteem by reading about it or attending a course; people heal and grow by being in relationship, by hearing about their impact on others, by reflecting, practicing, and learning to express themselves differently. This is true the world over: our innate social nature as humans means that we grow and develop *in relationship*.

Life Skills in Daily Living

Regardless of how long a woman will stay at Maher, whether a few weeks, months, or many years, there are certain life skills that will help her be a better, stronger, happier woman, wife, and mother. These include hygiene, childcare, nutrition and food preparation,

---

CASE Basic life skills can help save a family

For one woman who sought reconciliation with her husband, early meetings and a home visit uncovered that a major source of conflict had been that she did not know how to cook or keep the home clean. In this case, part of preparing for successful reconciliation was coaching her in these areas. For another woman, all she had known was violence, having grown up in a home where fighting, yelling, and hitting were the norm, so she behaved this way too with her husband and children. In this case, her case management plan included coaching on nonviolent communication, meditation, alternate forms of disciplining children, and other skills needed to help make this family stronger.

---

basic home management, and managing money. Many of the women who come to Maher have been disadvantaged for a long time. They have had little training and few role models for these skills that many of us take for granted. Even for the women only staying a short while before reconciling with families, Maher seeks to expose them to as many of these skills as possible, providing more guidance in the most critical areas of hygiene and childcare. As each new woman arrives, part of her assessment as she stabilizes is which of these life skills she possesses and which she does not. Then staff prioritize which basic skills are most critical for her, and these priorities are recorded as part of her case management plan. Obviously, the longer a woman stays, the more she will learn.

As a woman and her children begin to settle in at Maher, no matter how long her anticipated stay, she will be assigned

work to do based on her interests and abilities. She may begin in a housemother role (specific duties are described in Chapter 7) or she may help with office work if she has these skills. Additionally, she may engage in classes (music or art) and specific training, as they are available. She may go with staff to village self-help groups sponsored by Maher, or on exposure visits to other institutions. These activities all serve to keep her mind busy (not dwelling on her fears, anger, or other troubles), to teach her these valuable life skills, and to help her put her own experiences into perspective by hearing the stories of other women and children.

Regardless of what work the women do, they are coached in a range of basic skills required to run a household and to raise children. These skills are applicable to women on short-stay, women reconciling and going home, and women remaining at Maher long-term or until they find work elsewhere. Training occurs daily and often in the moment, as things come up; staff continually guide and encourage each woman.

Below is a general list of the life skills women learn while at Maher. These skills are also required in their roles as housemothers (or in any staff position). Women who remain at Maher long-term continue to master the rest of these life skills and to learn additional skills for their specific roles. (It is assumed that staff hired directly from outside know and can perform all these life skills, although perhaps they will become more skillful while at Maher.)

Sample list of essential life skills

1. Cleanliness and hygiene (for self, clothing, food, dishes, house, and yard)

   - Understand importance (disease prevention, pleasantness)

   - Toilet habits (such as washing afterward)

   - Personal hygiene: bathing body daily, washing hair weekly, nails clean and trimmed, check for head lice, teeth brushing (prevent tooth decay, sweet breath)

   - Clothes washing: how to do properly, also pressing (ironing) and folding

   - Clean and neat appearance: clothes in good repair, learn basic hand-stitching to make repairs

   - Housecleaning: how, with what materials, daily care and cleaning, such as dishes, counters and workspaces, floors, windows, and food storage areas

   - When and how long to boil water for safety

2. Food preparation

   - How (and why) to correctly prepare healthy balanced meals (beyond rice and dal), including fruits, vegetables, greens, eggs, milk

   - How to shop for, clean, prepare, and cook fresh vegetables and leafy greens

   - Use of spices both in terms of health benefits (Ayurveda) and for good flavor

   - Measuring quantities so there is no waste

3. Care, development, and discipline of children

   - How to teach or guide children in good hygiene (doing for younger children, and supervising for older)

- Proper dressing for children, including proper undergarments, neat and clean appearance, clothes clean and in good repair

- Guide children to eat all foods, not just one or two

- Understand value of education for *all* children, completion of homework, being on time to school, and more

- Engage appropriately with school principals and teachers, and positively resolve issues regarding children's education

- Nonviolent discipline and guidance for children; alternatives to force, yelling; how to guide and teach good behaviors and choices in children

- Basic first aid for cuts, scrapes, and other injuries, as well as fevers and common nonthreatening illnesses; know when to consult a doctor (See Chapter 6 for more details.)

4. Other house-management skills

- Safe use of electricity, gas cylinders, and clothes iron

- Bed-making

- Pick up and properly store personal items

- No trash left out

> **TIP** Vipassana meditation is a critical part of women's emotional development. With its focus on the breath, Vipassana supports emotional stability by teaching a reflective (as opposed to reactive) stance. Women learn to feel emotions (joy, anger, sadness) but to no longer let these emotions overwhelm them; they learn to let go and return to breath. Slowly they develop inner resources and strength to deal with strong emotions, setbacks, and stress. Every woman at Maher begins a daily practice of 10 minutes at the start of the morning housemother meetings. Sometimes a short class is available that teaches why Vipassana meditation is beneficial and how to do it. Otherwise, the other women teach newcomers the basics. They build up from 10 minutes sitting to a half hour. If a woman decides to stay at Maher, she is encouraged to go to a 3-day, and later a 10-day, Vipassana training.

5. Emotional development and effective relationships with other women and staff, and with men

- Basic self-esteem and respect for self and for others, regardless of differences in caste, class, religion

- Curb tendency to yell or continually criticize; learn to speak up for own needs and desires, and for children's needs

- Emotional development and self-awareness (includes how to settle the mind with meditation)

6. Other life skills essential to living outside Maher

    - How to use a mobile phone, buy a railway ticket, post a letter, make bank deposits and withdrawals, manage money

    - Awareness of their rights as women, the dangers of alcoholism, and how to seek treatment

7. Maher's core values as "guiderails" to help build more satisfying and peaceful lives and relationships. Be creative as you help these women learn to be better mothers. Maher often uses "street plays" as a way of teaching values and behaviors. In street plays, women can see an issue in daily life acted out, with good resolutions suggested by the play. In one case, the food was not prepared well, and the children were not finishing their food. So Sister Lucy asked the older children to prepare a street play about this topic. They

acted out the situation (the children weren't eating), and the possible whys (too salty, not fully cooked, or overcooked). The women saw the play and understood. The bigger children make up these plays easily because they have seen it all. Sometimes the housemothers too make up street plays: to create the plays they must discuss the issue, and so they learn. Creating and performing these plays (on a wide variety of topics) is one method of raising awareness in the villages too.

House rules

Maher has a few house rules whose principle goal is to develop and reinforce all the life skills above, rather than simply to get compliance. Therefore the approach when someone breaks a rule is to teach, not to punish. This is true for residents as well as staff.

Examples of a few rules (more in Chapter 6):

- No personal calls on mobile phones when women should be caring for the children; limit usage.

- No visitors of the opposite gender.

- Be on time, both in maintaining the house schedule and to meetings and programs.

CASE Breaking a rule is an opportunity for learning

Some of the housemothers were buying mobile phones with their money. The children came to complain that the housemothers were in the showers at night talking on their phones, making dates with men for their time off, for example. In reaction, some staff members wanted to have a rule of no phones for housemothers. Sister Lucy reminded them that these women had gone from being under the control of parents to being under the control of husbands. They had never had freedom, their own phones, their own money. Now suddenly they had all these choices, and the women needed to learn how to manage these things. So let them have the phones, watch them, and then guide them in appropriate usage, Sister Lucy advised. Taking away the phones would not help them learn, and most of them were not abusing the freedom anyway. The same approach applies to teaching them the value of money, how to be role models to the children, and how to be in "right relationship" with men.

Examples of some of the life skill topics as they may arise in daily Maher life

Money management

Each woman remaining beyond a couple of months will have a bank account set up for her. Maher makes regular deposits of her salary, plus any earnings from her work in the Production Center[18]. Each account will have a staff name plus the woman's name, and signatures of both are required for

---

[18] Maher constructed the Production Center so residents could learn skills while producing items for resale such as stitched cards and purses, crocheted items, candles, and jewelry. Residents may work here in off hours, earning a small amount per piece created. Much of the work is handwork and its repetitive nature is soothing to many of the women.

TIP Sister Lucy says, "In India, when we are children, we are naturally dependent on our fathers. When we are married, we are dependent on our husbands. And when we are old, we are dependent on our sons. None of our women have a bank account; they do not even know what a bank account is. They don't know how to write their names. At Maher we teach these things, and then the women really see that they can support themselves. I see them changing their lives."

withdrawals. This protects the money from being taken by her husband. The woman must ask staff if she wants to withdraw money, which provides an opportunity to talk about the value of saving, about choosing between wants and needs, and about making choices that likely she has never had to make before.

Relations with men

These women often have the double challenge of general low self-esteem due to cultural views in India, and of having been abused and degraded by their fathers, husbands, in-laws, or others. They have had little education or exposure to strong and independent women role models. Therefore Maher seeks to impress upon these women that they are equal to their husbands, and not to feel bad for being women, regardless of cultural tradition. These messages must be repeated in many ways, over and over. A great deal of effort is made to boost women's self-esteem, through daily life and through specific courses. Sister Lucy has made sure to hire male social workers, so the women learn how to interact with men as peers and equals. Even so, often she must coach these men too to overcome the traditional male attitudes regarding women's roles. The women must learn also to deal with male authorities, shopkeepers, and others without becoming intimidated. They must know and be able to speak up for what is

---

CASE Good listening story

At a daily housemother meeting the author attended, a newly arrived woman and a housemother got into a conflict; one was hurt, the other was angry. As one woman began talking, the other started to interrupt; a staff member gently stopped her. The first woman was allowed to finish speaking; then the other spoke and was listened to. As the two women spoke back and forth, feelings were strong; there was even some shouting and some tears. The staff member then intervened, advising: "This is not the Maher way. You love her [the older housemother] as your mother, and you love her [the new woman] as your daughter. No one has to change—we bring our bodies, minds, hearts, and hands with us wherever we go, so we must love each other as we are." Both women listened intently. Then the other women in the meeting began offering solutions and advice. Even with the raised voices and tears, it stayed respectful and everyone listened. After this everyone was fine, the new woman was smiling again, and all were laughing as they moved on. The other women have all been there and there was no judgment.

correct for themselves and their families.

Maher introduces the idea that it is okay to be friends with men, but without "spoiling" the men's family life. That is, they must learn appropriate boundaries for friendships between men and women. At Maher this is talked about openly, which in itself is unusual in India. Sometimes a woman may become entangled with one of the older boys. Sister Lucy advises care in selecting the housemother to the older boys, and then to watch closely. If a woman becomes entangled sexually or is simply unable to stand up to the boys, then she is transferred or a job is found for her outside Maher.

Emotional Development

The women, as well as most of the staff, need to be supported in general emotional development. This includes how to experience and express feelings in a timely and appropriate manner so nothing is buried. It also includes good

---

CASE Bottled-up feelings

Two of the housemothers (sharing a house of 20 children) were fighting in front of the children, and the social worker was concerned. The situation was brought to Sister Lucy's attention and they all met.

The context, Sister Lucy knew, was important: both women had come to Maher seeking refuge, both were widows, and each had three or four children. As widows traditionally barred from remarrying and as young women still, they had many frustrations. Also, Indian women are taught to keep in their feelings, to bottle them up.

Sister Lucy recognized the natural leadership qualities of both women, but noted that neither seemed able to compromise with the other. Even though her heart was full of love and compassion for the two women, she deliberately used a strategy of "scold and provoke" to model "getting it out" to let them fight a little bit. In this way they were able to show their anger and feelings so that these could pass and resolution could be found. Both women were able to settle and slowly learned to air differences more constructively.

Sister Lucy later coached the social workers to learn to tolerate a little fighting, so things did not get bottled up. Only if it got to be too much should they intervene while still encouraging the expression of feelings. "After all, if they do not show their feelings here at Maher, where will they go to let them out?" Sister Lucy pointed out.

listening and how to practice compassion and nonjudgment toward all. Bottled-up feelings are part of the source of tension in marriages and other relationships, including at Maher.

Women living together, many under stress from unresolved questions about their futures, may easily get upset or feel hurt by another. The daily housemother meeting, which includes all women residents, is one place where they can begin to learn to work through conflicts as a normal part of daily living. Staff must be prepared to address issues "in the moment," both to help resolve the immediate conflict, and to demonstrate and teach those involved

how to live with feelings openly expressed.

Additional Programs and Services

The women will be exposed to and taught a great variety of general life and vocational skills, many of which add more depth to the essential life skills listed above. All these opportunities have the goal of helping these women become all they can and might wish to be, as human beings, as women, and as mothers. Some topics are taught by Maher staff; others are taught by outside resources.

CASE The children watch and learn from the adults

Two staff members got into a conflict over a set of keys. Lakshmi (a recently arrived woman) needed a key to do a task assigned to her by Sister Lucy. Meera, a much older, very stubborn woman who had been on staff since the early years, had her own set of keys but hated to lend these keys out because they so often got lost. So when Lakshmi asked Meera for the key, Meera refused. After much haggling, Meera finally gave over the key. After the job was done, Lakshmi did not want to return the key because she knew she would need it again soon. But Meera demanded the key back. Lakshmi was so upset by this time that she skipped the evening meal and hid away.

At the evening meal, Sister Lucy heard the story and immediately called Lakshmi to her and quietly scolded her for skipping dinner due to the conflict (which, as in any family, everyone knew about). Sister Lucy told her, "You are not setting a good example for the children. You are upset and you go away. Do not do this! You must let it go and go on with things. Children watch how you deal with things, as an adult and as a mother: you are always a teacher and you need to set good examples."

CASE A better life

One of the housemothers learned computer skills and took on a lot of the recordkeeping at SOFKIN (many hours' journey from Pune). After a few years, she was able to get a good job at an office back in Pune where she will be closer to her family. Of course SOFKIN let her go, knowing they would have to find and train another housemother to do that work, or possibly even hire a bookkeeper. "This is what we want for these women—a better life," says Chaya Pamula, founder of SOFKIN.

Lifelong learning: sample topics

- Adult literacy classes in reading, writing, even basic school equivalency if desired, to open new horizons (Many women who were illiterate when they came to Maher have begun to sign their names and read newspapers.)

- Additional training related to health, self-care, and mothering

- Interpersonal skills training such as nonviolent conflict resolution, listening, behaving compassionately toward others, and building appropriate relationships with children, peers, men, and staff

- Self-esteem workshops

- Vocational and professional training and guidance (see list below)

- Meditation and spiritual guidance

- Yoga and exercise

- Dance or music as therapy

- Different types of celebrations such as religious holidays from an interfaith perspective, and Indian and international events

- Awareness of current events, politics, the wider national and international community

- Awareness programs on issues such as AIDS or legal rights of women

Other support

- Rehabilitation: gentle assistance to get back into the social mainstream and to lead a meaningful life

- Marriage, remarriage, or divorce assistance

- Assistance with correspondence to family members (phone calls or letters)

- Exposure visits to similar institutions

251

A note about exposure visits

Maher takes women residents, housemothers, and even social workers on exposure visits to other organizations and institutions where women or children might live or work, to see alternatives to being at Maher. Maher may seem like "hard work," but the women (and staff) see how good it is at Maher in comparison, the love that is all around, and the increased opportunities. These visits provide a great chance as well to talk about the impact of living and working according to Maher's values.

Learning that the Maher way is better—the hard way: One woman who had been a prostitute was being hassled by other housemothers who said she was not fully into the Maher way, for example, leaving her children alone. She asked to go to a different organization. Sister Lucy advised her it would be better for her and the children if she changed her ways, but the women refused. So Sister Lucy arranged for her to go to another place that takes in women and gives them work; after a while they threw her out. She called Sister Lucy, begging for another chance. Three times she made mistakes, and three times Sister Lucy allowed her to come back. Now she is back at Maher and making the necessary changes.

Training and job placement

Maher provides as many opportunities as possible for residents to learn skills that they can then apply to support themselves and their children, beyond Maher. Most of the women who stay at Maher have little or no education. Without this, usually a woman cannot

---

CASE From despair to a full life

Marala first came to Maher as a widow with her son. She remembers: "I was always crying. My mind was dull. I did not know how to relate to the other women, children, and the world. The staff were always guiding and encouraging me. I started learning how to cook, how to measure and make the right amount. The staff were always telling me I could do it, the way a mother encourages her daughter. I have learned so much here, more than I could have learned at home. I went with the director to see and help the women in the villages, and to see the self-help groups. I saw how other women lived. I always kept busy. I became a housemother-cook, then a housemother, and then got training as a para-social worker. Now I never feel tired, and I am always smiling. I saved my money and bought land in my village. Someday I will build a house there!"

CASE Professional development: Manju's path

Manju arrived about 12 years ago with her baby boy. She was unmarried and had been abandoned by both her family and the boy's father. Other institutions would not help her unless she gave the boy up for adoption. So she came to Maher to raise her child and create a life for them. Sister Lucy warned her that it would not be easy being a single mother, that the world would judge her and her child. Manju was determined, and so they settled at Maher.

Manju was one of the lucky ones who had completed her basic education. Like most women who arrive, she worked first as a housemother. After several years she completed Maher's para-social worker training, and eventually was placed as a social worker at Maher's Ratnagiri-based home for 30 girls. Recently she returned to Pune to work for a new joint-venture project between Maher and another local NGO, working for the rehabilitation of mentally disturbed women. This organization interviews and selects women who, with counseling plus medical and home care, can get jobs. Manju now manages the home (a halfway house, essentially), caring for these women so they can work. Manju is also taking classes, studying for her MSW. Her salary has grown over the years to match her growing capabilities. Her son, a teenager now, is doing well at Maher, and she has a good career.

---

manage on her own outside. She cannot earn enough to support herself, let alone raise and educate children. The most common outside job placements are factory work and domestic work. Maher has developed a reputation for providing good, dependable workers, and prospective employers now call Maher when looking for people to hire.

Other women either have some education and can build on that, or they choose to develop some of the vocational or professional or other training programs that Maher is able to offer.

Vocational training provided at Maher or in Maher's Production Center

- Housekeeping (for own home or for future employment in other homes)

- Tailoring

- Henna patterning

CASE Job placement and living support

Rekha and her children fled to Maher because her husband, a drug addict, became violent. He stole her hard-earned money and used it to buy more drugs. When the author first met Rekha, she had been at Maher at least two or three years; by that time she was the cook for staff and guests. Her children lived at one of the homes in Pune so they could remain enrolled in the same school. Then her mother- and father in-law came to Maher saying it had grown worse with their son and they also had had to flee, and so she must care for them. Rekha agreed. Maher found her a job at a local factory and helped her rent a small home for herself and her in-laws near her work. Her children remain at Maher, although they come to live with her on holidays and vacations.

- Cooking and food preparation
- Handmade greeting cards
- Fancy candles
- Ready-mixed curry powders
- Incense sticks
- Paper bags with tribal paintings
- Crocheted and fabric bags

<u>Professional training provided by Maher</u>

- Para-social worker
- Kindergarten teacher

<u>Specialized training provided at other institutions and training centers</u>

- Cooking
- Baking
- Nursing

<u>Job placement and referrals</u>

It is Maher's aim to help each woman achieve financial independence. Maher is known for high-quality referrals and regularly receives calls from people seeking women for domestic work, for example. There are often more domestic placements available than there are women who want that work. Maher also has relationships with several large local factory employers who hire Maher women, teens who have completed their education, and also men from families with whom Maher is working.

Comments from some women residents about Maher:

- "I came here and received love and closeness."

- "Maher sees and uses my talents."

- "My own people never gave me the love I get here."

- "Mother Lucy cares for me. There is so much togetherness, and sisterly and brotherly love here. And understanding."

- "I have got my own self-respect, my own living, and there is no need to beg. I can work and stand on my own two feet."

- "My children get more opportunities here: schools, dance, travel, and more."

- "I like the interfaith love and understanding for each other. There are no differences between senior and junior women; people are equals here."

- "I have become bold here!"

> ## CASES Becoming change agents
>
> *Women trained at Maher are working as staff and also working out in the villages. They have gone from being oppressed, abandoned, and worse to active change agents for the future of India. Komal, a social worker in Kandur, was so traumatized when she first came to Maher that she could not speak—yet now she is working to stop the sale of alcohol in Kandur, where it is a big problem. She has organized 3,000 women! Another woman, Mongul, became a model social worker in another village, and has started many self-help groups and also her own business.*

Conclusion

Maher helps all women coming to its doors heal and transition to a better life. Families are sometimes successfully reconciled, and a whole family's life is changed for the better. Housemothers are Maher's best success stories; they were largely healed not through talking, but through caring for children and other women—that is, doing the work of Maher. Loving others, being loved by others, building relationships, and belonging: these are the core of healing. The women then go out into the villages, starting self-help groups, running awareness meetings, and creating other programs. As they are transformed, they help extend Maher's reach and transform others.

Women stay here patiently, working here until they can stand on their own. Most thrive. Their children are also helped, and in the end they take care of their mothers. This is "the end of the story," part of the meaning of Maher's slogan "Rising to New Life:" the children grow up and eventually provide a new, better home for their mothers, as well as for their own children.

Summary of Recordkeeping and Copies of Files

Summary of All Paperwork Relating to Women

Women's forms, files, registers	Stage begun	Stages when updated
Admission form	1	2
Admission application letter	1	
Admission file (all admission-related papers, including form)	1	2, 4
Admission register (paper and online)	1	2. 4
Medical file	1	2, 3, 4
Receipt for valuables	1	as needed
Case file	2	2, 3, 4
Marriage application form		as needed
Leave form	4	
Feedback form	4	

Copies of files

Below are copies of forms and files where these may be useful. In Maharashtra state in India, these are standard; elsewhere you will have to check and adapt as needed. Downloadable copies are on the book's website www.replicatemaher.wix.com/tools where noted.

Women's admission form

(List of contents only: you will need to add appropriate spacing for data to be recorded.)

Attach photo
Admission Date
Name
Full address
Age
Birth date
Marital condition: married / unmarried / divorced / widowed
Religion
Caste
Languages known
Education
    Illiterate
    Literate
    Training
    Graduation
Income resources: Income (yes / no)
Children's information
    Total number boys and girls
    List names, ages, education, occupations, handicaps
Husband/father information
    List name, address, age, education, occupation
    Private service / government / unemployed
    Income
Family history
    List names, ages, education, occupations, handicaps
Assistance being received? (lawyer / institution / organization / person / other)
Reason for requesting admission to Maher
    Husband harassed physically or mentally
    Addicted husband / father / brother
    Trouble from family members
    Death of husband
    Thrown out of house
    Unwed mother
    Other
Referred for admission by: (institution / person / social worker / friend / neighbor / other)
How was the woman's condition, physically and mentally, at the time of admission?
Name and address of person accompanying woman for admission

Things woman brought with her at admission
    Money
    Personal belongings
    Food
    Important papers
Address and phone number for communication
Reason for leaving Maher
    Unhappy at Maher
    Reconciled with family
    Got job
Reason for readmission
    Unable to adjust
    Trouble started again
    Cheated
    No cooperation from relatives
    Left job
    Other
Date of readmission
Expectations from Maher
    Basic needs
    Training
    Job
    Legal help
    Other
Beneficiary—name and signature
Person accompanying woman to admission—name and signature
Social worker— name and signature

Sample Admission Application Letter

Date

With my own wish and will I came to the institution and I will follow the rules and regulations of the institution. If I do something wrong, the institution may say this is okay or may ask me to leave. I have some things, gold, money, or papers, that I am keeping with the institution, and I have been given a receipt for these.

Signature

Miss / Mrs. _____

Admission Register (spreadsheet on website)

Column headings include case number, first name, family name, address, date of admission, year of admission, year of discharge, sex, number of children, religion, caste, cause of admission, current year, current age, sent by, final disposal, date of discharge, still at Maher (Yes/No), staff role/house. Notes: Most will not know the year and date of their birth, which is why current year and current age are collected. Also, the government requires caste and religion be recorded.

Case File

Ideally each woman will have one case file with everything in it:
- Admissions form and file
- Case history (her background and why she came, what steps have been taken toward reconciliation, monthly summary)
- Medical file (although more often now all the medical files are kept separately, all together)
- Case management file, updated regularly with goals, activities, progress, accomplishments, issues (such as conflicts or behavioral issues that arise)
- Leave forms

Marriage proposal form (for perspective husbands)

Attach photo
Name
Age
Date of birth
Local address
Phone number
Permanent address
Does he have own property? (yes / no)
    Details
Education
Religion
Employment
    Place of work
    Designation
    Salary
    Business
    Monthly earnings
    Is job permanent?
    Shift duties (yes / no)
Family member information (List names, relations, ages, occupations, monthly earnings)
Facilities at home (TV, gas, fridge, etc.)
Referred to Maher by
Reason for coming to Maher
Hobbies / spare activity
Habits
Food habits (vegetarian / nonvegetarian)
Married / never married / widowed
If married, reason for remarriage (describe)
Expectations for a wife
    Religion
    Caste
    Age
    Years
    Education
    Height
    Color
    Nature (describe)
    Other
    Remark by interviewer (observer)
Interviewer signature

9 | Assessment, Healing, and Development of Children

You have escaped the cage.
Your wings are spread out.
Now fly.

                    —Rumi

Children who come to Maher have the chance to develop rich, full lives, a chance to flourish, a chance to live out hopes and dreams they would perhaps never even have dared to dream. And you have a chance, through them, to give something to tomorrow, to the future. This is an incredible privilege— and lots of work.

Each child will have already suffered hardships and even horrors, whether from poverty and malnourishment, fear and abuse, death of one or both parents, or any of a host of other disadvantages that face children without stable homes and families. Most come from poor families that either simply cannot afford to educate their children or that suffer from the violence common in desperately poor families. They may have had some schooling, but not consistently. These children tend to adapt to Maher fairly well.

But many other children have had to learn to survive on the streets; they may have been arrested or cycled through several institutions before coming to your NGO. Many have had little or no schooling. These children from the streets are unlikely to have good personal hygiene habits, may be unused to things like shoes or underclothes, and have no idea why or how to clean dishes, clothing, or floors. They may not even know how to use a toilet or wash their hands properly. Some have never even lived in a building. Most of the daily living habits you take for granted they have had limited, if any, experience with due to their circumstances.

263

Many have learned to survive by fighting, stealing, lying, or running away. A mother's or a father's love may be completely unknown to them. Therefore, great care must be taken to first gain a child's trust, then to lovingly, with patience and understanding, guide him or her into a new life. Maher doesn't coerce compliance, but helps children to slowly make better choices within a loving environment. And somehow, through the resilience of the human spirit perhaps, they respond.

Whether you decide to run a project focused only on children or you plan for women who then bring children, how you work with the children who come to stay will be mostly the same. Of course, children who come with mothers who are then shortly reconciled and returned to families receive less developmental attention. The main focus of this chapter will be on the children who live at your NGO through the years of their growing up and education. Short-term stay children who come and go with their mothers will be more briefly discussed.

Goal for Children: More Than Survival

At Maher, children get so much more than food, shelter, clothing, and a government education: they learn values and life skills, they develop hidden talents and potential, and their wounds are healed as best they can be. Ultimately, the goal is that:

TIP At Maher, the goal is for children to thrive, not merely survive. One definition of "thrive" is "to enjoy meaningful relationships, be caring and compassionate, do well in school, work hard and be responsible, and feel good about who they are."*

* Daniel J. Siegel, M.D., and Tina Payne Bryson, PhD, The Whole-Brain Child. (NY: Delacorte Press, 2011),vii.

- Children walk together toward wholeness

- Children, having grown up in loving and safe Maher homes, are prepared to create similar homes for themselves and their future families

- Children discover their power within and develop self-reliance

- Children are prepared to become economically independent and self-sustaining adults

- Children reenter society well equipped to face the challenges that lie ahead, even to seek to "give back" and become the leaders of tomorrow

- Children feel grateful for what they have today

Research shows that early intervention can make a great deal of difference in a child's life, and this is why Maher's approach is so critical.

> *For children born and raised in deep poverty (defined as half or less of the income of the poverty threshold), often other factors are present as well, such as single parents, abusive adult-adult or adult-child relationships, drugs or alcohol, violent neighborhoods, and little access to health care and good nutrition. Concentrations of deep poverty in a neighborhood lead to an "exponential increase in related forms of social dislocation," according to University of Chicago sociologist William Julius Wilson.* [19] *Additionally, "neuroscientists and developmental psychologists describe how early stress and trauma disrupt the healthy growth of the prefrontal cortex . . . and [the] absence of strong and supportive relationships with stable adults inhibits a child's development of a crucial set of cognitive skills . . . leading to trouble controlling impulses in school, trouble getting along with classmates and following instructions. Intensive early interventions make a great deal of difference."* [20]

Maher believes that stable two-parent or extended families are still the best environment for raising children. If you cannot stabilize and facilitate reconciliation for families, then you work to provide stability and healthy relationships through life in the NGO. This is a crucial difference between institutions that merely house children and Maher-inspired organizations.

Overview of Working with Children

As a result of the work done in previous chapters, you have identified the groups of children the NGO plans to accept, their ages, and whether to serve both boys and girls. Children may arrive from six possible channels[21]:

1. With the mother, who is also seeking refuge

2. Referred or brought by police or other institutions

3. Found on the streets (orphans and others staff may pick up)

4. From families who are intact but too poor to send their children to school, so they ask Maher to take them (these families remain active and visit, and the children return home on holidays)

---

[19] Paul Tough, "The Birthplace of Obama the Politician," *The New York Times Magazine* (August 12, 2012): 28.
[20] Ibid: 44.

---

[21] Note that your NGO may choose to select children from only certain channels, such as orphans or poor children who have known family life and are easier to work with.

5. Children bring themselves to Maher (requires checking with police to discover their status)

6. Referred or brought by neighbors or relatives when parents are dead or missing

Every child who arrives at Maher is unique, but it is both possible and useful to think about guiding each child through a process, following a map that applies to all. Certain steps come in a certain order. Just as it is necessary to add spices to a dish you're cooking early on to allow the flavors to mature, similarly in working with these children, certain steps should happen before others. Even the challenges that arise usually occur at predictable stages and ages. If you recognize this, you can more easily anticipate and plan for these challenges. Workflow tools are also useful for training staff, showing them an overall orderly flow and then adding details as they gain more experience at Maher.

All children follow the same workflow process over their years at Maher. The exceptions are children who come with their mothers for a short stay and then return to live with reconciled parents or other family members. A discussion of these children follows the main workflow narrative. How long it takes a child to adjust will vary depending on what life circumstances they have come from. Children from poorer families in the villages are the easiest to work with and the quickest to adjust. Children who come from the streets will need extra

attention and socializing to be able to live in a home. Those who come from an abusive family situation or are newly orphaned will need additional/special counseling. Usually the first 6 to 12 months involve the hardest adjustments; this is the time when failure is most likely. Once they settle, learn to trust, and begin to feel loved and safe, then the children can blossom.

The children who arrive at your NGO will likely have similar backgrounds to the children who come to Maher. Maher's workflow, services, and guidelines are offered here so that you have some idea what to expect and can model the practices of your NGO after Maher, adapting these as necessary to local culture and circumstances.

Grandmother and three grandchildren

CASES Where children come from

1. A year and a half ago, two sisters were on the streets. A car ran over the older one and completely crushed her leg, leaving the bone sticking out. The car did not stop and no one helped them. The younger girl tried to take care of her sister on the streets. Finally a man stopped and asked their story. He took them to the police, who took the older girl to the hospital for surgery. Police then brought the smaller sister to Maher. A social worker took her to the hospitals to try to find her sister, but they did not know under what name she had been admitted and could not find her. So for three months there was no word. The small one was very withdrawn. Sister Lucy kept her close. Then the police arrived with the older girl from the hospital. She still had pins in her leg from the surgery and had to remain immobilized. No one visited her in the hospital or looked for the girls through the police, so their family and history is still unknown. Now they are settled at Maher and happy, both playing with other children. The older one still has to mind her leg.

2. A grandmother who has four daughters came to Maher with one of her granddaughters. Two of her other granddaughters (from a different daughter) were already living at Maher. She told Sister Lucy that she could not keep this child, that she had two others already. She had planned to take this one to an orphanage; she was afraid what Sister Lucy would say. In the meantime, social workers brought in her two other grandchildren so she could see them. These girls reassured their grandmother that Maher was a good place, and one of them sat on Sister Lucy's lap and snuggled. Seeing this, the woman sat down with Sister Lucy and told her more of the story. The girl's father was mentally unfit, so her mother remarried. Then the new father had tried to kill the little girl because he did not want to raise another man's child. (This is common in India.) So Sister Lucy said the girl could come to live at Maher, and told the grandmother to arrange the paperwork with the CWC. But the child's birth had never been registered, and the grandmother was afraid to go to CWC. (Unregistered births are common for poor people.) So Maher sent a social worker. They had to estimate the child's age, create papers, and get what was needed to register the girl for school. (See photo previous page.)

Maher's director, a guest, and several childen

Workflow for Residential Children

Below are three formats, showing five stages, with progressively more detail:

- First is an **Overview Map** showing the high-level overview for all children coming into Maher.

- Second is a **Summary Flowchart** with all the steps from above but with more detail about the work, who is doing what, and how long each stage might last.

- Finally is **Narrative Support** with a great deal of detail about the work itself.

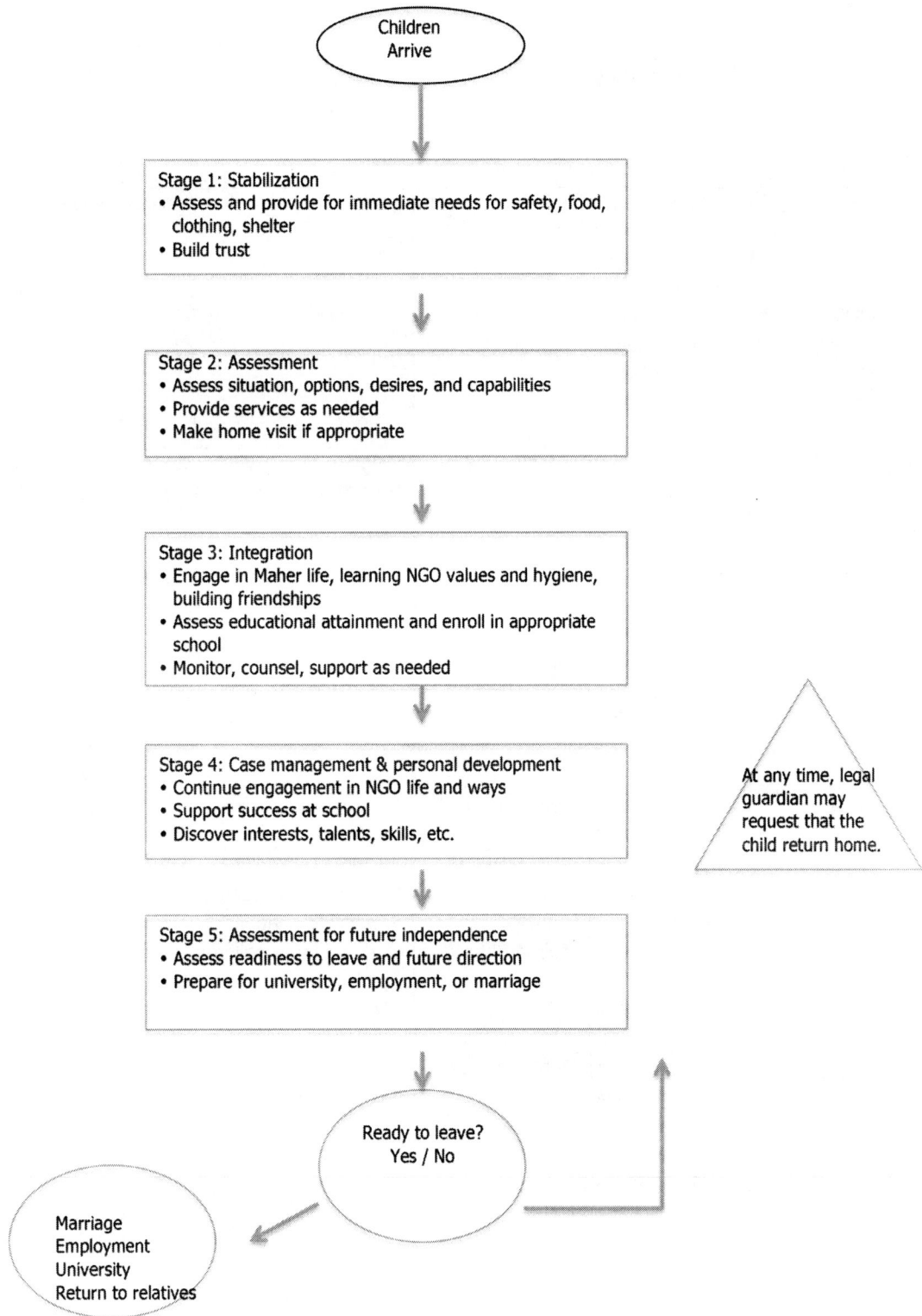

```
                          ┌─────────────┐
                          │  Children   │
                          │   Arrive    │
                          └─────────────┘
                                 │
                                 ▼
```

Stage 1: Stabilization
- Assess and provide for immediate needs for safety, food, clothing, shelter
- Build trust

Stage 2: Assessment
- Assess situation, options, desires, and capabilities
- Provide services as needed
- Make home visit if appropriate

Stage 3: Integration
- Engage in Maher life, learning NGO values and hygiene, building friendships
- Assess educational attainment and enroll in appropriate school
- Monitor, counsel, support as needed

Stage 4: Case management & personal development
- Continue engagement in NGO life and ways
- Support success at school
- Discover interests, talents, skills, etc.

At any time, legal guardian may request that the child return home.

Stage 5: Assessment for future independence
- Assess readiness to leave and future direction
- Prepare for university, employment, or marriage

```
                          ┌─────────────┐
                          │ Ready to    │
                          │ leave?      │
                          │ Yes / No    │
                          └─────────────┘
```

Marriage
Employment
University
Return to relatives

Summary Flowchart

Stage	Focus & Key Tasks	Special Issues & Concerns	Staff Responsible
Stage 1: Stabilization 1-2 days	• Assess and provide for immediate needs for safety, food, clothing, shelter, medical care • Build trust • Medical evaluation • Begin admission form and file, and medical file • Enter into admission register	Safety and physical wellbeing	Social worker primary
Stage 2: Assessment 1-4 weeks	• Determine child's background, parent or legal guardian status • If child is "found" or from police, seek any family members • Home visit and/or communication with family and school • Provide services as needed • Complete all CWC and admission paperwork • Begin case file	Listen to the child's full story; hear what is said *and* not said; build trust Assess school/education level	Social worker for all research and paperwork, and interface with CWC[22] Social worker begins transitioning care to housemother Director and social worker agreement re: admission.
Stage 3: Integration 1-6 months	• Enroll in appropriate school • Engage in NGO life, learning hygiene and values, building friendships, taking part in activities • Monitor, counsel, support as needed • Update case file	Tutor or enroll in school session Observe interactions and developing relationships with staff and other children	Social worker monitors and reports Housemother primary in daily care and discipline
Stage 4: Case management & personal development To age 17	• Continue engagement in Maher life, learning values, etc. • Support success at school • Discover & develop education, skills, interests, special talents	Note developmental needs and provide	Housemother primary Social worker problem-solves, handles periodic review and direction of housemother

---

[22] CWC refers to the Child Welfare Committee, a government office in India that issues licenses for childcare, reviews and approves every admission, and is responsible for ensuring the NGO meets all government requirements for facilities and care. In other countries there will be an organization with a similar function, as you will have discovered in Chapter 2.

Stage 5: Assessment for future independence From about age 15-18	By 10th standard, assess life goals and readiness to live independently: • Assess future desires, including any desire to marry • Develop plan for path to self-sufficiency and good life after Maher • Provide learning and services per plan • Help procure job, further education, or marriage	Find creative ways to provide living space to continue the child's schooling, and part-time work	Social worker guides development of future plans
DECISION: Ready to leave? Yes / No	If **YES**, child leaves Maher for university, employment, or marriage, or returns to relatives If **NO**, assign to work at Maher so child may remain; continue developing toward eventual self-sufficiency Client completes feedback form, social worker completes leave form and admission register	If a legal guardian requests that a child returns home prior to age 18, assess safety at home and ability to complete school; take appropriate action whether to allow child to return home or petition CWC to be able to keep child at Maher	Director with staff input

Narrative Support for Workflow

Children arrive by one of the above six channels. Note that some of the steps below refer to Maher with its multiple homes and the fact that Maher takes children from all of the channels. If your NGO is only a single facility, or only accepts certain groups of children, then some of these steps may not apply. This process is based on admission requirements in India. Check with your local child welfare organization for specific requirements in your area.

Stage 1: Stabilization

- Assess and provide for the child's immediate needs for food, clothing, and medical care. Whether the children arrive with a parent or not, they may feel scared, sick, or hungry, or they may be only partially clothed. Do what you can to help them relax a little and begin to gain their trust. Treat them with love and patience.

- Take a photo of the child as soon as possible after arrival (make five passport-size copies). Take a second photo of the people who brought the child.

- Begin the admission form, gathering items for admission file (complete list included at the end of Stage 2 below), and other paperwork. A list of the content required for the

---

CASE Keeping families together

A man came asking Maher to take the children of a woman he wished to hire as domestic help. He claimed that her husband was an alcoholic, the home was not good for the children, and the woman needed work. But he did not want to take her children with her, and resisted all suggestions for keeping the family together. Sister Lucy suggested, "Why not have the woman come to work during the hours the children are in school, letting all stay living at home?" (A little investigation had shown that the husband drank but was not abusive; he was just not working. If he had been violent or there were signs that the children were in danger, Maher would have taken them.) Because the would-be employer was very selfish, he did not want this; he wanted the woman for more work and more hours. The woman was also talking of taking the children to an orphanage. Sister Lucy asked, "Why do you want to make the children orphans when you are still alive and well?" She encouraged the woman to find other options so she could keep her children, and referred her to other institutions that could help.

admission form that Maher uses is at the end of this chapter.

- If the child arrives sick or injured, take him to a hospital. In the case of an injury, also file a police report.

- If child is not with at least one parent (or have appropriate paperwork from a referring institution or the CWC), register the arrival with the local police station, providing a photo of the child.

- Decide whether to admit. There are times when admission may not actually be in the child's best interest, such as when there is some way for him or her to stay with at least one parent in a family home. If the family has some economic hardship but is otherwise stable, for example, Maher may provide a periodic food supplement (such as rice, flour, and oil) or other assistance to help the family get by. In this case, a social worker may do a home visit and then decide. (See case at left for another example.)

- Show the child around the NGO. Give her bedding, toiletries, clothing as needed and show her where she can keep her things and where she will sleep.

- Arrange a medical evaluation (a government requirement in India) within a day or two of arrival. (It is advisable to have a relationship with a local clinic where staff have been prepared ahead of time to work respectfully and gently with these

clients.) Begin a medical file for each child.

- Enter the child into the admissions register, assigning a case number (paper, computer, or both).

TIP As Maher has grown, staff have begun keeping all the medical files in one place, so that if a resident needs to be rushed to hospital it is easy to quickly grab her medical file and go.

The timeframe for this stage will likely be only one or two days.

Stage 2: Assessment

- Assess each child physically, mentally, and emotionally. If he or she does not have a stable parent present and seems traumatized, a social worker may be assigned to stick with that child, build a relationship, help with adaptation, and see that the child eats, sleeps, and feels safe and loved. This is intended to help the child stabilize while the situation is reviewed. (If you do not have a social worker on staff, you may wish to seek a professional evaluation. Any staff member can be assigned to focus on a new child, to build that first critical relationship and assist with the transition.)

- Keep children with any family members with whom they arrive, as they will feel safer together. If a child arrives alone, she will be assigned to a home with a social worker in residence, or at least an experienced housemother who has extra time to spend gaining her trust. The housemother also then provides input to the assessment based on her observations.

- Begin the admission process: for every child admitted in India, there must be a CWC order allowing the child to become a resident under care of the NGO. (Check with your local child welfare organization for requirements in your area.)

  o If the CWC brings the child to Maher, then the CWC will handle the inquiries about the child's situation, gather the necessary papers, and send the final order to the NGO.

  o If the child comes directly to the NGO with a parent, the parent is instructed to go to the CWC and initiate the paperwork, and gather necessary information for the child to come under the care of the NGO.

  o If the child is brought by someone other than a parent, and if the parents are either dead or missing, then the person bringing the child must bring a letter from the local police. Individuals who can keep the child with them during the application process may do so. They are requested to go directly to the CWC, complete the paperwork, and bring the order back to the NGO. Then they can bring the child to live at Maher. Otherwise the child can stay at the NGO (with letter from police), and the social worker will assist with the admissions process.

CASE Reuniting lost children with parents

Maher staff found a girl on the streets and brought her to Maher. After posting ads, they located the parents, who were looking for her, in Karnataka. The girl was taken home to her parents, but staff continued to check in with her to assure she is okay and attending school. They told her if she has any trouble to call Maher and someone will come to either help solve the problem or return her to Maher.

- o If the parent, guardian, or other support person is illiterate or otherwise unable to go to the CWC and complete the paperwork, then the social worker will take them with the child to the CWC and request an order for placement of the child.

- Research and learn the child's situation, including an in-depth history of how he came to Maher, the nature of his previous home(s), his history with other institutions, school attendance and records, what happened to the family and whether his family members are alive, and what, if any, support or resources are available from the family. Gather the remaining papers for the admission file.
- o Make a home visit and write the report.

- o If a child is found on the streets or arrives on her own and does not know (or will not say) who her family is, Maher must register this child with the police, and then try to find out where the child came from. Put up photos, ask around, and put a notice in the newspaper.

- o If family (usually parents but sometimes grandparents or uncles) is found, then do a home visit here to ensure the home is safe and the child can be cared for appropriately and sent to school. Find out how he came to be lost or on the streets. If the situation is satisfactory, such children can be sent home. Check on the child after a month, and again at three months: see if he is being well cared for, if he is sick, and if he is going to school. Assure the child that he can always call Maher for help.

- o If no family is found, then complete all the CWC paperwork and meetings to keep child at the NGO.

CASE Sometimes children lie out of fear

Sister Lucy was shopping and saw two children begging. She brought them to Maher. They told many lies about where they had come from. Finally, after a year, they explained about their situation: their mother was dead and their father was an alcoholic, living behind a shop. They could not be left with a father who was continually drunk, so Maher completed new paperwork allowing them to return to Maher to live up to age 18.

- Complete the admission file (see full list on next page).

- Once an order is provided, admit the child. Although the order is sometimes for only six months, it is generally issued for a year. The CWC will review the case for the child's continuing stay at Maher at the end of each order period.

- As the child is ready, gently begin teaching the basics of health, hygiene (for example, how to use the toilet, how and when to wash hands and body), appropriate interpersonal relations, and even values. (This training may begin even while the admission process is being completed.)

- Perform education-level completion assessment: determine whether a child has attended school, where, and at what grade level. If there are no school records, perhaps provide paper and ask him or her to write to see what the child knows. If the child is staying at the NGO, there are government tests to help determine grade level.

The first two stages may take anywhere from a few days up to several weeks if a child is traumatized or the stories and origins are unknown. Give her time, counseling, and love, to let her feel safe enough to open up and tell her story, and to begin to adjust to this new life. Note that sometimes children do not tell where family is, or they lie about it because, for example, the mother is

dead and the father drinks. The children want to live at Maher. Assure each of his or her safety, and eventually the children will open up.

The admissions file becomes the start of each child's case file. Case files are broader, containing all the observations, accomplishments, issues, and other information regarding the child for the entire stay at Maher. Each year at least there should be an assessment of the child's status, wellbeing, development, and case management goals.

Note: In India, both the school mark-list (see next page) and the school leaving certificate require a fee if Maher applies on the child's behalf. Generally a parent can obtain the mark-list for free. If a child has a mark-list from the old school, then the new school may obtain a school leaving certificate free from the old school. In many cases, however, the women and children flee from dangerous situations with no time to gather such papers, and cannot go back for them without the risk of exposing where they are. In such cases, Maher or the new school will simply request the mark-list and school leaving certificate once the situation is under control and the woman's and children's safety is assured. Unfortunately, under these conditions, the child will lose more time out of school. Be sure to check your local requirements for children to change schools. Private and government schools may have different requirements.

Final contents of the admission file with assigned case number

- Photo of child at arrival (updated every 3 or 4 years as children grow up)

- Admission application from family or guardian OR, if referred, a letter requesting admission on letterhead of the requesting institution (hospital, orphanage, police)

- Admission form (see end of chapter for list of information required)

- Copies as available of child's birth certificate, school leaving certificate and mark-list* , caste certificate, and ration card. (Ration card shows permanent address and provides access to subsidized food.)

- Mother's and/or father's death certificate if they are deceased (If death was not registered, village leader can sign attesting to parent's death.)

- Copy of the police report if child was abandoned (if no report was filed, the NGO must file with the police)

- Five passport-size photos of the child

- Medical evaluation form (admitting medical exam)

- Counselor's evaluation (if applicable)

- Case report (child's mental, emotional, and physical states; reason for taking the child; family details such as living situation and siblings)

- Home visit report (if applicable)

- Other papers such as bank, land, or house papers (In cases where parents have died, the children may be heirs to money or property, so Maher will attempt to obtain this on their behalf.)

- CWC papers, CWC code for why child is at Maher, and final order (formal permission for Maher to keep child), including how long he or she is approved for (after which renewal is required)

* A mark-list is a report of a child's attainment in his or her current grade (exams completed and marks obtained). Additionally, to enroll in a new school, a child must have a school leaving certificate from the old school.

Case file for children

- Admission file

- Residential certificate

- Case management plan, including monthly reports on child's progress and status, and annual developmental goals

- Observation records

- School records

- Copies of any awards or recognitions

- Records of visits from parents, guardians, relatives (from visitors" register)

- Medical records (unless kept in a separate file)

- Girls' menstruation data

- CWC "spot review" form

- CWC final status form (for when children either return home or "graduate" from Maher)

Stage 3: Integration

As a child integrates into NGO life, the housemother gradually takes over primary responsibility and care, with direction and assistance from a social worker as needed.

- Social workers begin to develop a case management plan for each child, addressing physical, social, emotional, behavioral, and educational needs, as well as discovery and development of any interests or special talents.

- When the child is ready, enroll him or her in the best school possible. To ease the child's entry, arrange meetings with school administrators and teachers.

- Provide for tutoring as needed to catch up to an age-appropriate grade, or to make up for a partial missed year. (See education section below for more information about schooling.)

- Support the child's adaptation to NGO life and values, including ways of social interaction, management of emotions, hygiene, and daily life.

Provide interventions, counseling, mediations, talks, role-plays, and more as needed.

- Encourage the child to try a wide range of activities, and identify special interests and talents. Introduce new activities such as drawing, dance, music, and tae kwon do, and place the child in classes as these are available.

- A social worker tracks each child and reports weekly, then monthly, then every three months. Each child also has an annual case review. Social workers speak regularly with housemothers for input.

Case management plan outline

As noted above, as each child begins to integrate and settle at Maher, a social worker develops a case management plan for that child. These plans can follow a similar format to those you have developed for the NGO and for your staff. The example below shows the start of one such plan. Fill in goals and activities appropriate for the child's age, stage of development, and individual needs. As goals are completed, new ones will be added. Activities should be specific.

Start of a sample case plan

Name, admission case number, admission date

Goals and Activities	Resources needed	Timeframe (include dates)	Accomplishments and notes (with dates)
Goal 1: Mental and emotional stabilization, and acclimation to Maher **Activities** • Support adaptation to NGO life • Refine personal hygiene practices • Support better management of emotions *[Continue with further goals and activities as appropriate.]*	Social worker assessment, counseling, and guidance as needed with assistance of housemother	Immediate, until completed	

The timeframe for this integration stage will depend again on the child's circumstances. Signs that a child is integrated include eating and sleeping well, engaging with other children of the same age group, regular attendance at school and completing school assignments, and engaging in the NGO's everyday life. This could take a few months or, in the most difficult cases, up to a year.

Stage 4: Case management and personal development

By this stage the child has integrated fully into NGO life. From this point on, housemothers are mostly in charge of the children, who require less monitoring and intervention. The focus now is on ongoing development.

- Every three months at least, review and update the child's case management plan. Record accomplishments, issues, troubles, and so on as they occur.

- Identify special aptitudes, skills, and strengths, and help increase the child's capabilities.

- Develop interests and capacities via extracurricular activities such as sports, writing competitions, art, music, dance, and projects around the NGO.

- Continue to help the child to learn NGO ways; to socialize well with other children, staff, and teachers;

and to become well-adjusted and happy.

- Teach additional life skills and develop leadership capacities and poise (see details below).

- As the child becomes a teenager, coach him or her in thinking about future plans past the 10th standard: College and university? Technical training? Job placement? Marriage?

Stage 5: Assessment and planning for future Independence

- By age 17, the child should have a plan for where he or she will go at age 18, and understand what is needed in order to be a successful, independent adult. If the child desires to seek further education, help with a plan to cover financial needs and living requirements.

- Place the child in a suitable job, help her apply for advanced schooling, or arrange a marriage, according to the child's ability and wishes. (Maher encourages girls to wait until they have completed their education and are at least 20 years old before marrying.)

- Some children will return to live with parents, relatives, or a guardian. This may happen after the completion of 10th standard or at any time the legal guardian decides. If the guardian requests that a child come home to live, the NGO must let him go, unless there is concern for his safety or if the completion of education through the 10th standard is at risk. In this case, the NGO can report its concerns to the CWC, petitioning to keep the child. The CWC will review the case and must agree to let the child return home, since the guardian signed over responsibility for his welfare and education to the NGO through the CWC. Otherwise, he may remain at Maher.

- Complete the exit form when child departs.

Workflow for Short-Stay Children

Children who arrive with a mother who is seeking refuge and reconciliation or only a short stay (no more than three months) are considered short-stay children. In these cases, the children may need only to be occupied. Or they may need counseling as well, depending on the family situation. Mother and children will live together, although older children may be placed in more age-appropriate Maher homes, yet still close by. Preschool children remain with their mother. Other women (and older children) assist with their care. For older children, schoolwork is provided, whether from their own school or via tutoring from a social worker. They might even help with work at Maher (for example, food preparation) or in the Production Center. They will also be exposed to Maher values.

CASE Family matter

Several years ago, twin girls came to Maher after their parents died. Their two uncles were fighting and the girls were left alone. They settled and were doing well in their studies. One day an uncle came, claiming to be the girls' guardian; he said he hadn't known where they were until now. Sister Lucy challenged him, saying that if he loved the girls he would have found them sooner. Later she told this author that the girls' father had a rickshaw license (these are hard to obtain), which this uncle had been using. He needed to renew it and wanted to do it in the girls' name. Maher must be very careful, even suspicious, when family members show up like this. Are they here because they want something? What is best for the child? Situations like this require further research.

If the woman's family situation is complicated and reconciliation is slow or unsure, it may be best to have the children settle at Maher for a longer stay so their lives can be more stable and their education as uninterrupted as possible. In cases like this, Maher can offer to have the children stay for a school year while the family stabilizes, and then everyone can "see how it is" and decide what to do next. These children are integrated into Maher life as any child would be, seeking to provide them as much stability and support as possible. Once family reconciliation is successful, parents and a social worker discuss and agree when these children should return home. Ideally the family will have had time to stabilize, so the children do not get bounced back and forth. Older children may be asked their preference.

School continuity is a key factor. Maher's staff is well aware that missing big chunks of school lessons can add stress for a child already challenged at home. If the child is not getting a consistent education, then arranging for some form of schooling is a priority. If a child was in school but fled with the mother, staff will often contact the school on the child's behalf so he or she is not penalized for missing school (unless this notification puts the mother or child at risk). Sometimes arrangements can be made for children to continue going to their school, or to have homework sent over. If they transferred to a new school near Maher, most children wish to finish out that school year rather than transfer again midterm, and possibly go home to

more fighting. If a child wants to stay beyond the school year, even though the home situation is now satisfactory, Sister Lucy explains that it is better for the child to be with family and let others who have nowhere else to go have a place to stay at Maher.

Basic Services for All Children

Basic services are available for the wellbeing of all new arrivals, including children who will only stay a short while. These include:

- Food, clothing, shelter

- Medical evaluation and care

- Counseling for trauma

- Basic hygiene as needed

- Educational assessment and support

- Home visits

- Participation in daily life, such as celebrations, games, and all programs

- Maintaining family relationships where possible

Counseling with Families

Given Maher's respect for the family unit, support services that can help a family remain together are a key element. For example, if a family is stable and safe but poor and cannot afford to send the children to school, then Maher may help with money. The social worker checks monthly with the family and with teachers. If all is okay at home and school, then the child can remain living at home. Maher also encourages the families to save, even just 20 or 50 rupees per month, in an account for the child to pay for studies after the 10th standard.

Services and Developmental Programs for Residential Children

Once it is determined that a child will be at Maher for more than a few months, then the full array of developmental programs is added to the above basic services.

TIP When any children arrive, whether for a short or a long stay, they are given clothing as needed and a place to keep their clothing and personal items. Sometimes this is a shelf, sometimes a sort of locker or suitcase. They are expected to keep their clothes neat, clean, and in good repair. By age 7, children are taught how to wash their clothes under the housemother's supervision. This is a simple way to begin to teach hygiene where it is needed.

Formal Education

Education is a deeply held value at Maher. Having a good education will provide children with opportunities later in life. A lot of work is done to assess children's abilities, potential, and progress, to get them the best education possible. State education goes through the 10th standard in India, when the child is about 16 years old. College is 11th through 12th standard, at which point the child is generally 18 and an adult and no longer eligible to stay in a children's home. Vocational programs are an alternative to college. Maher encourages those with interest and ability to attend college or a vocational program so that they have as strong a foundation as possible before they go out in the world on their own. By the time a child is in the 10th standard at the latest, he will be in conversation with a social worker about future plans and how he will support himself as an adult (see Stage 5).

School selection

Children get the best education and have the most access to better future opportunities if they can attend English-medium schools (medium here refers to the language of all teaching at a given school). But children must start in this type of school in kindergarten. Once they have begun school in the local language, they cannot catch up enough for English-medium, so they cannot transfer at a later age. If a child shows

283

strong potential to excel in school, you may seek admission to an appropriate private school, even if it is not English-medium. There are many private schools in India run by nuns that are often very good. In India, no school, public or private, may teach religion, so this option does not interfere with Maher's values. Other children may attend local government public schools. As you'll recall from earlier chapters, one of the factors in site selection for your NGO is access to good schools so that all the children can receive the best possible education.

Catching up

If an older child has never been to school, a choice must be made about which grade level to start in. If she is 10, for example, one option is to start her in the 1st standard and provide tutoring to

help her progress as well and as fast as she can. However, this can be hard and

> **TIP** When helping children with their homework, help them learn—do not do it for them! With a math problem, help the child understand the question, and then to reason through to the answer; help her learn the thought process. If she does not know a word in a reading assignment, help her sound out the individual letters until she discovers the word. If you tell her the answers or write them for her, you are only harming her because then she will never learn. This requires time and patience.

CASE It is hard to adjust

One newly arrived boy had a great deal of anger and was not doing well in school. He was embarrassed that he did not know things, but he had not had regular schooling before Maher. This, of course, was not his fault. Because the new teacher would beat him, the child refused to go to school. So the social worker went to school, talked to the teacher and told him just enough of the boy's story to provide some perspective: that his parents were always fighting, and then he had witnessed his father murdering his mother; now no one else in the family would take this boy. The social worker asked the teacher not to beat the child, but instead to be patient, to work with him so he wanted to go to school and could learn. After this, the teacher was easier on the boy. Now he is going to school again and getting caught up.

embarrassing for children who are older than their classmates and may be teased. Often it is best to enroll the child in a life stage–appropriate classroom and to provide tutoring and lots of help to catch up. As one social worker at Maher said, "It's not the child's fault she never went to school—so help her!" Sometimes a child might be placed in between her age level and her assessed grade level and, again, helped to progress as quickly as possible. Housemothers are expected to spend extra time with these children helping them with homework and learning to write.

Working with schools and teachers

Maher works to build good relationships with the local schools and teachers. Social workers and housemothers both meet school principals and teachers for all their children, helping to smooth the children's entry and progress. Often the social workers have to coach the schools to be patient with children who are new to attending school, as they can be disruptive and difficult at first. In Vadhu village schools there are so many Maher children that the principal requested that staff come to meet with all the teachers and tell them about the children at Maher. Staff members came and told many stories of these children's lives and homes before Maher. The teachers were in tears. After that, instead of being

---

CASE Theft—the street children are not always to blame

One child stole from another child's school bag. The school identified a culprit and phoned Maher planning to expel the child. The social worker had to walk a fine line between protecting the child and helping the teacher understand what was going on and the child's need to feel loved. The social worker explained that these children had survived on the streets by stealing and begging, and even though they did not need to do so now, it was part of them. She asked the teacher to be patient and to show that he loved the child and not the behavior. She also asked, as diplomatically as possible, if he was sure that this child had done it (whenever there is theft, teachers tend to assume the Maher children did it, which makes all the Maher children stand out and feel bad). The boy remained in school—and three days later, it was found that another (non-Maher) child had committed the theft. The teacher did not apologize to the Maher child he wrongly accused. The boy came home upset and Maher staff had to console him: "You were good and right. Be proud of yourself. And let it go."

angry and frustrated with these children, the teachers were staying after school to give them extra help.

National Open School

Some of the children who arrive will have had large gaps in their education or it stopped altogether. For children too old to catch up, you will need a program for them to earn an equivalent diploma. In India, this is the National Open School system. Social workers register the children, books come by post, and staff help the children with the lessons as needed. When they are ready, a staff member arranges for the children to appear for the appropriate exams, 4th, 7th, and/or 10th standard. Those who pass the 10th standard exam can then apply to college. This program is specifically intended for deprived children, helping them to gain knowledge without the embarrassment of having to attend regular school classes with children who are much younger. (Some of the women at Maher have earned their diplomas this way.)

College, vocational training, and university

Some of the children will want to go on to college for training in fields such as nursing or secretarial work, and possibly even on to university to study for degrees in such fields as teaching, medicine, graphic design, business, and law. Others may not have either the interest or the aptitude for this, in which case helping them learn a trade where they can earn a good living is the natural choice. Vocations may include para-social work, kindergarten teacher,

---

CASE Finding work that suits each child

Ambha, a senior social worker at Maher, has a son who did not enjoy school and dropped out after the 8th standard. He did not seem to be interested in much of anything, and Ambha worried he would follow his father and turn to drinking. She discovered he had some interest in running a restaurant, so he completed a six-month restaurant management certificate. Ambha then retired from Maher and used her savings to lease a nearby flat for the family plus a small plot of land across the street for the restaurant. Her husband built a simple shed with a small kitchen and seating area. Ambha and her son work every day in the restaurant. He does all the marketing, cleaning, and food preparation, and Ambha does all the cooking. The restaurant is steadily busy and the Maher volunteers report that she makes the best "veg noodles" ever! Her husband continues to work at Maher. (see photo on the next page)

beauty school, tailor, or trades such as electrician, welding, carpentry, restaurant business, baking, or computer technician. Courses of study can range from a six-month certificate program to a two-year diploma to a four-year university degree, and even graduate school.

Ambha and her son

TIP Guide each child, helping her make good choices for herself but without telling her what to do. Lila thought she wanted to be a teacher. Sister Lucy thought she would be happier as a nurse, but did not want to tell her what to do. So she arranged for Lila to talk to a teacher about what the job was like and what skills and types of work were involved. Then Lila spoke with a nurse about her work. Lila then made her own decision that she wanted to be a nurse. She completed her nursing schooling and is now completing a nursing internship at the nearby Vadhu hospital clinic, where she hopes to work full-time. She loves nursing!

activities are formal programs and some are simply part of Maher life.

Life skills for children

Children who grew up in slums where the homes are open with dirt floors, on the streets, or in tribal villages—and sometimes even those who have lived for a while in a family home—will need to be taught many basic life skills that we take for granted. Each child must be observed and assessed, and then have a developmental plan made. Many of these skills and knowledge, such as hygiene, respecting others, and being on time, are taught in simple day-to-day exchanges with housemothers and social workers.

Beyond School: Programs for Developing Children

In addition to school, the children's days are filled with activities that keep them busy and channel their energy, and that develop them physically, mentally, emotionally, and spiritually. The focus is so much more than just providing food, clothing and a place to sleep: Maher aims to raise the children to be tomorrow's leaders, to be the best humans they can be. Some of these

General hygiene

Children need to learn the most basic things, both the how and the why, especially if they come from the streets or the slums. For example, they must be taught to wipe up a water spill on the floor because someone could slip, and to clean up crumbs and bits of rice after eating as these draw flies, which can lead to many diseases. Also important is the pride in a clean, neat space—even straightening the pictures hanging on the wall if they are askew has value. Because many of the women residents, and even some staff, need to learn these things as well, staff must continually model and teach the most basic care, hygiene, and maintenance.

Hygiene practices include:

- How to use a toilet and clean oneself afterward

- Washing hands before eating

- Why and how to bathe

- How to comb hair (and for girls, how to braid, etc.)

- Fingernail and toenail care

- How and why to blow one's nose

- How to care for and wash clothing (no chewing, tearing, etc.)

- How and why to pick up after themselves

TIP Instead of using toilets, many of these children are used to going in a field and using a stone to wipe. So now they must learn them how to use the toilet, to use water to clean themselves and then to wash their hands. Maher has learned to teach hygiene to groups of children and then to continually reward and therefore reinforce the new behaviors. When a child is doing this well, praise him in front of the other children. When the child is new and still learning, teach the others to be supportive and helpful, like brothers and sisters, and remind them not to scold or tease.

General "good citizen" behaviors

- Do not throw things or destroy others' things; teach how and why to take care of books and household items

- No lying or stealing

- No tantrums

- Do not use "bad" words (explain which words are bad)

- Be respectful to adults, parents, and guests; explain that a child's behavior reflects on himself as well as on Maher

- Play or share with more than only best friends

This list is a start; more behaviors are covered in the discussion of Maher values in Chapter 10, "The Art and Genius of Maher."

Money management and bank accounts

Every child who comes to Maher for more than a short stay has a savings account opened in her or his name and co-held in the name of a Maher staff member (so that parents cannot take it). Maher begins each account with a small

> **TIP** Be patient with these children—for example, regarding the expected behavior not to destroy things, Sister Lucy reminds staff that these children are not used to having things. And, in the end, they are children; and children play hard and destroy things! So find a balance, as would a loving mother.

contribution, and then directly deposits Rs. 25–50 per month as long as the child is at Maher. Parents and family are invited and encouraged to make a monthly contribution as well (even if only Rs. 50). Maher staff, when they can, also put a little into orphan children's accounts so they too have something. This teaches the value of saving, and the child has money for when she wants to go to university, start a trade, or get married. Some of the older teenagers earn money from their work in the Production Center (making purses, candles, jewelry, cards, and more) or from staff jobs at Maher. Their wages and Production Center earnings are deposited directly into their bank accounts. To withdraw money, a child needs a check signed by the staff member in charge of the banking and also by herself.

College student painting bags

CASE Learning to save

Ashok lived at Maher for a while with his mother and then went to live with his grandparents. During a school break, he worked 15 days in the fields and saved all his money (Rs. 100 a day), knowing his granny was poor. She bought new clothes for him, but he saved some, not wearing them all, out of respect for how much they cost. His mother related this story to the author with obvious pride in her son.

Every three months the children are given pocket money (about Rs. 10) to spend as they choose. They may buy snacks in the village, or they may be taken to a village festival and can choose whatever they like. Social workers observe what the children buy, and may have a discussion about unwise selections, so that the children learn how to make good choices with money. When they leave Maher as adults, the money is all signed over to them. If they go home with parents or guardians as younger children, then the parents get the money. The parents are told it belongs to the children for their education or to start a career and that they may not spend it, but there is no way to enforce this.

Sexuality

Sexuality is an important topic and is addressed once or twice a year for all children over 12 years old. Maher uses a DVD about sexuality designed for children of this age group. Sometimes a younger child who has had early exposure to sex (for example, in the slums, or if his mother was a prostitute) may also come. Both boys and girls need to learn about pregnancy, sexuality, and responsible behavior. The boys are taught to respect women, and to value and respect the girls. They are friends, like brothers and sisters. This is rare and new in Indian village life. The Indian holiday *Raksha Bandhan* is an opportunity to reinforce this idea. A description is included later in this chapter.

It is also critical that none of the girls get pregnant, and to assure there is no "funny business" between teenagers. Social workers and housemothers must closely monitor the children. This is another reason developing trust is so important. When the teens do have issues or questions about sexuality, or about boyfriends/girlfriends, it is important that they feel free to come talk to staff about their confusions and choices before it is too late.

Street or slum children may have been exposed to too much at too young an age and they will not know how to handle it. They are often confused about

---

CASE Learning about sex too young

A boy at Maher, about 14 years old and the son of a prostitute, was showing some of the other boys how to have sex. The smaller boys told Sister Lucy. She called this boy to her and told him that what he was doing was wrong and that he should be ashamed of himself. She threatened to post his photo and what he had done all over Maher. (This was merely a threat; she would never actually have done it.) Sister Lucy also told him not to be ashamed of his mother, that she had been doing a job, and she had done it so he could eat. She repeated that his behavior was wrong, then told him that she loved him. He was given counseling as well. He has since become a good boy and perfectly behaved. As Sister Lucy explains, you must know the background of these children; in street children it is not surprising that these issues arise. You must handle them with love and patience: if you keep your heart open and have faith, then solutions will emerge.

---

what is wrong or right. Teach them with patience and creativity.

Programs to further develop children

Over the years, Maher has devised numerous ways to develop the children mentally, emotionally, physically, and spiritually. The first three listed below, dance, meditation, and yoga (and later tae kwon do), are at the heart of programs designed to enrich these children.

Meditation: emotional and spiritual guidance

All of the children are introduced to meditation. Vipassana is the primary form because its focus on stillness and breath is appropriate for followers of any religion. Basic training, *Annapana* (Vipassana for children), starts at age 5 or 6, and by age 9 each child will have one day of Vipassana training per year, taught by a traveling teacher. By the 10th standard, staff begin explaining the longer Vipassana retreat (silent meditation) and how it will benefit the children mentally, emotionally, and physically. By age 16 they may go to a full 10-day Vipassana training. Boys and girls are sent separately; some have even elected to go twice. However, if someone does not want to go, that is respected. All staff attend these trainings and retreats, so they can speak from personal experience.

Vipassana meditation supports emotional stability by teaching a reflective (as opposed to reactive) stance. Children learn to slow down and consider before acting. It also helps them pay attention to, but not cling to, emotions. They become able to feel emotions (joy, anger, sadness) and then to let them go and return to breath, and ultimately to no longer let these emotions overwhelm them.

Yoga and tae kwon do

Teachers, often volunteers from the local community, are brought in to teach classes in yoga or tae kwon do. Or a housemother may know enough yoga to lead the children in morning breathing practices and basic movements. Yoga is useful not only to keep the body balanced, strong, and fluid, but also to cultivate self-awareness and focus of attention. Tae kwon do is more physically and vocally expressive and can be useful for channeling the high energy and emotions of street children

or abused children. Maher had a visiting tae kwon do teacher for several years, and now one of the boys who progressed to the higher levels teaches the children at the main Maher site. They have class every morning before breakfast.

There are also periodic competitions where masters come and the children who pass the tests progress to the next level. A number of Maher groups compete locally and regionally in tae kwon do and consistently bring home awards. Both programs provide discipline in movement, attention, and breathing. Girls and boys participate in both.

Tai kwon do

> **TIP** When the children win local competitions and go on to regional, state, or even national competitions, whether in sports or academics, it is encouraging to them and to the other Maher children—and the outside world learns that these "throwaway" children can achieve greatness. This is yet one more example that Maher is so much more than a roof, a bed, and food; it is a family that sees each child as an individual and helps each to discover and reach his or her potential.

Gardening

Each child is given a plant to care for, or at least helps in the garden, both to learn about caring for another life, and to learn about gardening, composting, and water management. Sometimes garden work is used as therapy for more traumatized residents. Most Maher sites, even in Pune, grow some vegetables and flowers for their own use.

Dance program

A professional dancer came and lived at Maher for several years. She taught the women and children classical Indian dance (Odissi and Kathak), choreographed dances for them, and created costumes. They learned and practiced and then did small local performances. As word spread about how wonderful they were, there were more requests for performances. Local corporations like Mahindra, Weikfield, and John Deere also invited the children to come perform at corporate events. There is a new dance teacher now, and some of the older children who started with the first teacher are themselves teaching some of the younger children. These teens also do their own choreography and combine traditional dance with modern moves in creative ways. Some of the teens have also traveled as far as Mumbai and Delhi for state and national championships. There is a video link on the book's website of a short performance.

Dance teacher and class

The therapeutic aspect of Maher's dance program is described in *Women Healing Women*. The performances are also wonderful exposure and outreach for Maher to both locals and foreigners, plus they are helping to preserve Indian culture and history. Preparing for the performances is good discipline for the children and requires a lot of practice.

Dance performance

Music class

When they perform in full costumes before an audience, they feel a sense of accomplishment, gain self-confidence, and are proud of their efforts. Finally, as the children choreograph their own dances now, the collaboration builds good relationship and team skills.

Music

All the children learn to sing the interfaith songs of prayer and welcome. Additionally, a music teacher comes on the weekends and teaches singing of traditional Indian music and playing the harmonium to small groups of 5 to 7 children, one group after another. A teacher also comes to teach *tabla*, traditional Indian drumming. Any interested child may take lessons.

Sports Camp

In late January, Maher holds a three-day Sports Camp, now organized and run by the college and university students and supported by the social workers. All the children travel to the main Maher

---

CASE Maher tour to the United Kingdom

Jaya (then in the 10th standard) greatly admired Gandhi and wrote a script for a Gandhi dance and drama. She and the other dancers (both children and women) put this to music and Indian dance, and ultimately Maher performed this in Mumbai and the United Kingdom.

The tour to the U.K. was life-changing for all who went (31 people, including young children, women, and several staff). They flew in an airplane (a first for all of them), captivated the crew and passengers, and even performed a dance in the plane's kitchen! They rode "electric sidewalks," used western toilets and showers, ate strange food, went to a zoo and water park, met British schoolchildren, stayed with British families, and were exposed to life outside their village and outside India. They did 32 shows, sometimes 3 or 4 a day. One of their hosts helped them make photo albums, which they passed around for all their new British friends to sign.

---

campus at Vadhu to stay and are assigned to mixed age groups. Each group has a color, and the children wear a wristband of that color to help keep track of who is in which group. Social workers and housemothers are assigned to each group to monitor the children as well as their scores. Organized teams play different games from about 10 a.m. to 5 p.m., with scores collected by color groups (like countries in the Olympics). Evenings are devoted to cultural programs (such as dance, singing, speech competitions, and fashion shows.). At the end of the camp, the winning group gets a trophy. Throughout the three-day camp, children learn to support their teams, not just themselves.

Outings

Every month children go somewhere for different experiences. Sometimes foreign visitors will hire a bus and take a whole house (or two) on an outing. Each year there is at least one big outing where children go somewhere both fun and educational. While 1st through 4th standard children mostly just play, the older children have an educational element where they learn something for their future, for example about Indian history, or the environment, or simply about life!

CASE Outings are easily arranged and fun for all

The author and another foreign guest organized an outing for all the children and staff at the Maher home in Ratnagiri, a port city on the Arabian Sea coast. Everyone had a buddy, pairing small children with either an adult or two older children. Nearly 30 of us packed into the (already full) local bus, causing quite a bit of entertainment for the rest of the passengers. We rode into the city and as close to the sea as the bus route went. We walked the rest of the way to a beach on the Arabian Sea. None of the staff or children knew how to swim, so the author went out with several of the older girls and taught them how to hold their breath underwater and how to float. Lots of shrieking and laughing was shared by all. Others played in the sand. Later we all went home for dry clean clothes, and then the final treat of the outing was dinner out. It was the first time the children had been to a restaurant, and the first time many had sat on chairs at a table to eat. The restaurant staff were nervous at first, but soon waiters were captivated by these wonderful, well-behaved children and invited them all back whenever they wanted.

Potential Development

Staff members continually introduce the children to a variety of activities, and then pay attention to identify the strengths of each child and increase his or her capabilities. There are many formal and informal ways to do this, such as:

- Hold weekly gatherings with all children to talk informally about different activities. Soon the children start asking to try dance, or karate, or to learn to draw. Teachers for these extra subjects observe how the children are doing and encourage ability. Children who are sitting to the side are encouraged to try something. If they like it, okay. If not, then a staff person encourages the child to try something else.

- If the children try things at school or are in a special program, offer words of praise and a small gift in front of the other children.

- Ask children to participate in celebrating a holiday or exploring a subject. In preparation for Mother Teresa's birthday, for instance, Maher staff spoke briefly about Mother Teresa, then asked each child to prepare something special (a small speech, a dance, a drawing). These activities foster expressive skills and poise. After presentation, a small gift was given in front of the group to recognize good work. All the children encouraged each other and the competition was friendly.

Developing responsibility and poise

Create opportunities for children of all ages to begin to develop responsibility, leadership and management skills, and poise. They must learn how to influence their peers, younger and older children, and adults. Here are a couple of examples:

Children's Parliament
Each year six leaders are selected from among the children in each house to be the following ministers:

- Education Minister: sees to the discipline of the children's studies and homework, (for example, noting to staff when a child is struggling or not doing homework)

- Health Minister: sees to hygiene and cleanliness practices (for example, sees that garbage is picked up and all areas are kept clean)

- Agriculture Minister: sees to the gardening, vermiculture pits, and biogas production (for example, sees that watering is done and pits are clean)

- Sports Minister: sees to sports and games for his or her house and is part of the planning team for Sports Camp

- Culture Minister: participates in planning all cultural events

- Chief (or Prime) Minister: oversees the other ministers

Each house has its own set of elections. Children apply for a minister position, presenting their candidacy to the other children, describing their skills and reasons why they are the best choice. Elections are held by secret ballot. Each ministerial term begins with the new school year.

Event planning

The teenagers are given leadership roles in the many festivals and holiday celebrations. A group of boys and girls (usually college- and university-level) will be in charge of an event, working with a primary staff person. They must develop a proposal for the event, including which activities, at what time, who is invited, the order of ceremonies for formal events, food provisions, and decorations. Sister Lucy must approve all plans. Next the group organizes all the work and enlists other children for projects, such as creating a writing contest, organizing a game, writing a play to be presented, or developing a dance performance. Then at the event, these teens are often the emcees, using the microphone to welcome guests, invite speakers to speak, and talk about the purpose of the event. They may do this in both the local language and in English when some of the guests are foreigners. This is a great way for children to learn planning and responsibility, to develop the ability to speak in front of groups, and to feel "ownership" of Maher programs. Some of these young people are astonishingly articulate, poised, and funny—a joy to behold!

TIP Perhaps a volunteer or someone on staff is able to teach English, especially for the children not in an English-medium school. Learning to at least speak English is a valuable skill for all the children. The author has observed that the most successful of the Maher "graduates" taught themselves English—creatively using the Internet, interacting with foreign guests, taking advantage of any classes available at Maher, and working hard.

Miscellaneous projects, classes, and skill development

Maher is constantly devising ways for the children to learn, or at least be exposed to, as much as possible. The more children are exposed to under positive circumstances when they are young, the more open they will be as adults, and they will continue this lifestyle of continuous learning (one of Maher's core values). Staff are skilled at finding online projects, local or even foreign volunteers, and other resources to create learning opportunities for the children. (One example is the Canadian-based Kapoor Foundation who sponsor the Youth Excellence Awards.)

Ad hoc classes

There may be classes in English, drawing, computers, and other subjects, depending on local resources available to teach. Sometimes foreign guests have skills to share with various ages and groups of children and so volunteer to teach them.

TIP It is vital to find ways to challenge the children and to find or create opportunities for them to push themselves, perhaps to compete with other children. Through dance, music, art, school projects, tae kwon do, and more, they learn the value of working hard on something and doing their best, even more than they thought they could. For example, the group practiced for the U.K. tour from 8:00 p.m. until 11:30 p.m. every night for the last month to achieve perfection—and they still attended and kept up with school!

Household jobs

Each child is assigned some household job, as would occur in any family. The jobs are rotated so all the children learn all the jobs. Job assignments are age-appropriate and fit within the requirements of the school timetable. Consequences for not fulfilling these responsibilities include denial of a privilege until the job is done. Below is a sample jobs chart used in a home for teenage girls. Every week names are filled in for each job on each day, with the assignment rotated daily.

TASK	Mon	Tues	...	Sun
Sweep & wash floor a.m.				
Wash toilets a.m.				
Pick up garbage outside				
Wash dishes/ breakfast				
Wash dishes/ lunch				
Wash dishes/ supper				
Sweep & wash floor 4 p.m.				
Make chapati dough				
Sweep & wash floor evening				
Wash toilets p.m.				
Fill drinking water				
Make chapatis				
Cut vegetables				

Other skills

Girls learn how to do *rangoli* (Indian decorative floor designs), make *chapatis* (traditional Indian flatbread), and help to prepare food as part of daily life at Maher. They may also learn the art of henna designs on hands and feet, hair cutting and styling, hand sewing to mend clothes, and other useful skills. Boys learn some of the maintenance tasks by following and assisting the handyman. Any boy who is interested may learn cooking as well. (Maher's handyman is known for cooking large pots of food for celebrations, usually surrounded by a group of boys!)

Additionally, many of the teens choose to work in Maher's Production Center, where adult and teenage residents receive training in various skills such as decorative ceramics, stitching, knitting, painting, candle making, paper making,

etc. The teens are paid a small amount for each piece they make, providing them a bit of pocket money, which the college and university students use to help pay their bus and transport fares to classes. The finished pieces are sold to guests, tourists, and benefactors in the Pune area. Some foreign guests buy larger quantities and take them home to sell, thereby raising money for Maher. In addition to building marketable skills, the teens learn about work ethic. Since the items are for sale, each piece must be of acceptable quality and finished in time to fill orders. Maher's Production Center is briefly summarized in the final chapter.

Arranging Marriages

Many of the girls want to be married, and for orphans there is often no family to arrange this. Although many Indian families encourage very early marriage for girls, and girls may ask for help to be married while in their teens, Maher does

---

CASE Seeking a bride

A woman came to Maher seeking a bride for her 29-year-old brother. Their father was mentally disturbed and she was the oldest child of the family. The woman's husband was being transferred overseas, and she wanted to see her brother married before they left. Sister Lucy thought through the girls who might fit and also want a situation like this. Sister Lucy thought they seemed honest, but of course she arranged a home visit to "learn what they aren't telling us" and also to find out whether the father's mental troubles are hereditary. If they were, then the marriage would not have been pursued. Since the family situation seemed good, Sister Lucy did find a girl who had asked to be married, and who was interested in this situation.

not usually support marriage until a girl is at least 20 years old. Boys should be at least 22 to 30 before Maher will recommend them for marriage.

Maher will arrange marriages for the girls who want it. This is one circumstance in which Maher pays attention to caste and religion. Even if a girl is raised at Maher and is therefore

respectful of all faiths and castes, she will need to fit into her husband's family. While Maher has made great strides in helping local villages become more tolerant, matching a bride and groom in religion especially gives the marriage a better chance to work well. Orphans generally are considered as having no caste, so assurances must be obtained that whatever the girl's background, this

---

CASE A dream of marriage fulfilled*

Uma, 22 years old, had grown up at Maher, arriving when she was just 14 years old. She wanted to be married. So Sister Lucy arranged a marriage with a young man from a nearby village.

Both the bride and groom were Hindu, so the ceremony followed Hindu customs. Uma looked beautiful in her colorful, sparkly sari, with bangles and mendhi (henna designs) up to her elbows. She sat on the stage and, according to local tradition, people placed things on her head, around her neck, in her hands, and on her face: flowers, powders, pastes, coins, leaves, grains, and sweets.

When Uma said goodbye to Sister Lucy after the wedding, it was a tearful embrace. Lucy loves her like a daughter. Then Uma and Nandu got into the backseat of a car that was decorated with their names, real flowers, and a lot of glitter.

CASE A young bride

A young girl arrived at Maher at age 15. She was pregnant by her sister's husband, who had died, and she and the baby were not accepted by the family. She was too young to understand the consequences of her actions. Then a man came seeking a wife. He was sad and disheartened after his wife left him for another man, taking their baby. Then he read in the local newspaper about Maher arranging a marriage for an orphan. So his brother researched Maher online for him, and he came to Maher to see if Sister Lucy would arrange a marriage for him. Sister Lucy told him about this girl and her baby, then told the girl about this man. They agreed to meet, and decided to marry.

*adapted from personal writings of Maher visitor Mikaela Keepin

will not be held against her. The man's background and story are all checked for accuracy. For more information about how to arrange marriages and plan weddings, see the section on arranging marriages in the previous chapter on women.

Emotional and Developmental Issues and Discipline

Maher has learned a great deal working with children from many different backgrounds over the years. Some issues arise at predictable stages and ages, or in certain circumstances. How to discipline children from difficult backgrounds while still being guided always by the heart is a difficult balance. Here are some suggestions from several of Maher's best social workers.

New Children Trying to Adjust

Newly arrived children face challenges adjusting to life at Maher whether they are suffering trauma, are scared or homesick, or are overwhelmed by too many new people and ways of doing things. You must help them all. Given time, patience, and love, most will adapt.

Certain standard policies are designed to support children's adaptation to life at Maher, and to help distract them from their sadness, anger, or homesickness:

- There is a welcome ceremony for each child (or family).

- The children are involved in the daily routine as soon as possible, helping the housemother and doing schoolwork, to keep them busy.

CASE Attention seeking

A new girl came to Maher. She was sweet, yet "underhanded" in seeking attention. She complained regularly of a tummy ache due to menstrual cramps. Staff gave her medicine, and even took her to a doctor to see why she had cramps so badly, but she was not satisfied. The staff grew frustrated with her, especially when her brother (living outside) called Maher to complain about the lack of care for his sister. Finally this girl came to Sister Lucy, saying that her tummy hurt and "no one is taking care of me." Sister Lucy told her, "Don't spoil your future by small things like this. I have great expectations for you! What do you want? Do you want to be sitting by the fireplace caring only for children, or do you want to fly high [a paraphrase of a local saying]?"

- All the children are continually engaged in group games and activities.

Homesick

If a child is homesick and thinking about parents or siblings, staff can help him use a phone to call his family and talk. Also, explain again to the child why he is at Maher (for example, mama or papa is sick, or not looking after him well). If phoning is not possible, have the child write out on paper, confidentially, all his inner feelings. It may take several tries to write all the feelings and thoughts before the whole story comes out. This helps the social worker better understand what is going on for the child. (If a child cannot write, invite him to draw pictures of his story, anything to help him start to talk with the social worker.)

TIP After school, play a ball-passing game with the children to help them open up and tell you what is happening. Pass or toss a ball around the circle from child to child. When the ball stops, the child holding it tells what he or she did that day, or which teacher did or said what.

Withdrawn or closed

Some children do not mingle; they are quiet and do not play with the other children. Begin to learn their interests by inviting them to play a game, music, or some other activity. Find another child with a shared interest or a similar family background, and give them a task to do together.

Angry

If a child is angry, take this as a good sign: at least the feelings are not buried. The anger can come from many places—a child may be angry at her parents, perhaps, for not protecting her from the sexual attacks of a relative. Yet she cannot express this anger directly, either because the parents are not available or because she fears losing even the slight connection to her parents she does have. Such children are just looking for somebody with whom to fight! It is understandable.

Be careful to not respond to the child in anger. Talk to him politely and explain why he is here, what will happen, why he has to learn new ways; help calm him. If he is hitting another child, or shouting at someone, stop the behavior and ask what he is doing and why. Do not scold. Build a relationship with him; try to understand him, and to help him understand Maher. If he is acting out his anger at school, talk with the teacher. Some children may also be sent to professional counseling, especially those coming from homes of violence and abuse.

You might also hold a small group session for the children who are struggling with anger. They talk about their anger and then try "laughing therapy" where each child has to make her or his partner laugh, and vice versa. This helps to release the anger. Participation in tae kwon do can help channel the anger too.

> **TIP** When a child is having a hard time, tell the child to think of all the good things that she did today, not the bad, as she is lying in bed at night. Help her to go to sleep recalling the good things and the fun things she did, things she is happy about and proud of. Suggest that tomorrow she try to do positive things, not to do wrong things, one day at a time. You can help build her self-esteem this way as well.

Running away

Take immediate action to search for the child. When he is found, draw him out and learn more about his situation, his feelings, his fears and hopes.

Whatever an individual child's issues, the social worker talks to the housemother separately, explaining what she is learning about a given child, and coaching the housemother how to work with him or her. Over six months, little

changes can be seen, day by day. Slowly each child settles and adjusts.

Problems by Age Group

Once a child settles at Maher, then troubles are typically related to age and are more predictable developmentally.

Small children

In the morning they start out clean; by evening they are messy and have dirty clothes, fingernails and hands, like any young child. Let them be children, and teach them how to clean up. If they are unused to wearing shoes or having a book bag, they may easily leave these at school or somewhere along the way home when they stop to play. And they will play with anything, even if it is not clean or safe. They are still learning about hygiene and need frequent reminders and patient guidance.

Older children

As children grow up, they seem to have less capacity to listen. (This seems to be an international phenomenon!) Their speaking tone is different and they are more likely to "talk back" instead of being polite. It is harder to make them learn and pay attention. And they have a lot of energy that must be channeled or they will get into trouble. Since most of them have learned better hygiene habits, one way their energy can be channeled is in helping the younger children wash themselves and their clothing. And teenagers will have 101 excuses not to do work. Impress upon

> **TIP** One way to handle older children who tend not to listen is to mix the small and big children together for activities in the daily timetable. Have the bigger children teach and guide the younger ones. This keeps them all busy, and the big ones learn when they realize they have to guide and manage the little ones.

these older children their responsibility as role models: just as they learn from and watch Sister Lucy and the staff, so the younger ones watch them.

Also, as they get older, pay attention to friends they make at school: are these youths who will be good or bad influences? While you cannot control who they choose for friends, you can keep reminding them of core values, and that you love and trust them. They will make mistakes (all children do) and they must trust you enough to come tell you when they find themselves tangled up in something or needing advice. If there is a problem with a particular child, the housemother can try to talk to him or her, and she may seek out a social worker to ask for help.

Teenagers

By the time children are becoming teenagers, it is appropriate to teach them about sex, as noted earlier in the section on sexuality. They need to have a place to talk about appropriate relationships between boys and girls, and about new feelings that might arise. At this time, trusting relationships with staff are critical so they have people to whom they can turn with questions or confusion. Remind the boys to treat all girls with respect, as sisters. Remind the girls of the risks of inappropriate relationships with boys, and to hold onto the dreams and goals for their lives. (See case next page.)

Discipline and Tough Love

At Maher the focus is to guide women and children morally, both by setting an example and by continual counseling, advising, and teaching. Children come from trauma, abuse, and other difficulties. Staff must recognize that they have had horrible things happen to them and they have bad habits (mostly from ignorance or desperation). Through love and patience and lots of help from everyone at Maher, they will slowly exchange these bad habits for good ones. Women too come from trauma, and often have to learn how to be loving mothers and how to discipline from love. Maher has to teach them how to reach out to their children, and then to other children, with love. Some guidelines for discipline:

- Make sure love for the child has been clearly expressed and demonstrated in staff behavior.

- Mild scolding tells the child that the behavior is wrong. Make sure that the child understands that you "hate the behavior and love the child."

304

CASE Discouraging young love

A teenage girl, who had only been at Maher a few months, started seeing a boy. She was Hindu; he was Muslim. A staffperson found out and yelled at her and told her to stop. The girl became afraid she would be kicked out (as she had been from a previous institution), so she arranged with the boy to run away in the night. She asked for help from a new girlfriend at Maher. The friend wrestled with what was right, but she trusted Sister Lucy. So when the new girl left, the Maher girl told Sister Lucy everything right away. Staff members were able to find the girl immediately, before anything happened. Sister Lucy talked to the new girl much of the night, holding her as she cried. She told the girl how hopeless it would be for her and the boy, that neither family would accept them, and that she would end up pregnant with nowhere to go. She explained why the girl should wait, finish school, and then get married. The girl cried and said no one had talked to her about all of this. She took Sister Lucy's hand and said she would never do this again. They then called the boy on Sister Lucy's mobile phone. The girl told him to never call her again, and Sister Lucy also talked to the boy, explaining why this was right for him too. The girl is now completing her education at Maher.

Sister Lucy used this as an opportunity to coach the staff. She told them "This will be happening more, as our children grow up. You must build their trust, so they will come to you with their troubles. Teach them with love why not to run off or get married so young. Teach them why marrying outside their religion will be so hard, that family and society will not accept them. Even though Maher teaches and lives interfaith, remind them to be practical about the world they live in."

- Punishments, along with firmer scolding, come next; this often involves extra work or a restriction of privileges. Sometimes punishment is designed to help the child understand the effects of his actions. (See accompanying case examples.)

- Only when love is clear, and scolding and other punishments have not worked, will Sister Lucy sometimes slap a child, just hard enough to get his or her attention. She does this always from love and never from anger or frustration. "It is what the child has experienced culturally in the past," she explains.

CASES Helping children understand the effects of their actions

Chili Powder Revenge
Some of the children fought during the day and one boy lost. That night he went to the kitchen, stole chili powder, and put it in the eyes of the other sleeping children and the housemother. The housemother called Sister Lucy in the night: "Sister, all the children are crying!" When Sister Lucy came, she saw the chili powder bottle and the one boy sleeping nicely. This boy had done many other things before this incident. So this time she told him to put the chili powder in his own eyes. When he refused, Sister Lucy put some in, so he could see how the others felt. Staff have continued to constantly correct him over time, and slowly he has come around.

Inky Prank
One boy put ink on all the school uniforms. He had been doing lots of pranks and making trouble. At first, staff had told the other children not to react to his pranks, to "turn the other cheek." The children went along with this. Finally with this ink prank, staff told the other children to put ink on the boy's uniform. He too is settling in now.

Stolen Buckets
At the home for teenage boys, the boys kept leaving the buckets lying around and then they were stolen. Maher had to buy more to replace them many times. On Maher Day when everyone was at the celebrations, the buckets were left out once again and were stolen. This time, Sister Lucy told staff, "Don't replace them—let them struggle a bit first! Let them learn from their mistakes."

Corporeal punishment, including slapping, is avoided at Maher if at all possible. Sister Lucy says that when she hits children, they already completely know she loves them, and that if she hits them it is with love. Even two star Maher boys who both have completed university studies with high honors had to be hit once each. "It's what they know," she says. Children see those in power hitting (such as police and fathers), so if you scold and do not hit, they still think they are right. Slapping a child is always a last resort. If you need to hit, always do so with love for the child and in his or her best interests, and

---

CASE Temporary stop to privileges

When this author was at Maher on Christmas Day, all the children, staff and friends of Maher were gathering for the big Christmas program (games, presents, and more). As we prepared to leave Vadhu, I saw two boys who looked very sad. When I asked what had happened, I was told that they had been causing a lot of trouble—and on Christmas morning, they even kicked and hit the housemother when she asked them to roll up their beds. So those two were not allowed to go and were left back at Vadhu. Eventually the two called Sister Lucy and said they were sorry and that they would never do that again. They told her they understood their mistake. Then they were allowed to come for the rest of the day. My next trip back, I asked about these two boys: they have shaped up now and are doing well.

CASE Sometimes one slap is needed

The local school called about one of the Maher girls who kept sneaking out. Staff discovered that she was sneaking out to engage in prostitution. (Her mother is a prostitute.) Sister Lucy told her not to do this, explaining that it was bad for her and that she was a bad role model for the younger girls. Yet the girl kept on doing it. When asked why, she said, "Sister Lucy did not hit me—so I am not doing anything really wrong." The next time it happened, Sister Lucy slapped the girl two times. She stopped and is now doing well, excelling in school, and loving Sister Lucy. This girl later told Sister Lucy: "If you hadn't slapped me that day, I would be a professional prostitute now; I was ready to go."

---

never out of anger or frustration. Children will know the difference.

Children from alcoholic homes
Many of the children come from homes where alcohol is part of the family troubles. Sometimes only the father, sometimes both parents, and often other family members drink. They have grown up with role models who use alcohol socially or to avoid dealing with problems, and also as an excuse for bad

CASE Alcohol troubles

Five boys got alcohol and took it to school. The school expelled them. When they went home to Maher, the staff evicted them from Maher as well. Sister Lucy was furious when she learned this. The staff thought that to allow them to stay at Maher was to encourage the use of alcohol. Absolutely not, Sister Lucy said. "You have to understand these children. They all come from alcoholic families. Now you have sent them home to alcohol! You threw them from the river to the sea!" She added, "What if this was your child? No second chance? They need our help!" Two boys came back; three did not. We are here to help these children lead different lives and make different choices, Sister Lucy advised. "We help them learn how to fix mistakes."

behavior. It is what they know. Often this addiction is in the blood, and the children can grow up wanting it. Again, you must be able to be patient: expect mistakes and strive to correct them. How else will children learn and have a chance at a different life? Approaching this issue in the Maher way can require a major shift on the part of staff and even professional social workers, who must focus on helping residents learn and not rely on strict rules and authoritarian methods.

Working with Street Children

These children have likely run wild, doing whatever they want whenever they want, and have developed the ability to lie and steal in order to eat and to survive. Even if they lived in a slum with families, likely the parents were away working during the day, so the children were unsupervised and did not attend school regularly. If they have spent time in another institution, they may have been expelled for rebelling against the rigid rules and structure.

TIP Discover what the child may have learned on the streets, to understand him and whatever "skills" he may have developed, such as stealing or lying. Then see if any of that can be leveraged. Learning how he got to be good at stealing, for example, may show that he is clever; perhaps you can channel that ingenuity toward school or other projects.

308

CASE Planning ahead for smooth integration

Maher invited 65 slum children to come live at Maher. They all came from a desperately poor slum village where, until the year before, there had been no clean water, people lived mostly outdoors, and none of the children had attended school. Maher had begun a kindergarten there, so their parents had come to know and trust Maher. They were excited for their children to have opportunities no one in their village had enjoyed before. Staff recognized that these children would need extra care in preparing them for successful integration at Maher and so they would not be teased by the other children when they met. Planning ahead, the staff brought this group in over school holidays when the other children were not there. They worked intensively with these seriously disadvantaged children, teaching them the basics of living indoors. Most had never used a toilet before and were frightened to enter such a small space. When they did go in, they went in groups of four or five children! Sister Lucy advised the staff to let them be, since at least they were using the toilet. Slowly the children acclimated, became less fearful, and learned. All became part of the Maher family.

In general, street children have very short attention spans, whether or not they have lived with their families. They cannot sit still or do the same activity for long, while Maher children can concentrate somewhat longer due to their meditation practices. The daily schedule must reflect this by filling time with activities and not leaving too much unstructured time. None of these children are used to a schedule, and while they resist it at first, as they grow up they are thankful they learned the discipline of keeping to a schedule. As one older Maher teen reports, because she learned how to discipline herself, she can create her own timetable based on the times of her classes, bus times, and so on. If she needs to study and is sleepy, she knows it is okay to sleep and then study later. She can make good choices for herself.

Discipline of children from the streets or from institutions is trickier than with children who grew up in a stable home. These children need to be reminded again and again that you love them and hate the behavior. Teach them the consequences of their choices. Be loving and firm, punish as needed, and practice forgiveness. If you are too soft, these children will play you. They need to learn love and slowly learn to trust your love. And they need firmness.

Maintaining Family Relationships

Maher values family, and so encourages families to maintain connections. Staff work to support good ongoing relationships in a variety of ways.

Family and Home Visits

As much as Maher tries to create the experience of mother's home at Maher, children do best when they are loved and supported by their birth families, even if this comes from extended family such as grandparents, older siblings, or an uncle or aunt. Maher encourages visits and seeks safe opportunities for all children to experience a safe, loving family home.

Children with family

Family members are welcome at any time, and one Saturday a month is a regular family visit day. Parents and grandparents are encouraged to come and visit with the child, to hear stories child about school and their child's life at Maher. They are also invited to leave a little money for the child's savings account, or perhaps to bring toothpaste or some small necessity. Family members may also be invited to some of the holiday celebrations at Maher.

Children may go home for school holidays, as well as religious holidays observed in their family. Staff will want to be sure the children are safe (whether from violence or from sexual assault),

and also are not confused if their family habits are different from what has become familiar while living at the Maher. Often these families live in slum conditions, or do not have the hygiene habits the children have learned. And while a home visit is done ahead of time, not everything can be predicted in advance. Perhaps a neighbor is a risk to a child, and the social worker does not learn this during the home visit.

Before sending children home for a holiday, teach them what to expect. Remind them that their family members or neighbors may not think like Maher adults do. Remind the children how to behave and how to dress, still consistent with Maher ways. Also, for their protection, tell each girl to stay only with her mother, not to let anyone touch her, and to tell her mother right away if someone does touch her. If a man is inappropriate or hurting the child and the mother supports the man, then the child is told to go right away to a call box and call Maher. A social worker will come immediately to pick her up. Social workers visit each child's home at least once every holiday to see how the child is doing.

If these holidays go well and the parents come regularly to visit, then work with the family to develop a plan for when the child can go back home to live there. Of course, it must be clear that school will continue, and it must also be what the child wants.

310

Orphans

While Maher does its best to provide a loving family home atmosphere, ideally all children will at least briefly experience living in a single family home that is loving and safe. Therefore the staff works to find ways to create this opportunity for as many of the children as possible.

Orphans may have family members, such as older siblings living on their own, or aunts and uncles. After relationships are verified, family members are encouraged to visit. If these visits go well, the children might be able to stay with a relative for a holiday or summer vacation. Staff will conduct a home visit before a child is sent home to visit.

For school holidays, trustees, the dance teacher, and other benefactors in Pune may take two to four orphan children home for a week or two, so even these children have an experience of home life. It is best to keep the children in groups for their security and comfort, especially the girls. But first a social worker will check all the homes to be sure the children will be safe, and that there are no boys nearby who would hurt the girls. Sometimes a social worker or housemother will take two or three children home for a week. Another option is to send a child to a different Maher house for a week for a new experience. Also staff may take orphans, or other children who cannot go home, on outings or arrange special games.

Responsibilities of Parents

Maher has a list of responsibilities for parents while their children are at Maher to help encourage ongoing involvement. It may be appropriate to request any or all of these things from guardians, or other family relatives when the parents are no longer available.

General communication

- Communicate with the housemother or social worker.

- Please inform the NGO if you have a new address or phone number.

- If you want to phone your child, do that on Sundays between 9 a.m. and 5 p.m. at Maher. If it is an emergency, you may call anytime.

Schooling

- Take an interest in your child's schooling and encourage the child to do his or her best.

- Do not go meet your child at the school.

- Do not take the school leaving certificate from the school without the NGO's permission.

- If you take the child home to live during the school year, you must pay any new school fees, since the fees the NGO paid will not be refunded.

311

- When the child is in the 8th or 9th standard, prepare the "cost and income certificate" for the child. It is needed for further education in college.

Visits at Maher

- Come once a month to visit the child and for parent meetings with staff. When parents do not come for visits, the children struggle emotionally.

- Always meet on the premises of the NGO.

- When you come to visit, please bring personal items such as hair oil, soap, or toothpaste.

- Do not bring oily food or snacks.

- Do not give money, toys, or other things directly to the child without telling the NGO office.

- Do not tell family problems to your child. It may be difficult for the child to hear.

Financial support

- If possible, contribute a little bit (even Rs. 50) to the child's savings account every month. When your child leaves Maher, he or she can take that amount, and it will be useful for higher education.

- When you come to visit, bring the child's savings account book, if you have one.

- If your child is a boy, please submit money for haircuts.

Home visits

- When your child comes home for the holidays, please give him or her a daily bath and oversee cleanliness. (Some families, such as those living in slums, may be unable to do this.)

- Keep a proper environment in the house. Limit time for TV and videos.

- If you work outside and will send the child to a relative, please think of how this will affect the child. Will she be safe? What will she do all day?

- Do not send children alone to swim.

- Keep an eye on your child to be sure she uses equipment properly and safely, such as gas, iron, fan, refrigerator, and mobile phone.

- If your child is sick while home for the holidays:

  o Keep the child at home until he is well enough (for his wellbeing and to safeguard the other children).

  o Please bring any medication to the NGO when the child returns.

Teaching Values

In addition to the conventional school curriculum and the developmental programs above, an important part of the children's development is to receive a solid base of ethics and values. The foundation is laid at a very early age, when even the toddlers observe and imitate older children. Without bias or prejudice, there is a healthy respect for all religions and castes. The children are taught to guard against superstition, bigotry, and fanaticism. They are also taught to be clean in thought, speech, and action, and to be helpful and cooperative. All of the core values are taught through daily living and discussions.

Learning Values Through Daily Life at Maher

Below are a few examples of learning values through daily life that are especially relevant for children. In Chapter 10, "The Art and Genius of Maher," you will read more about creating a values-based NGO.

Holidays

All of the religious and secular holidays are opportunities to teach values that are consistent with Maher's core values; these are really universal spiritual values found in most traditions. For example, the Hindu festival of Raksha Bandhan symbolizes a sister's love for her brother, and a brother's lifelong vow to protect

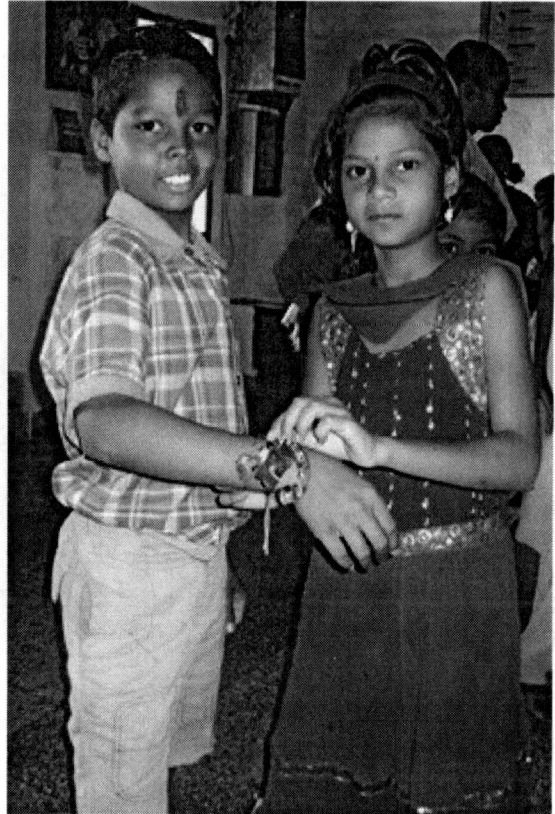

Boy is given about 8-10 threads!

his sister. *Raksha Bandhan* literally means "bond of protection" and signifies the responsibility of brothers to protect and respect their sisters. On the day of the Raksha Bandhan, a sister ties a decorative thread on the wrist of her brother after performing the *aarti* blessing. At Maher, all the boys and girls are sisters and brothers to each other. Maher provides enough bracelets for all the girls to tie on the wrists of as many of the boys as they want. After each boy is offered *aarti* by one girl, then it is chaotic and fun as many more threads of protection are tied. Some of the boys end up with a dozen or more of these threads! As a secular example, Gandhi's birthday is an opportunity to teach about nonviolence.

CASE Using satsang to reinforce good sportsmanship

During one visit by this author, Krishna's birthday was celebrated. Following Indian tradition, a clay pot filled with curd (yogurt), coins, and treats was strung up high. A few other treats such as packages of cookies were attached to the rope suspending the pot. Divided into a boys' team and a girls' team, the children took turns trying to reach the pot and pull it down for all the children to enjoy. There was a great deal of competition to see which team would succeed in cracking open the pot. It was not easy! The children had to build a pyramid of people standing on each other's shoulders. Some of the boys started throwing buckets of water on the girls and throwing their slippers (sandals) to distract concentration. The girls soon followed suit. Eventually the girls won—for the first time in 13 years! (photo below) Afterward some of the boys asked that next year the boys and girls be separated and not compete against each other.

The next morning the whole community gathered for this author's farewell, and Sister Lucy took the opportunity of everyone being together to hold satsang. She asked first if they had all had fun at Krishna's birthday. "Yes!" they yelled. "Wonderful, she said." Then she said there were two things she did not like. She asked the children if they could guess what those two things were. Immediately the children named the water throwing and the slipper throwing. "Then why did you do it? And why didn't I like it?" she asked. Someone could have been hurt, they said. Some of the children said they'd done it anyway "because others did it." They all laughed at themselves when they saw her face, knowing that was a really dumb reason. They apologized and promised they would not do it next year. Then Sister Lucy gently scolded the boys who'd asked for a separate competition, telling them to be good losers and to congratulate the girls. All heard, all learned, and all were happy.

(A chart of all the holidays, including suggestions for underlying themes that reflect Maher values, is included in Chapter 6.)

Games, sports, and competitions

All the competitions and games are a chance to teach values of transparency, fairness, not cheating, and respecting all, regardless of who wins or loses. Children are taught to respect all the abilities of their peers, to support the team rather focus on themselves, and to embrace the joy of winning without cheating. Teaching through games and stories works better than just telling children how to behave.

"In the moment" lessons and *satsang*

To be most effective, praise must be specific and so must correction. Children are told clearly when they are acting stupidly or wrongly, and where it will lead. Staff do far more than lecture and try never to yell. They guide children to think for themselves, and to not follow adults, older children, or peers blindly. Indian culture can overvalue following directions or "following the guru" without pausing to really question the motives, wisdom, and outcomes of one's own actions. They praise and celebrate successes as well.

Role models in Sister Lucy and in staff

Maher's staff all point to Sister Lucy as a role model for themselves and for the children. It helps the staff and the children to see how she speaks to others and behaves. Sister Lucy is always open, loving, hardworking, and nicely dressed; she laughs or smiles a lot, and is happy much of the time. Staff point out how she always encourages others, and helps all who come to her. And they tell how she never gives up faith in people, but keeps trying because she believes things will work out. Children too are good observers. The more they see that the housemothers love them, even when they misbehave or make mistakes, the more they will love and forgive others.

Examples of what the children say they have learn from Sister Lucy:

- "When I am happy, others will be too!"

- "Didi [Sister Lucy] gave to me, so when I grow up, I will take two children too and give to them what I received, and they too will pass it on."

- "What I have, I will give."

- "Learn to face your problems and work through them, then good things come from that. It does not work to avoid or run from problems."

Ultimately love is the defining value and quality at Maher

Teach the children with loving ways. Once they feel you love them, they will move mountains for you. Keep strict

315

study and homework times. At playtime, play with them; have fun and be with them as children. Let them know that we learn through mistakes. It is good to make mistakes here at Maher where it is safe, and they can learn and become confident to do right in the outside world.

Dreams of a Full, Vibrant, Loving, Productive Life

The four young people described here were raised at Maher. The first three came when Maher was still small and Sister Lucy cooked for them, did the shopping, and handled much of their care. She came home late at night, so the children would wait up for her to come in to say good night. To them, she became a second mother. All four have expressed the desire to give back to others, in gratitude for all Maher gave to them. Also, all four attended Marathi-medium government schools up to the 10th standard (Marathi is the local language of that state in India). English is only nominally taught, and is mostly rote memorization of some vocabulary. Most colleges and all universities conduct classes in English. Therefore, all of these young people learned English on their own to be able to continue their education. They required no translator for these interviews.

Jaya

Jaya, who was 20 at the time of this interview, came to Maher when she was 12 years old. She has four sisters and one brother. All of the children were bright but, while their mother worked and wanted them to go to school, there was not enough money. Their father was an alcoholic and beat their mother. A trustee of Maher, leading programs in the village about alcoholism, heard about the family and told them about Maher. The mother went to Maher, and eventually the three younger girls were admitted. At first Jaya was excited to be there because she could attend school regularly. Then she got homesick and cried a lot. But there were so many other children at Maher and people took such good care of her, she says, that she quickly adapted. After the 10th standard she attended college and university, working toward a law degree. Her younger sisters are still at Maher (one completing her teaching degree). The family still gathers for visits and holidays, and later Jaya moved back home with her mother while still continuing her studies. At the time of writing, Jaya was in Delhi working on the final step of her law degree, completing her internship year at India's Supreme Court.

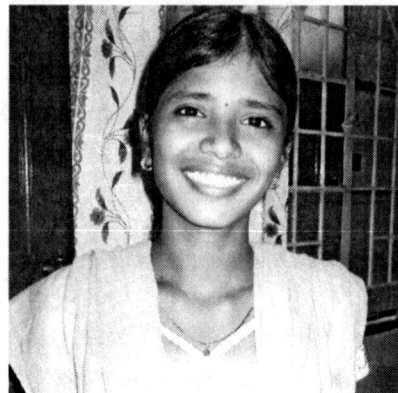

Jaya

316

Jaya says she never had dreams before Maher—but now, after so many amazing experiences (including travel to the U.K. to perform with Maher's dancers), she has many dreams. The first is to become a lawyer and to help people get justice, especially those who cannot afford lawyers. She wants to help people like the women who come to Maher. She plans to create a group that will make more people aware, fight for justice and work to change the laws. Eventually she expects to get married and have a family, but only after finishing her education and developing her career. Her mother understands and supports her. Sister Lucy hopes she will come back to Maher to work full time as a lawyer.

TIP Getting these kids passports is a challenge, taking much perseverance. Many do not have birth certificates, since they were found on the streets or their families come from poor areas where births are not regularly recorded. Friends of Maher in the government ultimately helped the process along so that the performing group could travel to the U.K.

Manu and Ghauth

Ghauth

Ghauth, who was 19 at the time of this interview, came to Maher when he was 8. He has two older sisters. Both his parents worked at Weikfield Company. Then his father had a stroke and became bedridden. His mother took a second night job in a hospital, but there was no longer enough money to send Ghauth to school, even though he was clever. Ghauth began working in a garage. His teachers offered to pay his school fees, but it was not enough: the family needed his income. Then a woman in the village told his mother about Maher and she brought him here. Ghauth returned to school and quickly began winning awards: he was chosen "best actor" in the 8th standard and later selected for Maharashtra Social Forum, a government program for promising children from poor families. Ghauth and another Maher girl both went on to Mumbai and then were selected to continue to the forum's national competition in Delhi. Ghauth won first place there, and was chosen to go to an International Forum in South Africa, but could not get a passport in time. Sister

317

Lucy advised him not to be sad, that something else would come along. And it did—the trip to the U.K. to perform!

Ghauth too has dreams: a career in commerce, perhaps for a multinational company; an MBA; and then to start an NGO like Maher, to help others like himself. Or perhaps a career in politics, to act as a voice for change. In the meantime, he is teaching dance and drawing on Saturdays at a construction company's school for the children of its laborers. He saves the money he earns from this for his own schooling. Recently he was chosen to be one of 50 university students from thousands across India to spend a month with the prime minister of India. Ghauth will soon begin graduate school.

Manu

Manu, who was 18 at the time of this interview, was 8 years old when he first came to Maher. He has two older sisters. He never met his father, who beat his mother and sisters and even kicked his mother's belly when she was pregnant with Manu. She fled to her parents. She worked in a hospital to try to support the children. Manu went to school two or three days a week and the rest of the week sold sugarcane juice by the roadside. His sisters were also working. Manu had his schoolwork with him at the juice stand and read whenever he had a break. One lady came for juice and asked him why he was not in school. She took him to Maher to meet Sister Lucy. Soon his mother brought him back to Maher to stay.

Maher had only been in existence for three years then, with only one house and three staff members. At first it was hard, Manu recalls, but then everyone became family. He took an exam to see what grade level he was in school. They placed him in the 4th standard in a Marathi-medium school, and he caught up quickly. He loves meditation, and attended the 10-day Vipassana silence retreat after the 9th standard (earlier than most children) and again after the 12th standard. In addition to dancing, he plays harmonium and *tabla* (an Indian drum) and draws.

Manu's studies in college led him to create a one-year project in Shirur to study water usage in agriculture. Shirur village has about 20,000 people. He surveyed 15 homes and taught the residents how to use water more effectively: how to filter it, how to store it, and how to use it efficiently in the fields . He successfully taught them how to measure groundwater and rainwater, and then to use that information to add water and increase crop results so they could earn more income. This project won awards at the college, university, and state levels. The day after this interview, Manu was off to Delhi for a national competition regarding his project. Even after the project was officially completed, Manu still traveled to the village (over an hour by bus each way) on his own time to help them. If he were to stop now, they would go back to the old ways, he explains.

Inspired by his trip to the U.K. with the Maher dancers, where he saw the British road system and GPS, he chose to study environmental geography in university. Manu dreams of helping to design a GPS system for all of India, including rural areas. After this interview, Manu received a full scholarship to prestigious Pune University's MBA program.

Lila in her nursing uniform

Lila

Lila's story is a different one. She comes from the remote tribal village Thakar Wasti, where Maher has a small home for about 25 children. Both her parents live at home and she has two younger siblings. The family is very poor. There is no education beyond the 10th standard available in her village. At that point she would have gone to work in the fields, herding animals. (Her younger sister is already now an unwed mother, not uncommon for young girls left alone and vulnerable while the parents work.) Lila's parents sent her to the Maher home in their village at age 8 so she would have better opportunities. She failed 10th standard English and wanted to quit

school then. But Sister Lucy brought her to Vadhu Badruk then, to study and to sit again for the 10th standard exam. She passed this her first try. After that she agreed to continue at Vadhu and go to college. It was hard for her to fit in at Vadhu; life was very different in her small village. She was lonely. But Maher taught her the value of education, and she came to enjoy life at Vadhu, she says. She was shy, but she smiled a lot and was very quick to help others. And as she became accustomed to Maher, she sometimes felt awkward with the very different way of living when she went home to visit. This is a common challenge for these children of Maher who learn new values and new ways of living.

In college Lila studied Marathi, Hindi, English, geography, politics, and history. Hindi was her favorite, and she hoped to take teacher training to teach Hindi at a primary school, or possibly at Maher, to give something back. However, after interviewing both a teacher and a nurse about their work, she decided nursing was a better choice for her.

Recently Lila completed an 18-month nursing program. She graduated in the top tier of her class. She was accepted at the Vadhu Hospital for her internship. If that goes well, she expects to be employed there afterward. The author first met Lila when she was 18 years old, had only recently come to Maher. She was shy and not at all confident. Three and a half years later Lila appeared confident, spoke English well, and was brimming with enthusiasm.

Summary of Recordkeeping and Copies of Forms

Summary of all paperwork relating to children, referencing workflow stages.

Children's forms, files, registers	Stage begun	Stages when updated
Admission form	1	2
Admission application letter	1	
Admission file (all admission-related papers, including form)	1	2, 5
Admission register (paper and online)	1	2, 5
Medical file	1	as needed
Receipt for valuables	1	as needed
Case file	2	2, 3, 4, 5
Case management plans	2–3	3, 4, 5
Marriage application form		as needed
Leave form	5	
Feedback form	5	

Copies of Forms

Only some of the above forms are included, when these may be useful. In Maharashtra, India, these are standard; elsewhere you will have to check local requirements and adapt as needed. A final list of admission file and case file contents are summarized at the end of stage 2. Downloadable copies are on the book's website where noted. (www.replicatemaher.wix.com/tools)

Content of children's admission form

Photo
Name
Date of admission
Date of birth
Blood group
Permanent address
Phone number
Name, address, relationship of contact
Place of birth
Religion
Mother tongue
Language spoken in home
School class, at present
    School where studying; medium (language) of instruction
If repeater, number of times and classes repeated (list school, class, times repeated)
Family history
    Description
List names, ages, educational qualifications, occupations, and income
Details of mother's and father's death
    Description
    Date of death
    Cause of death
Any family member who is alcoholic, TB patient, or suffering from leprosy or venereal disease
If no parents, details of guardian (list name, employer's name, address, phone number, type of accommodation, details of accommodation—owned or rental)
Recommended by: (list name, designation, address)

Admission Register (spreadsheet on website)

Column headings include case number, first name, family name, address, date of admission, year of admission, year of discharge, sex, religion, caste, cause of admission, date of birth, current year, current age, sent by, final disposal, date of discharge, still at Maher (Yes/No), House, class (school). Notes: Many will not know the year and date of their birth, which is why current year and current age are collected. Also, the government requires caste and religion be recorded.

Sample admission application letter

Dear Director,

I, undersigned, request you to admit my son/daughter/ward in your NGO NAME. The contribution of Rs. ___ will be paid by me toward upkeep, by the 10th of every month, and the sum of Rs. ___ toward initial expense. In case of sickness or dismissal from NGO NAME, I assume the responsibility of taking my son/daughter/ward from the NGO NAME within 24 hours on receipt of notification. If during the stay in NGO NAME the child gets sick or meets with an accident, I will not hold the management responsible. If my child dies due to some reasons, you have my permission for further investigation.

Thanking you,

     Yours sincerely

     Signature / left-hand thumb impression of mother / father / guard

**Rising to New Life rangoli design,
some of the boys and male social workers**

10 | *The Art and Genius of Maher*

"If you don't know what's important to you, if you don't know what you stand for, I don't think you can lead. . . . It's not something you can see . . . the search for knowing what kind of leader you want to be. . . . It's inside you, and that's the interesting work, to recognize the sort of leader you want to be.

—Jenny Garrett, founder of
Reflexion Associates <http://reflexion-uk.co.uk>

One of the most often asked questions is, "Can Maher be replicated without Sister Lucy personally leading the way?" Is it possible to replicate the magic of Maher, the feel of the place, the people, and the results? Can another NGO also develop the incredible positive regard Maher has built both in its local communities and internationally?

This author believes the answer is "yes, absolutely!" This manual is intended to help others inspired by Maher spread the magic. Most of the chapters so far have focused on the "science" of Maher, indeed of running any NGO: details about planning, budgets, job descriptions, workflows, and case management plans. Some of the uniqueness, the "art" or genius, has

been noted earlier; here, the central qualities of that success will be made more explicit and expanded upon. While the science is important, it is not what drives Sister Lucy each day or what truly shapes Maher. Rather it is the art and genius she intuitively developed that create the essence of Maher.

What, then, are the "alchemical secrets" that make Maher feel so special and make it so successful at helping women and children thrive—both at Maher and beyond? Where is the right balance between the art and the science?

It Is All About the Vision and Mission

Maher is a vision- and mission-driven NGO. It began with a deep call in the heart of Sister Lucy. Her deep abiding commitment to truly make a difference, to end the violence and despair facing women in India (and their children as well), has shaped every decision along the way. Sometimes this means things are done inefficiently, from a purely business perspective. But when you look beneath the surface, there is often a good reason for the so-called inefficiencies that supports the needs of the women and children. For example, small homes are perhaps less efficient economically, but they are essential for the family feel and heart-centered focus of Maher. Sometimes too it has meant that the business side of running a now large NGO has suffered from being less a priority. Only in the last few years, for instance, has there been a concerted effort to computerize and organize the vast amounts of data collected in the seemingly endless paper registers, facilitating better data analysis and reporting. Most staff have very basic computer skills at best; most are hired for their desire to help women and children, not for their ability to run a business. In fact, some of this work is being done by the children raised at Maher, who are now attending universities.

Maher's Vision

> No matter who we are, we walk together toward wholeness. All have the opportunity for a decent life, dignity, and happiness irrespective of caste, gender, or religion. There is no longer any work for organizations such as Maher.

Maher's Mission

- *Develop and deliver services to address the root causes of violence and despair and their effects, so women, children, and families are healthy, happy, and self-reliant.*

- *Where possible, support family reunification, providing services as needed to support healthy and stable homes.*

- *When family reunification is not possible or desirable, provide safe and loving residential, educational, and developmental services for children and women.*

- *Enable sustainable communities by addressing economic, education, health, and environmental issues focusing on villages and slums.*

Seven Critical Elements

There are seven critical elements to the art and genius of Maher. They are listed below. Leadership is also critical to Maher's special nature and success; it is discussed in the latter part of this chapter.

1. Women Healing Women, Children Passing It On: Together Creating a New India

All Maher housemothers, as well as many of the other staff, were themselves once in need and took refuge at Maher. They intrinsically understand the harsh realities of many women's lives and can offer compassion beyond measure. Part of their healing comes from helping the next one who arrives. Through staff roles they are supported to do more than they can even imagine they are capable of doing. Previous chapters related stories of women who arrived desperate, in tears, with little or no hope left, who are now leading whole centers, training other women, and full of confidence in themselves and in the future.

Maher's children, as they become young adults, are infused with gratitude for the path their lives have taken at Maher. They know they are the lucky ones, and they are committed to sharing their good fortune with others. While still in school they volunteer their time teaching other disadvantaged children dance, music, self-empowerment, nonviolence, and more. They are studying for careers as lawyers, teachers, nurses, artists, computer specialists, and business-people with dreams of making a difference.

They have lived together as boys and girls, and as Muslims, Hindus, and Christians. From the highest castes to the lowest, they share daily life, and they have learned to love and respect all their Maher family members equally. And they are expanding this nonjudgment and compassion beyond Maher, to their classmates at school, local villagers, and others they meet. Not only will they never be part of the sectarian and gender violence plaguing India and other parts of the world, but they are already becoming voices for, and leaders of, a new and better future for all.

Having been raised at Maher, in this environment, with these values, these children in particular represent the future hope of India. They have learned

---

CASE Children creating the future

After a horrific rape in Delhi in December 2012 that caused an uproar, both in India and internationally, Maher organized a 1,200-person-strong protest march and rally decrying rape and violence against women, marching from Vadhu village to the next village. Maher boys and girls led the way; villagers, leaders, self-help group members, and others joined in. Later, Maher's college and university boys and girls shared a particularly poignant discussion. The boys and girls spoke about their feelings, and asked each other tough questions about how men and women view each other, about rape. This kind of cross-gender conversation is forbidden in village life, and nearly so all over India. Simply being able to talk is a start.

new ways of living and interacting that now are rooting out ages-old destructive social norms. Maher has slowly expanded its work (beyond only women and children who come seeking refuge) into villages and communities, and slowly the old ways are changing. As Father D'Sa, a Maher trustee, has said about the vision of Maher, "It's a huge task awaiting us"—but it has begun.

Maher-led march and rally to stop violence against women.

2. Core Values Drive Everyone and Everything

A values-based NGO is a living, breathing culture of core values shared among all employees and residents. The content and application of these values distinguish Maher from traditional institutions and organizations that have a more machinelike business approach and that rely on authoritarian relationships. In a values-based NGO, a clear set of core values provides a foundation and guiding principles for decision-making, actions, relationships, and a sense of community. Values *become* the management.

Without being beholden to any particular church, philosophy, or group, Maher overtly upholds universal spiritual values, such as unconditional love and respect for all; social justice for all; and truth, transparency and fairness in all interactions. As a reminder, Maher's core values are repeated below.

Maher's Core Values

- *Embracing all people of all faiths, regardless of caste, class, or ethnicity*

- *Spiritually infused interfaith daily life and operations*

- *Unconditional love and respect for all*

- *Social justice for all regardless of caste, class, or gender*

- *Truth, transparency, and fairness in all interactions and in distribution of resources*

- *Reawakening our personal relationship with Mother Earth and treating her as the Body of the Divine*

- *Lifelong learning and continual reevaluation and change*

Core values as expressed in daily life and policies at Maher

Your NGO will have its own set of core values. To help you see more clearly how deeply these values are embedded in daily life and how values become management, the following examples show just some of the ways each value is reflected in decision-making, actions, relationships, and the sense of community Maher has created. Your NGO will need to develop a similar set of practices reflecting its core values. It is important that these values are absolutely consistently applied in all situations, or they will lose their power, and cynicism will develop. Values generate the foundation of a community of staff, clients, guests, and others. Values are not rules or duties: they must be felt and lived from within.

<u>Embracing all people of all faiths, regardless of caste, class, or ethnicity</u>

- When new clients are admitted, they are not asked what caste or religion they belong to. Instead their immediate needs are attended to and all are listened to with compassion (although eventually

> **TIP** Values are lived and modeled all through Maher, from Sister Lucy to staff, residents, and even guests. You cannot tell someone to get up at 1 a.m. with a smile because a child is crying—that is love and commitment. You have to feel it!

caste and religion are recorded as required by the government).

- Maher's "circle of religions" design (a design with the symbols of the twelve most common religious groups in India) prominently welcomes all arrivals at every site. In this way, each person who comes sees a symbol of his or her faith on display. (See photo in Chapter 2; a similar image is shown later in this chapter.)

CASE Staying true to the values

A priest met Sister Lucy and loved the work she was doing and wanted to give Maher money from his church's charitable funds. This was in the early days when funding was particularly scarce. He understood and valued her interfaith mission, but his church required that all the children be given a Bible along with the much-needed funds. They did not even have to read it, he said. But Sister Lucy understood that this would convey exactly the wrong message to arriving women. She stayed true to her values, without "sliding down a slippery slope," and refused the funding offer.

TIP The children of Maher have learned new values, as well as to be practical. "We don't see each other as he's this and I am that," says one university student raised at Maher. "We ask what is your need, not what is your caste or religion." Later she says, "When I marry, some families may allow a son to marry outside caste and religion, but we have to pay attention to the parents of the husband, his brothers. I will have to see."

- All residents and guests eat together, the same food from the same dishes, regardless of caste or background; everyone lives integrated into one family. (Reflecting respect, foreign guests may be served less spicy versions of the food and offered chairs for their western hips unaccustomed to floor sitting.)

- All are treated the same, whether their clothing is torn and stained or clean and new. (Exceptions are women whose clothes are so tattered as to be revealing, or foreign guests who do not understand the culture and whose clothes are revealing; in such cases each is given appropriate clothes to wear.) Disability, marital status—none of these surface issues matter: *all* means *all*. If some are uncomfortable with this, they keep these feelings to themselves.

- Maher declines donations that come with stipulations in favor of any one religious practice.

- Staff come to Maher from many different religious backgrounds. Regardless, they help with preparations for, and participate in, all Maher religious celebrations in active demonstration of respect for all faiths.

CASE The commitment to interfaith must come from deep within.

Sister Lucy explains her commitment to interfaith work: "I have been insisting on 'One God, one people, and one world' because our Church teaches us that it is the same Spirit from which all truth and goodness emerges. It is Maher's way of interreligious dialogue. It is the Spirit that is prompting me to live with the people of different faith traditions and to embrace individual persons as members of one community. We are called to be the yeast in the bread, the salt of the earth, and the light of the world."

328

- Major holidays are celebrated for each faith represented in the community, with discussions of the positive value that the holiday stands for. The goal is to experience the best of each faith, and to learn how each addresses the universal questions of "Why am I here?" and "How should I live?" (Chapter 6 includes a list of most of these holidays plus a brief note of at least one universal spiritual value for each holiday.)

- Everyone is free to practice his or her own faith as well, whether that means going to Mass, wearing the Muslim headscarf, returning home for important religious celebrations, and so on. However, Sister Lucy does not wear her nun's habit at Maher, as even this could be taken as a subtle preference for

Christianity. Instead she wears a specially made cross that combines symbols of Islam and Hinduism into the design.

Spiritually infused interfaith daily life and operations

- Every day, every meal, and every meeting begins with prayer, and often also with silent meditation.

- God's grace is acknowledged daily with gratitude, and it is taught that while God may have many names and faces, it is all one God.

"Is God so small to be possessed by one religion?"

- Daily prayers, prayers to welcome guests, and prayers at events are all interfaith (that is, they do not address a particular name or form of God).

- Every Maher home has an altar with fresh flowers plus a Qur'an, a Bible, a Bhagavad Gita, and a Dhammapada. Here community

TIP "Religion has to be followed in mind and spirit," says Sister Lucy. "Following rituals without realizing the true message of religion is not faith. Maher is unique in founding the interfaith tradition of working. It does not look at community service devoid of religious context; it believes that the religious context need not refer to any single religion or ideology. We try to pass on this ideal to the children through celebrations of all festivals."

> **CASE** *The Indian custom of aarti (bathing one's guest in light) is performed to welcome guests, and a small bit of sandalwood paste is placed on the third eye. Aarti, while coming from the Hindu tradition, is truly now a national tradition, practiced all over India by people of different faiths. Sister Lucy grew up with this custom even though her family is Catholic. It represents several ideas, including the blessing of the light to overcome darkness (in the world and in ourselves), and reminds us to keep the Divine (in whatever form we hold dear) at the center of our lives and hearts.*

meetings, meditation, and prayer take place.

- Vipassana meditation (breath-centered meditation) is taught to, and practiced by, all residents. All adults, including children starting at age seventeen, attend a ten-day Vipassana retreat to deepen their meditative practice. In addition to its other benefits, it is also a way to communicate privately with the Divine if one so chooses.

- The core values are generally spiritual values and are reinforced daily, not as the "rules" of any particular religion but as the foundation of any spiritual life. The children are taught to apply these values (not stealing or cheating; being compassionate) at school, indeed anywhere, as life values.

- Says Father D'Sa, a Maher trustee: "In a nutshell, Maher is teaching the staff, women, and children to be

decent human beings—that is real spirituality!"

Sister Lucy leading children in meditation

Unconditional love and respect for all

- Mother's love is unconditional: each child is loved simply because he or she exists.

- Mothers and older children help the younger children, and lead by example (in hygiene, on-time attendance, following rules, attitude, and more).

330

- Maher follows the practice of "we see how it is," which means listening and learning first, before intervening or telling others what to do, whether with an individual, a family, or a village.

- Discipline emphasizes guiding and teaching children (and women) after "mistakes" rather than dispensing punishment, with second and third chances to get it right.

- Forgiveness too is unconditional.

- Sister Lucy advises staff to "hate the behavior but love the child."

- Staff are taught to seek responsibility and reconciliation instead of blame in families.

- Everyone practices heart-centered action in all interactions (with women, children, families, men, donors, and guests) whether in person or in writing.

<u>Social justice for all regardless of caste, class, or gender</u>

- All girls and boys get the same educational opportunities, play the same sports (even if on separate teams), and pursue individual talents as equals.

- Girls and boys equally take leadership roles at Maher.

- Staff men and women share the same work, and are treated and rewarded equally; promotions are based on abilities.

- Work in tribal villages and slums is done not only to bring services, village improvements (such as a well or biogas), or improved opportunities for the children, but also to teach residents how to advocate for their own rights.

<u>Truth, transparency, and fairness in all interactions and in distribution of resources</u>

- Maher pays no bribes, even though this may (and usually does) mean delays in building permits or passports for children, for example.

- Every rupee is accounted for and the records are available for public view.

CASE Learning to forgive
Says Sabita: "Sister Lucy always forgives us when we make mistakes, so now as a housemother, when a child makes a mistake, then I must forgive them too. This was hard for me when I first arrived. Now I can do it, after Sister Lucy demonstrated."

> ## CASE Maher pays attention even to small things
>
> *In Indian villages, only boys are allowed to ride bicycles. While this may seem small, it is related to the expectation that women's place is only in the home. So slowly, the Maher girls began to ride bicycles. Slowly the village got used to this, and now even village girls are seen riding bicycles. In another example, as Maher girls learn and compete in tae kwon do, this too helps to change expectations and age-old customs.*

- Each person is expected to follow all rules in games and sports, even when others may be cheating.

- Everyone receives a fair wage; no one enriches himself or herself at the expense of Maher's clients or donors.

- Maher staff live the same standard of living as do the residents. No one receives special food, housing, or clothing, not even Sister Lucy. A few of Sister Lucy's cousins are now Maher staff, but they get zero special treatment.

For example: the staff and children all eat the same food: three meals a day, always fresh. Most institutions, the author was told, cook breakfast for the children and give them leftovers the rest of the day, not three meals. "What crime did these children commit to not get the same as us?" asks Sister Lucy.

Reawakening our personal relationship with Mother Earth and treating her as the Body of the Divine

- Maher both follows and teaches environmental stewardship practices such as biogas, solar hot water, composting, vermiculture, solar lamps, not wasting water, and avoiding the use of plastic.

- Gardens and flowers are planted at all homes so the children (especially street and city children) learn responsible care for plants and soil.

- Everyone recycles and reuses whenever possible.

Lifelong learning and continual reevaluation and change

- Educational programs are central, from crèches and kindergartens to adult literacy programs and job training programs.

- Well over half of the staff are women who came to Maher seeking refuge and have been trained as housemothers, social workers, and in other roles. Even a few of the men on staff at Maher followed this path.

- The value of learning is expressed and rewarded daily. For example, contests and awards for performance are given to both children and adults, encouraging them to keep on learning skills, information, and languages.

- All staff, women residents, and college and university students go to workshops regularly. Topics range from self-esteem to women's legal issues to resolving conflicts nonviolently, among many others.

- Everyone is given opportunities to discover talents and interests and to develop his or her potential.
- Everyone is encouraged to reflect on his or her beliefs: where these were learned, what effects those beliefs have in practice, and whether each

person truly wishes to retain those beliefs or create new ones that lead to better outcomes, more in line with the vision of a better future.

Staff in a values-based organization

In a values-driven NGO, ideally staff find a match between their personal values and the organization's values, creating a unified and motivated workforce. This is challenging when many of the values are opposite to local customs and beliefs. At hiring time, Sister Lucy explains some of the key differences (especially the interfaith and caste-free aspects), telling new employees that they will be expected to comply with and even embrace these values. Slowly, over time, they learn and commit to Maher's vision, mission, and values. A few never become comfortable with the culture

---

CASE Modeling the practice of challenging your own beliefs

Sister Lucy knows that many of the values of Maher require the staff to challenge beliefs and practices with which they grew up. She knows this is not easy. She shares with them her own experience challenging some of the tenets of Catholicism as they were taught to her, seeking guidance from Jesus and from other faith-based teachers. She has found she can still be a nun, still love the church, and yet also fully live the values of Maher, even though many in her local diocese disagree with her. She has learned to walk a fine line, always guided by her heart but without breaking the rules of the church. This takes great courage, she says, and the ability to reexamine one's habits, values, and tastes to see if they really make sense. Even these may vary at different stages of a person's life. Sister Lucy can credibly encourage staff to do a similar reexamination because they all know she has done so and continues to do so.

and choose to leave. Most, however, see the wisdom and the forward-thinking nature of these values and come to embrace them wholeheartedly—even the local villagers hired as drivers.

Recently some of the staff attended a series of workshops to reflect on their own life vision and values and how this aligns (or does not) with Maher's vision and values. Many found that this strengthened their commitment and are now bringing a form of this exploration not only to others in the Maher family, but also to villages and self-help groups with whom they work.

Maher's values guide every facet of life, coming directly from Sister Lucy's heart. This is why the children who have grown up at Maher almost effortlessly live these values—even more so than the staff. These children have grown up with the values as the very air they breathe. This is India's future.

Values become management

When values are embedded, staff do not need to rely on their manager to direct certain actions or create certain outcomes. They know what is the right thing to do, and they do it.

Maher's doors are open 24/7, every day of the year. No appointments are necessary. All who come are welcomed graciously and served at least something to drink, or a meal if it is eating time. Regardless of what is going on, Maher finds a way to simultaneously respond to multiple demands; its staff and family have become amazingly flexible. When challenges arise, values guide everyone in the community toward correct action, often even without management personnel there to tell people what to do. This is particularly noteworthy in India, where the cultural norm is that no one takes initiative but waits for orders.

CASE Maher values are a lifestyle
This author, with a few others, had gone into Pune with Maher's director and a Maher driver from the village. While we waited for the director to finish a meeting at the university, a child came up to us begging. The driver asked her where her family was, and if she needed help. She ran away. Later he noticed she was with two other children; then we saw either a mother or big sister. He slowly wandered over to them, so as not to frighten them, and asked if they needed assistance. Did they have a place to live? He told them about Maher, and said they were welcome to come with us, or to come to Maher at any time. This author was astounded. Even the drivers carry Sister Lucy's desire to save as many children as they can! Even for this driver from the local village, Maher has become a lifestyle, not a job.

The following story demonstrates this well:

One day, there were two events scheduled for the same time, at two different sites. At Vadhu Badruk, a man from a local company had chosen to celebrate his birthday at Maher by catering supper for all of the nearly 300 residents and staff. Meanwhile at Vatsalydham (another Maher site about 35 minutes from Vadhu), a group of 30 college students and teachers from an American school of social work was scheduled for an informational tour and tea. Their bus, however, turned out to be too big to navigate the road into Vatsalydham, so they were rerouted to Vadhu at the last minute. When Vatsalydham called to tell of the change in plans, the staff realized that not only would the birthday dinner need to be relocated across the street, but dinner would need to be created for the bus group, who would now arrive near dinnertime! Everyone (children, women residents, housemothers, social workers, even foreign guests like this author) joined in to move the big birthday dinner out into the courtyard across the street. We also scrambled to prepare a full meal, including special Indian foods not normally served, for a group of 30 foreign guests. Meanwhile, a video about Maher was arranged, and a speaker to answer questions, until Sister Lucy and the director could arrive.

During all of this, a woman and her parents came in for family counseling just as Sister Lucy arrived. Her two children who lived at Maher were brought in by staff. The children were terrified of being sent away from Maher; one girl was literally shaking and clinging to Sister Lucy. Sister Lucy assured the children they did not have to leave, that Maher would always be their home. They all spoke with Sister Lucy for an hour, and were invited to come back again to continue the discussion. Of course, neither they nor the American busload could be turned away and asked to make an appointment!

What is perhaps most remarkable about this story, beyond the incredible flexibility of everyone, was that there was no manager onsite at Vadhu to lead all this. Here, the values *became* the management! The staff lived the value of heart-centered action: they sorted out what had to be done, and did it. No one got annoyed or short-tempered. All the guests were given what they came for without feeling the slightest bit of the stress that the staff was under to get everything done. Sister Lucy said later in the evening, "This is mother's house—how can you say no to supper guests or families in need?" And *she* did not have to make it happen. This is how a values-based operation works. (This kind of initiative is definitely not a cultural norm in India!)

The above values influence and help generate the remaining five elements of the art and genius of Maher.

3. Holistic Individual Development

Maher's programs respond to the physical, mental, social, and spiritual needs of women and children seeking refuge, including helping them dream of and then achieve a future. Most institutions focus on physical needs only—providing shelter, a bed, food, and the most basic of education—and then eject residents when they prove difficult, when some arbitrary time limit is reached, or (in the case of children) when they reach the age of 18. At Maher, women's and children's lives, even though often deeply traumatized, are made whole through unlimited love, nutritious food, regular exercise, education, and a range of innovative programs including development in the arts, self-esteem, and working to support and develop other women and children.

While love is clearly a primary ingredient in this transformation, so is attention to the residents' spiritual lives. As they learn to love, feel compassion for, and help others, they are seeking their purpose and place in the wider order. As discussed above, the core values are teaching them the essence of leading a spiritual life. Particularly for children from the streets or orphans who do not have a family religious tradition, this provides a rich base from which to choose a spiritual path when they become adults. Vipassana meditation is a crucial ingredient in their spiritual and emotional lives, helping cultivate both hopefulness and a resilience that will serve them the rest of their lives.

Maher looks after each resident, not just for the time they live at Maher, but considering their whole life span, their potential, and their dreams. Residents who arrive with no other goal than to survive are eventually helped to consider their future, to dream again. Everyone has opportunities to learn skills, self-confidence, and more to prepare them for independent, meaningful lives in their communities, whether with family members, on their own, or even marrying and developing new families.

4. Needs-Based Support for Healthy Family and Village Life

The value of respect for all is articulated in a favored phrase of Maher, "we see how it is" first, before acting. This phrase echoes around Maher in all parts of its operations. Being respectful change agents in families and villages means *first* we listen and learn, *then* we assist. Maher staff act as resources and guides, rather than as bearers of "the one way." Maher has no formulas to fix a family or a village. Needs are addressed as they are identified in the course of listening and talking.

In family life

Maher will intervene at the woman's request to reunite a family where this can be done, changing the fabric of family life for the better. Most women outside the larger cities would prefer to live in a family situation with children and husband (even if they are not "in love") if all can do so free from fear, despair, and violence. Maher makes no assumptions about who is to blame, or who is right and who is wrong. Generally the story is much more complex than that. Staff are trained to listen with nonjudgment and compassion. Each family is looked at in the wider context of their lives (including family makeup, where the home is, and backgrounds). Often this wider lens helps couples to see their difficulties with new eyes, and so new choices and options emerge. Blockages loosen, hope begins to bloom. Then actions and agreements can begin. As you read in the chapter on women, actions can range from job placements for the men to dowry renegotiations, from alcohol treatments to monthly food assistance. Agreements might include, for example, that all the man's earnings go into one shared bank account that requires both the woman and the man to cosign before withdrawals. The focus is on doing what is needed to stabilize the family, including monitoring and intervening as needed to help a new, better status quo emerge.

In village life

Maher has expanded operations and now also works to improve village life, bringing improved health, wellbeing, dignity, and opportunities for all. It does this through awareness meetings, classes on overcoming alcoholism, establishing local self-help groups, building wells and toilets, and much more. Through this work, families are stabilized and strengthened, and fewer women and children seek to flee to Maher.

The underlying "we see how it is" approach developed in working toward family reconciliations is behind Maher's needs-based way of working in the villages. Often an "expert" solution does not work because it does not fit the context in which it is applied. There are many reports the world over of aid projects where foreigners came in, applied an elegant solution they had "used successfully all over," and the villagers smiled for the cameras. And then when the foreigners left, it was back to business and life as usual. If a change agent expects people to do something differently, then all must work together on a foundation of mutual respect and trust. Solutions must be appropriate to the full context in which they are applied. Maher lives this truth. This is one reason Maher does not have failures in its work with villages: staff members and volunteers go slowly, pay attention, and build a relationship—and they stay. So when something does not work, everyone sits down together to see why and what to do next. Soon the villagers are asking Maher for the next step, rather than anything being imposed.

> ## CASE Signs of progress: the author's observation
>
> *We visited the small slum village of the Pardhi Wasti tribal people in Shirur district. These people are members of a caste that is the lowest of the low. Traditionally, they have no options for respectable work due to the rigidity of the caste system. The children receive no education and wear scant clothing, and all have very poor hygiene. The girls are generally prostitutes by age 14; it is nearly the only way their families can earn any money.*
>
> *We saw a small shed Maher had constructed as a kindergarten. They had begun with half a dozen children only a year before. Now there were about 20 children, all in relatively clean clothing (washed by the teacher at night). When we arrived we were taking photos. I had taken one of a young mother and her son. Later, as we were leaving, she came up to me and signed to me to take her photo again. Sister Lucy pointed out to me that while we were looking at the school, the woman had gone to the well (which Maher had installed). She had washed her own and her boy's hands and faces and tidied his clothing. It was with a shy pride that she asked me to take a better photo, in which she and her boy were clean and neat. Clearly the message about hygiene was getting to the village! (See photos on facing page.)*

If a village seeks out Maher's help, for example to build a well, then Maher will do so. Then, of course, the villagers need to learn ways to use the new clean water source to improve hygiene, but they have no experience with this. Maher can talk to them in awareness programs, but this has limited impact. Meanwhile the village is coming to know and trust Maher, so after a while, they ask for a kindergarten. To further build trust, Maher will seek a local teacher rather than sending a Maher staff person. Then Maher supports that teacher with materials and whatever he or she needs to be successful. The children are enticed to come to school with the offer of milk and a full meal, which Maher delivers each day. One rule is that the children must be washed and in clean clothes to come to school and have the meal. The teacher helps the children and their families learn how to wash. Often these teachers not only have the children during the day, but they then take home the dishes and even sometimes the children's clothing to wash overnight. Maher provides

Maher Kindergarten in Pardhi Wasti

Mother and her boy in Pardhi Wasti

dishes and donated clothing as well. Slowly the village learns to trust Maher and new behaviors begin. Villagers come to see that they and their children are able to have a better life. Throughout, Maher staff are loving, nonjudgmental, and trustworthy.

5. Small Home-Like Living Centers as Part of a Larger Community

Heart-centered operations

This practice is unique to Maher and arose organically from Sister Lucy's background. Guided by her personal experience as one of nine children in a secure, loving family, Sister Lucy began the first home of Maher to become "mother's home" to those in need. Soon she had nearly 70 women and children living together, and this was too much.

Sister Lucy had seen other institutions where children are "warehoused" and merely surviving and operations are strictly rules-based, with no room for individual needs. When it was time to add on to Maher, she built several smaller homes all in one larger complex to maintain the feel of a family home where each child is guided by mother and loved simply for being alive. (Photo in Chapter One.) And each housemother comes to love each child as her own. Each child's needs are attended to personally and specifically. At Maher, a child suffering cannot hide; instead staff take time to build a trusting relationship and to draw out each child. The relationships created between staff and residents, and also between residents, nurture and sustain everyone. This level of attention is not possible in large institutional homes based on efficiency and authoritarian relationships. Maher could not have the impact it has if the staff were each responsible for many more children. Even as Maher has expanded into Pune city and into nearby villages, the homes are all designed for 20 to 30 children at most, and all are actively part of the larger Maher family. This author observed that even at remote sites, Sister Lucy and her director knew each child's name, family situation, and current issues—even though at this time Maher had more than 600 children and nearly 200 women in residence. The women too live with the children, in the various homes. Their stories, families, and hopes and fears are all held by the staff.

> **TIP** Sister Lucy reminds staff again and again that loving the women and children is of major importance. She tells them she prays a lot for these women and children, prays that they will learn, that they will do well. She holds them all dear in her heart. Surely the children feel this love and her prayers: the children flock to her and she is surrounded by groups of them wherever she goes.

Heart-centered family life

The children too look out for each other as in a real family. For example, two boys from the streets, both about 10 years old, were acting out and skipping school. They had been given several chances to learn and change, but nothing seemed to be working. Sister Lucy was at a loss and upset. She decided to fast until there was a resolution. As in any family, every one knew what was going on. The rest of the children became worried about Sister Lucy. Some of the older boys realized they were the big brothers and these boys needed help. So they talked to the two boys, obtained promises and made plans, and then all went to Sister Lucy early the next morning. The older boys decided that a weekly meeting with all the boys in this vulnerable preteen group would be beneficial, to talk about how things were going and find out if they needed help with any problems at home or school. The younger boys settled down, having "older brothers" to look up to and lean on. The older boys had mostly grown up at Maher, so they understood the values not as rules but as guidelines for how to live a good life and do right. So they were well qualified to mentor the younger boys. This is just how children learn right and wrong in any family, from parents and older siblings! Six months later, these two boys had settled in and were attending school with no further problems.

Heart-centered discipline

Small family-style homes also provide the ideal environment for Maher's unique heart-centered approach to discipline. Large institutions, by contrast, rely on strict obedience with punishments to reinforce rules. Sister

Lucy says, "My heart connects to each child. I feel them as my blood, and so they want to obey me." The children feel her boundless love; they have radar for this, and know when it is not genuine. She says she sees herself more as a parent than as an administrator.

As a parent, Sister Lucy seeks a balance between structure and rules and letting the rules go for a special day or time. As a parent, she teaches about trust, and fosters trust between herself and the children. And just as in a family, as children grow and demonstrate trustworthiness, they are given more privileges, more responsibility, and more opportunities to demonstrate their trustworthiness. Children must have room to make mistakes and to learn

TIP One of the social workers suggests that when you feel irritated with a child—you have told her the same thing ten times—tell her again and with a smiling face. Do not get angry. Keep loving her. She will finally trust you and open up and tell you what is going on. Children need to experience adults who are patient and loving.

from their mistakes. "No one is perfect, not even me!" says Sister Lucy. "We can always correct ourselves."

CASE Punish or guide?

Some of the social workers were letting some older boys borrow Maher's motorbikes to get to a job or to university. The children were allowed the petrol for these trips. One boy gave in to peer pressure from other non-Maher children in the village and began stealing some of the petrol to sell. Maher staff caught the boy doing this. Some of the staff reacted by deciding he could never use the bike again. Others felt that none of the teens should be allowed to use the bikes again.

When she learned of this, Sister Lucy had to first coach the staff: "How would a good parent handle this? How do we teach these children who are our family? We should ask this boy, with love, 'Why did you do this?' We ask what he knows of right and wrong. We must give him a chance to learn and correct his ways." She advised them to curtail some privileges temporarily, allowing the boy time to demonstrate having learned. After this coaching, the staff worked with the boy in question, and with the boys as a group, to set clear expectations in the case of the privilege of using the motorbikes.

Discipline at Maher is guided by love and respect. Children who are loved generally will behave well and do the right thing if they know how. And, of course, they are still young and will learn through making mistakes, as is human. And often at Maher, what is right is not the same thing they used to do before Maher. They have a lot to learn and can get easily pulled astray by habits, peers, or desires. Sister Lucy wants them to learn not just strict obedience but *why* something is the right choice, so that they have guidelines for their future lives. This requires lots of patience, repeated expectations for behavior, explanations, and endless love and understanding. Sister Lucy must often mentor the staff first, so that they may guide the children. This is not how social workers are trained, and perhaps not even how most of the staff were raised themselves.

6. Addressing the Roots of Violence and Despair

All of Maher's work keeps in mind the ultimate vision of creating a world where there is no longer work or a need for NGOs or institutions like Maher. Achieving this vision requires addressing the roots of the violence and despair that Maher staff see daily. This requires a different view.

Learning to see systemically

One significant difference in the way Maher works is what can be called "seeing systemically." While Sister Lucy would not name it so, this perspective has developed organically from the Maher vision and its core values, especially the practices of "seeing how it is" and viewing others with compassion and within their larger contexts.

Cultural anthropologist and author Mary Catherine Bateson describes this new way of healing:

> *The point is that we need to see the connections between the parts of a system before we tinker too rashly and learn to see the analogies between systems of different kinds. In other words, we have to look for pattern, to look for connection, integration, and threats to integration and to the system. What's going wrong? Where is the pathology? It's not in the individuals: it's not the father, [or the mother] . . . it is a characteristic of the system. . . . [R]ather than only looking separately at individuals, how can we become, in some sense, [healers] of the society in which we live?*[23]

Families (including extended families) are systems; villages are systems; a culture is a system. If Maher were to see only individuals, it could only help individuals. Instead, as you have seen, Maher helps families and villages, and is influencing future culture. Below are a couple of examples of the effect of seeing systemically.

---

[23] Mary Catherine Bateson, "It's the System!" *The Center Post* Spring/Summer (2013): 5.

At the individual level of system

When an individual's behavior, wellbeing or lack of, and issues are seen out of context of his or her system (such as the family or the village), then options are necessarily limited. The accompanying case is a wonderful example of how children carry their parents' stories within them.

At the family level of system

Earlier you read about working with families by looking at the bigger context in which the family problems occur. "We see how it is" leads directly to a growing understanding of the range of issues in daily Indian life that contribute to the violence and despair. Maher recognizes and addresses the larger patterns in the lives of these families. Without this systems perspective, behaviors and individuals get identified as "the problem." From that narrow perspective, there are few options for healing. One of the reasons so many reconciliations are possible is that Maher does not focus on blame, and the families feel the difference and are open to change and the healing process.

At the village and cultural levels of system

Maher has identified a number of cultural patterns that are causal to the

---

CASE The problem does not come from within the individual

A 13-year-old boy was having a hard time adjusting to a new Maher home and school. He and his mother had just moved from Ratnagiri back to Pune. He was having seizures and daydreaming in school. Neither his teachers nor the housemothers knew what to do. Maher took him for a full medical evaluation and found no reason for the seizures. So Sister Lucy considered his history: His mother had fallen in love and gotten pregnant, but the man did not want her. Even after she and her baby came to Maher, his mother was unable to let go of the man in her heart; she always told her son that someday his father would come back for them. So Sister Lucy talked to him. She told him that he did not need to feel guilty or ashamed that his father had left. "It was before you were born and has nothing to do with you," she pointed out. She suggested he could tell the other children his father was dead or just gone. After several discussions with Sister Lucy, the seizures stopped and the boy was again doing well in school. Sister Lucy also advised his mother (a social worker now at Maher) that she should go for counseling. She must not feel guilty anymore; she must let go of this man in her heart, both for herself and the boy.

violence and despair. These patterns include the rigid caste system, which reinforces poverty and lack of opportunities, and also a pervasive lack of education for the poor. Another of these patterns is the deeply entrenched gender inequity; it is one of the root causes of violence and despair that Maher consistently addresses. Maher teaches the children, women, and staff to respect both genders equally. Boys are not revered or valued more highly at Maher, nor offered any more opportunities than are girls. They have the same choices in dance, computer training, school and university, leadership responsibilities, travel, and so on. For example, Maher was offered two scholarships to the MBA (master's in business administration) program at Pune University for qualified university graduates. Sister Lucy encouraged several boys and girls to apply and asked that one boy and one girl be selected from among those qualified.

The housemothers and other staff have to be taught gender equity too, as valuing boy children is deeply embedded in Indian culture. This view is too bold for some of the staff and they argue with Sister Lucy. She listens. They too need to learn, and some may need to leave if they cannot manage this. Sister Lucy's goal is bigger than just helping children survive until they are 18.

Sister Lucy's vision is an integrated world where men and women are equals and partners. Maher children have freedoms and ways of being with each other that generally their peers do not have. So they sometimes feel out of place in school and elsewhere. Says Sister Lucy: "But if we conform, nothing will change. Yes, it is confusing to them and for the staff too, who are also used to separating boys and girls. But if we separate them, the sexual energy is taboo and stronger. Let them be together, and watch closely, but let them learn, do sex education, talk about

CASE Learning to love more widely is at the root

One of the senior staff (herself a Maher rescue whose father and brothers were alcoholics) suggested that the teen boys from Rising Star home, next door to Vadhu Badruk, should no longer be allowed to come to Vadhu Badruk gatherings, to keep them separate from the girls. Sister Lucy told her to look into her heart: Did she not love her six brothers? They made mistakes. Why not love these boys? "Seeing the negative will cost you in your life—you will shrivel," advised Sister Lucy. "You must keep seeing from the heart, from love, or people will avoid you and you will be alone." Slowly, slowly this housemother is learning. Sister Lucy tells her that to not love jeopardizes Maher.

consequences of choices. They will soon be in the world and need to deal with all of this "out there," so let them deal with it here where we can guide them."

This is why the boys and girls learn tae kwon do together. This is why the teenage boys and girls together are masters of ceremony at the programs, from Christmas Day to International Children's Day. This is why they choreograph and study dance together.

Maher is creating India's leaders of tomorrow—both men and women!

Staff need to change too

If India is truly to become that place in the vision, where everyone can walk together toward wholeness, then not only the clients need to learn and change and adopt these values, so do the staff. Sister Lucy patiently and lovingly guides the staff to question their reactions and choices. For example, one of the male social workers still struggles with gender equity. He supports Maher's

girls, yet does not allow his wife to work (she is educated and wishes to). Slowly Sister Lucy works with him; she knows that the children see his actions with his own family and do not understand the inconsistencies. These are challenging messages, but also transformative.

Breadth of programs

While starting with a focus on women and children, Maher has developed organically to address a broad array of interrelated social problems. Every one of Maher's now 24 programs was designed to address one or more of these roots and patterns and to respectfully challenge and bring change to some of the traditional norms that lead to violence and despair. Theories did not drive Maher's expansion: experience did. Maher brought this perspective into the villages as well, with both respect and nonjudgment, and the solutions tried came from experience and listening in the villages. The resulting programs aimed to improve life in villages and in individual families so

---

CASE Bending the rules

Maher had plans to build a whole new building, to house the Production Center and extra classrooms. Normally it would have taken three years to get the permits from the town planning office without a bribe. So Sister Lucy got the approval and support of the village leaders, and went ahead and built the building. Eventually, she says, she will probably have to pay a fine for building without a permit, but this is preferable to waiting three years or paying a bribe.

that more families may remain together without needing to come to Maher.

A complete list of these 24 projects with a brief definition of each is included in an appendix to this book.

7. Anticorruption

Maher has done all of its work, since day one, without surrendering to the corruption that is so prevalent in Indian society, thereby demonstrating both the value of a fair practice and the courage needed to undermine this leech on Indian growth and sustainability. India, like many other developing countries, has a long history of paying bribes and of corruption at all levels. This is ingrained at every layer of doing business, hurting the poorest people the most. Sister Lucy has a practice of "zero bribes, ever." Period. Building permits have been delayed, sometimes for years, as corrupt officials attempt to extract their cut. Many have advised Sister Lucy at various times to give in and pay. There is a story about one building permit that had been stalled for nearly two years. Sister Lucy again went to the office and asked for her permit. They said, "Sister, just pay a fee and we can hurry it along." She held her ground that there were no "fees" due. She graciously invited them to come to Maher to visit. When they arrived, evidently expecting that now she would surely pay, she showed them around, and then said, "To pay your 'fee,' I need to send three women, with their children, back onto the streets. You choose which three." They fled, and she had her permit in two days.

The value of truth and fairness is taught to young children as they learn good sportsmanship. Both children and staff need to learn to "play fair"—for example, all use the same equipment in games,

---

CASE Winning fairly feels much better!

Maher was invited to bring a team to a sporting event to compete against other 14- and 15-year-olds from several different NGOs. The social worker in charge of the Maher group wanted to bring a couple of 16-year-olds who were good players and were small enough to pass for 15. Sister Lucy said no. The social worker took the two older boys anyway, who upon arrival refused to play because they knew it was wrong. What courage for two 16-year-old boys to stand up to an adult for what they knew was right! Maher still won more medals than any other NGO, and without cheating. When they came home, the two boys told Sister Lucy. She severely reprimanded the social worker, placing a note in his file. If something like this happens again, he will be fired.

and breaking the rules is taboo even if no one will catch you. These values are taught in all games at Maher, whether they are played competitively or just for fun. Then the values become habits when the children go outside Maher, even when the outcomes are perhaps more prestigious or the stakes higher. The children feel the pride of knowing they won fair and square.

TIP When a question about following rules arises, this is the perfect time for the staff to have a discussion of the core value of transparency, what this means, and its purpose as a guide for the children and the NGO. A discussion about why it was important that Maher not cheat, even though the other NGOs might do so, might have influenced the social worker to make a better choice in the example above. In this case, a similar discussion was held in the aftermath. This is how the staff learns the values in action.

Leadership

> *"A leader is someone with the power to project either shadow or light onto some part of the world and onto the lives of the people who dwell there."*
> —*Parker J. Palmer*[24]

Leadership, as demonstrated by Sister Lucy, is also part of the art and genius of Maher. You have read many examples of Sister Lucy in action, but now we will look specifically at her leadership, inspiring you to think about your own role. If you do not think about yourself as a leader, you need to. However, as there are literally thousands of books and courses on leadership available, the intent here is simply to highlight a few special considerations, especially relative to replicating the success of Maher.

What Is Leadership?

There are many definitions of leadership, and one common denominator is the ability to *socially influence others* and to *adapt environments*, in order that *desired results are achieved, through others*. Leadership of an organization is distinct from simply doing the work. Everyone will develop his or her own unique style of leadership; the more attuned that leadership is to the desired results, the better the leader.

---

[24] Parker J. Palmer, *Let Your Life Speak: Listening for the Voice of Vocation* (San Francisco: Jossey Bass, 1999), 78.

Further, in a values-based NGO, management and leadership set the examples for staff and residents, as well as those in the communities they serve. They live the values they preach. Staff and other adults are also reminded that they too must continually set good examples for the children and new residents.

What Does Values-Based Leadership Look Like in Action?

Above all, leaders like Sister Lucy are a living embodiment of the vision, mission, and values of the NGO. To Sister Lucy, these core values are not a list, they are *her*. The list did not exist in written form until this author began to collect them, through observations of Maher and Sister Lucy. Even so, they were easy to observe because of the incredible consistency of application. Every day, in every way, whether in welcoming a new client or a new project being launched or an annual financial report being written, the core values are the guides, with the vision as the goal, and the mission defining the activities.

This does not mean a leader must be perfect. Indeed, one of Maher's values is lifelong learning, and Sister Lucy has had a steep learning curve at Maher. She will be the first to say she has made mistakes and, more importantly, learned from those mistakes. Values are the guiderails: they support the numerous course corrections as you learn to crawl, walk, and then to run, as a leader. Similarly, staff have their own learning

curves, and Sister Lucy is constantly coaching them, challenging them to *become* the values. When a staff person refuses to go along with the values and acts contrary to them, he or she will be reprimanded and may even be fired.

Qualities and behaviors

A few leadership qualities and behaviors have been selected that are most relevant in the context of running an NGO like Maher. Examples of many of these have been shared throughout this volume. Below, they are divided into three groups: those that must underlie all you do throughout the life of the NGO; those especially critical in the first stages of the NGO; and those you will need to develop as the NGO matures and becomes more complex. That said, any of these may be required from day one!

Overarching leadership qualities and behaviors

- Begin with a deep heartfelt and soul-felt call; anything less will make it difficult to sustain the work.

- Have courage. Be willing to stand alone for what you believe and know is right.

- Define and keep the vision, mission, and values *always* before you, so that you are always aware of the effect of moment-to-moment choices on long-term success; always "see where you are going."

- Have a strong inner life, whether through prayer, contemplation, or meditation, that connects you to the larger reality. This will be a well you return to over and over.

- Maintain unflinching optimism:

  o There will be many obstacles, and you must be able to come up with an alternate plan and keep moving.

  o You will help many, but not all who need it; pay attention to what you *can* do instead of the staggering need.

- Keep a sense of humor. "If you take every things so seriously, you will be miserable and make others miserable," advises Sister Lucy.

- Have passion, but tempered by love and acceptance.

TIP Sister Lucy says that her deep faith in God guides all her actions, including "doing what is right and needed, without counting the rupees." She explains that "at the convent and at home, I learned to worship Jesus; working at Maher I learned to walk in his footprints, to live his example, and to be Jesus to people."

Leadership qualities and behaviors particularly useful in start-up and early years

- Dare to dream, yet have the clear-eyed ability to assess what is. "Hard-headed reality must ground dreaming,"[25] according to Margaret Benefiel. Focus on what you can do *now*.

- Favor heart-centered action and compassion over rules, yet within the guiderails of the core values.

- Practice "tough love"—sometimes acting stern or even angry to communicate the seriousness of a situation; also making tough decisions when these are for the woman's, child's, or NGO's best future, even in the face of arguments to do otherwise.

- Model and teach behaviors and core values 24/7.

- Routinize and delegate work as you are able.

- Build and maintain good community and stakeholder relations; be a "diplomat" for the NGO. Maher has established such vital relationships with local businesses (Weikfield, John Deere, the Rotary Club); local authorities and governing units (the CWC, village leaders); and friends around the world.

[25] Margaret Benefiel, *The Soul of a Leader* (NY: The Crossworld Publishing Company, 2008), 53.

Leadership qualities and behaviors requiring focus as NGO matures

- Think strategically and plan for the long-term strength and growth of the NGO, developing and directing the big picture.

- Make the tough choices. The needs will always be greater than your resources; stay focused on your mission. (If you overextend, the NGO could fail and then the mission fails too.)

- Manage and oversee operations, leaving staff to cover more daily tasks.

- Develop others into supervisors, managers, and leaders. (See definitions in accompanying box.)

- Do what needs to be done without seeking personal fame.

- Develop "management intuition:" know when to change and what to change.

- Welcome differing viewpoints.

TIP As Margaret Benefiel advises in *The Soul of a Leader*, speak what is true, from your heart. Seek resonance in key early stakeholders (watch for people's eyes to light up as you speak), and invite them to join you as partners (whether as trustees, volunteers, staff, or major donors). As you dare to dream together, your collective inner hope and outer partnerships will complement one another.

Sister Lucy: heart-centered

DEFINITIONS

In India (and elsewhere), titles are given sometimes as honorifics, without clear descriptions of new and higher expectations. For example, someone who is loyal or of long-standing service to the NGO may be given a new title as a reward. But if such people continue to do as they have always done, then there will be no one in the organization carrying on the critical higher-level functions. As the NGO grows, chaos can result from too few people with the higher-level perspective to guide the organization properly.

Supervisor A supervisor is one who is personally proficient in the tasks of the people he or she supervises. This person very likely has been promoted from among other workers because of exceptional ability in all parts of the job. Supervisors oversee and help to assure work quality according to NGO guidelines. They help train others and assist with, or even handle themselves, the more complicated cases and issues that arise.

Manager A manager often oversees a wider section of the NGO, including more than one function. One manager might oversee the daily running of a large site (such as office functions, supply procurement, and maintenance). Another manager at that site might oversee all the client work. Both may contribute to planning, and both will have areas of recordkeeping for which they are responsible.

Director A director oversees all of these people (managers, supervisors, staff) as well as all operations. This person does planning, allocates resources, and creates and analyzes reports (both quantitative and qualitative) for stakeholders, among other responsibilities. Where there are multiple sites, an executive director may oversee the entire operation.

The image below helps show how the perspective and work focus gradually change in the progression to higher-level roles:

The image below helps show how the perspective and work focus gradually change in the progression to higher-level roles:

Tactical worker supervisor manager director executive director **Strategic**

Task focus	Strategy focus
Today and now focus	Future focus
Single part of NGO focus	Entire NGO and stakeholder focus
Current issue	Vision, mission, values

A metaphor of perspective: Imagine you are standing on one of the lower levels of a building. You can look out the window and see a group of workers on the ground below doing various tasks. From this slightly higher perspective, you can observe them all, assess what they are doing, and give direction or tips to improve performance. That is a supervisor. Now imagine you are several floors higher in that building and there are windows all around. From here you can see both the workers and the supervisors below. This gives you more perspective than either those on the ground or those on the floor below you. That is a manager. Next imagine you are on the roof of this building, and can see all sides, all layers, even the surrounding areas and what is coming down the road. You will have information none of the others can see, both about what is inside and what is outside. This is a director. Finally, imagine that you are in a small plane and can fly over this tall building as well as several others that are all part of the organization. You, the executive director or leader, can see multiple sites at once. And while it is harder to see the workers on the ground, you get regular reports from the managers and directors. And, of course, sometimes you all gather for shared events, to tell stories, and to celebrate.

Developing as a Leader

As the NGO grows, the founder must grow with it. At the beginning, you will be a worker, a supervisor, and an executive director all at once.

- You will be doing all the day-to-day tasks while figuring out how best to do them, learning as you go (mostly tactical).

- If you have help, you will be delegating specific tasks to others, but you will be overseeing the work.

- You will also be reporting to trustees and stakeholders on current operations and planning for future needs and operations (mostly strategic).

As time passes, it will be critical to create routines for the more repetitive tasks that must be done day after day (such as admissions, cooking, cleaning, and recordkeeping). Slowly, as staff is added, others can take over not only specific tasks but whole areas of responsibility.

This is when the role of the founder becomes focused more on leading and managing and less on doing. Recall that part of the definition of leadership is accomplishing *through* others. A useful metaphor for this stage is perhaps "manager as conductor." [26] The conductor manager focuses on setting the goals and priorities, and on ensuring that staff are supported and have the

---

[26] David Bradford and Allen Cohen, *Managing for Excellence* (NY: John Wiley and Sons Inc., 1984).

resources they need, but makes no pretense of being the lead doer.

The only way to accomplish this is to develop other staff to carry out the daily work without your direct supervision. Two specific leadership skills are needed: delegating and developing others. Work must still be done correctly and in alignment with values.

> **TIP** Sister Lucy advises: "Listen to the staff! Hear what their troubles are, their frustrations and wants. Sometimes they just need to be listened to. You don't have to do everything they ask."

Learning to delegate

Delegate instead of do: it is a choice. Supervisory and managerial staff *must* learn to delegate. Once a staff member, a helping resident, or a volunteer has worked with you and demonstrated some of the skills required to do a task, then you can delegate it. The newer or less skilled the person is, the smaller the part of the work you can delegate at one time.

For example, ask someone to wash the clothes, and to come get you when it is done. Then you can see how she has done, and if it is satisfactory. If there is,

for example, a stubborn stain, ask what she has tried so far to remove it, and demonstrate perhaps a special method for this case. Then ask her to hang the clothes up to dry. Instruct her to keep an eye on the clothes, rehang any that fall, and collect them and bring them all to you once they are dry. Next you ask her to fold the clothing, sorting out any that need repairing or pressing. Again check to see she has done this correctly, teaching as needed when there are mistakes. Next ask her to press the clothing that needs pressing. And so on. Once she has completed all these parts, then next time you can ask her to do the washing, knowing that all of these steps will be done correctly. Tell her to come ask if she has any questions. This was a very simple example, but the process applies to almost any task. Breaking it down into parts helps assure success the first time around. Give plenty of positive feedback, especially noticing and stating to the person exactly what she did well at each stage.

If you see that something was not done correctly or not finished, do *not* do it yourself; find out whose job it was and see if the person needs a reminder, or perhaps needs help with a problem. Stay focused on the bigger picture and do not get caught up washing the clothes yourself. Otherwise you will be unable to handle the more strategic responsibilities—and no one else can do them.

Sometimes, too, as people take on responsibility for tasks, over time they may come to do them their own way, perhaps organized differently. You must learn to let it go; see this as a sign that others are "owning" the work. "Let them have it their way," says Sister Lucy. Pay attention, instead, to the results.

When you are delegating tasks, it is important that people understand not only why they are doing the steps required, but how each task fits into the NGO mission and how its performance reflects the NGO values. In the course of teaching someone about washing clothes, for example, you will refer to health and hygiene (mission-related). And she must do all the clothes washing even if some belong to a person of lower caste (values-related).

Developing others

Ultimately, delegation is only one tool used to develop others. Developing someone means supporting him through a learning path that helps him to become more than what he was, that helps him expand his capacities. Training generally only teaches a specific skill; development expands perspective. You will need to develop people to take on the supervisory and managerial functions to allow you more time to do the increasingly complex strategic work of the NGO. And they must be able to direct the daily work in perfect accord with vision, mission, and core values. You will need to hold frequent conversations with staff and residents about core values and why they are important all of the time, not only when convenient.

CASE Letting things go

"You need to learn to let some things go," advises Sister Lucy. "You will always see things to be done, or done differently, many more than you can do in a day. So do what you can and let the rest go."

One day this author observed Sister Lucy doing just this. We were visiting a remote site, and we saw some donated bunches of fresh mehti (fenugreek greens for cooking) on the kitchen floor. Sister Lucy told the housemother, "If you leave these like this, they will spoil." She suggested that the housemother could gather some children to clean and put it away. Later she saw it was still not done. Again she reminded the housemother. "It's a choice," she said, "remind the housemother or do it yourself." The housemother did do it later, and we all enjoyed the mehti as part of the evening meal!

CASE Growing by doing

Says Poonam, once a resident and now a housemother: "Doing outreach work helped me to grow the confidence to speak to men, to anyone. When I first came, it was hard to speak to men, but I learned and now I can speak to people one on one, in groups—it is all okay. I am confident now. I can go anywhere and succeed! And when I am happy, my children can be happy!"

Development follows training, that is, after someone is performing the basic tasks of an assigned role well. For example, to train a new social worker, you can fairly easily review the workflow for working with women as described in Chapter 8. You can show her a list of NGO values, and even point out some of the places in the process where expectations may be different than what she learned in school. She can easily learn to complete the paperwork. But it takes more than that to learn how to make a quick empathetic connection with someone who is afraid, traumatized, or wary of trusting, for example. It takes experience to hear "between the lines" what is not being said. This ability can be developed in people through coaching, through helping them pay attention to people in new ways, through letting them make mistakes and then helping them learn from those mistakes. Then, when someone is proficient in these nuances of the job, she may be ready to be developed and promoted to higher roles with more responsibility.

Keep your eyes open for staffers who show promise of developing beyond their current roles. Signs to look for:

- They see a bigger picture than what is right in front of them, seeing "in context" and using that broader view to develop creative options.

- They volunteer to take on special projects, and are able to organize these (what has to happen first or second, who needs to be involved, what must be coordinated) without relying on you to answer every question or direct the project.

- When a new situation arises, they can creatively, and within the bounds of NGO policies and values, come up with alternatives to address the situation.

- When they take an action, they can see four or five steps ahead to what the consequences of that action are, and use this to make good decisions.

- They seek out opportunities to learn and apply something new, such as computer skills, managing finances, or a creating a nonviolence program.

- They are able to develop others; for example, when training new staffers, they actually help them learn rather than merely directing or doing tasks for them.

- They are able to question the way things are done and speak up when they disagree.

- They are generally calm, flexible, and adaptable in different situations and in different assignments.

- They have a personal vision and mission that aligns with the NGO.

Looking to the future

Sister Lucy is looking to the future: she is seeking to develop a core group of people she can fall back on, to carry on Maher if something happens to her. Even if Maher must be divided into projects and regions, becoming a collection of separate NGOs, at least the core vision and values will survive.

Toward this goal, Sister Lucy has created a mixed group of 30 staff members and university children who were raised at Maher; they are engaged in a year-long process of self-reflection, examining their personal vision, mission, and values, and seeing how those mesh with Maher's. The older children who were raised at Maher are often more closely aligned to Maher values. After this core group does its work, then they will help bring along other staff. This process is led and financed by a local Indian company as part of its corporate social responsibility program. (The

CASE Developing a manager

On Maher Day—the organization's anniversary—more than 1,000 Maher residents, alumni, and guests were coming together for an awards program, several dance performances, and a full meal. Mala, a new manager of the Vatsalydham site where this event would take place, was overseeing all preparations. Sister Lucy called her on the phone while she and this author were driving to a meeting. As she explained to me: "It's a lot. Mala is capable, but I am checking in just to let her know she is not alone. I can answer questions, if needed. And I want to remind her she is appreciated!" The event was completed smoothly.

Indian government is now requiring all companies over a certain size to spend a small percent of their profits on such projects.)

Conclusion

It is sometimes a delicate balance that must be achieved between the science and the art of founding and running an NGO. For Sister Lucy, this has meant maintaining an equilibrium between "professionalizing" Maher and letting heart-centered action influence Maher's development. Outsiders come in and say she should professionalize, but they often miss the point of the great love that underlies all that Maher people do. Sister Lucy always seems to have a clear open line to both her heart and her head; any decision passes through both filters. Rules can be bent if that is what makes sense for the mission, but she never compromises on core values.

This chapter is meant to "lift the veil of secrecy," to reveal the sources of Maher's magic and demystify that magic so it can be replicated. Sister Lucy has always had a clear vision and mission front and center, plus clear values in her heart. And, critically, she has unflinchingly kept those values and vision front and center for staff, trustees, and residents. Sister Lucy leads from the heart with these values; it is not a calculated strategy that can be temporarily abandoned if they prove inconvenient. Indeed, abandoning the values would never occur to her.

It would be easy for the founder of an NGO (anywhere, not just India) to become overwhelmed by the volume of paperwork, the politics and corruption in the government, the frustrations of the court systems, and the sheer magnitude of the needs. In fact, one could become driven by these external factors. Instead, Sister Lucy's gift to Maher and to the rest of us is that she faithfully acts from her heart, pursuing her vision for the people of India. She is like water flowing relentlessly downstream to its goal: when rocks and blockages show up, she flows over and around them without getting smashed, and continues on. She never loses focus, she never loses faith and hope, and she never compromises her values.

Sister Lucy, author, and children

11 | *Where to Go From Here?*

God calls whom God calls, it seems, and the preparation comes afterwards when we actually do the task!

—Richard Rohr

Am I Ready??

Are you thinking: Am I ready to start and run a Maher-inspired NGO? Who am I to do this? The needs are so immense! Can I *not* do this?

Sister Lucy recalls feeling compelled to do more than she was doing, but afraid of going it alone, with no community, no one who even understood what she felt called to do. Her fellow nuns all told her she would fail. But Father D'Sa told her to go ahead and try it. "What is the worst that can happen?" he asked. "You might fail—but so what! You will be okay." If Sister Lucy had listened to her peers instead of to her heart, Maher might never have been born.

This attitude of humility in the face of such a large task is normal. A Native American friend of mine told me a story about grappling with just such feelings (note that Native Americans hold not only humans but all creatures as sacred and part of God):

I sat in my morning meditation, just before dawn, asking God if I could really do the work being asked of me. As I finished my meditation and prayers, I stood up and looked out my window over a broad plain. Just then a large bull moose (an impressive and very large four-legged wild animal with a huge rack of horns) stood up directly in front of me—he had been sleeping right outside my window, very unusual! We looked at each other, and then he slowly began to walk away. Then he stopped, turned, and looked back at me again. He did this several times, the last time as he was running up the mountain in the distance—looking back at me, as if to see if I really got the message. I did: 'Stay in your own skin. You have the capacity to do whatever is asked of you if you stay in your own skin.'

So as you respond to this calling, you may study and learn from Maher and Sister Lucy—but ultimately you must do it your way, from inside your own skin, one step at a time.

Other traditions say similar things:

Dr. Morsi Mansour found support as a leader from his Muslim faith:

> *"If you have faith in God, if your spirit is full of faith, then you will find hope everywhere. You will not give up. It will take patience. There will be obstacles. But you will be like the river, going around the rocks."[27]*

Do not be discouraged! Sister Lucy demonstrates that formal education is not mandatory—one can learn anything when one is motivated and willing to try things and fail, then learn and try something else.

---

[27] Margaret Benefiel, *The Soul of a Leader* (NY: The Crossworld Publishing Company, 2008), 56.

Deeply Rewarding Work

Challenges notwithstanding, Sister Lucy, in addition to being the hardest working person this author has ever known, is also the most joyful. In spite of all she gives to the residents, staff, and friends of Maher, she would say that they fill her heart with love and joy. Every day is a new possibility. Our souls call us to do work that serves humanity.

> *The Gita is a call to action. Its dialogue unfolds not in a quiet forest retreat but on a battlefield—the battlefield of life, of the human heart. We have no choice but to act, Krishna tells us. Even doing nothing is action. But we do have the choice of what to work for and how to work. We can work for ourselves or we can work for others. We can work in love and harmony or we can work in competition under pressure, goaded by petty motives like covetousness, envy, and pride. And the choice is ours. Living for others may not seem attractive, but it brings happiness, meaning, and freedom. Living for oneself promises to satisfy, but it only leads to increasing alienation and despair. So Krishna concludes, "I've shown you both paths, Arjuna. Now you choose what you think best."*
>
> *–Eknath Easwaren*

Developing Capacity

Start small, and develop your NGO's capacity—in yourself, in your staff, in your trustees, and in your stakeholders. Capacity is developed through doing the work, by learning from experience, including from mistakes.

You, your staff, and your trustees will need to become skilled with all the background work included in this book, including planning, fundraising, and financial management. You will need to develop a core of experienced housemothers and social workers, all with a depth of compassion, patience, and wisdom in working with clients. You will develop strong, mutually beneficial relationships in your community with residents, businesses, leaders, and other stakeholders. Slowly, as the NGO's operations streamline, housemothers and social workers will find they have extra time during the day while the children are at school, and can begin new projects, or expand the work of the NGO in some way. In this way, you will grow.

> **TIP** Sister Lucy shares this wisdom: "If I looked at all our 'crises' as problems, I would go mad. Instead I say these are challenges, and as we solve them, so we grow. Then it is okay."

Another part of developing capacity is avoiding "burnout," a phrase often used in the West to describe people who work tirelessly to help make things better for others. "Burning out" is when they are so exhausted, overwhelmed by the magnitude of the problems, and discouraged about making things right that they give up; they cannot do it anymore. And they quit, moving on to something else (or they blow up in anger or collapse in tears or ill health). It is hard when you know that for every one you help, there are dozens more that you do not even get a chance to help. Or sometimes you try to help someone and it is "too late:" either the person is in too much despair or fear and cannot accept the help you offer, or a family member kills her. Sadly, this happens the world around. This author asked Sister Lucy, "How do you keep going? How do you keep working all day every day, when still you see such suffering, you see children who go back to the street, women who return to abuse or prostitution and likely early death. Every day on the streets, in the news, you see and read of the huge need for so many women and children. How do you stay so energized and happy?"

Sister Lucy answered that she, as always, looks to God. "Look at the suffering in the world—do you think God wants it that way? Of course not!" she says. "But God too cannot make everyone safe and happy and loving and kind. Even for God, some go astray. So how could God expect me to do better?

God expects me to simply do my best, every day. That is enough. I feel such great love for all, and I do my best. And this is enough. I help whom I can help. I give them every chance I can. And then it is in God's hands."

Reflecting on this wisdom, the author notes that what Sister Lucy can do as her "best" has grown over the years. She works, she tries things; some work, some do not. So she tries something else. And she learns. Each year, her "best" is a little bit better. This is the way of things: as she learns, grows, and has more staff and resources, she can help more people. And there will always be those she cannot save. This too is the way of things. To despair about the one she lost or cannot help, means she is not available to help those she can.

Likely Growth Steps

Growth will ideally be organic: that is, reflecting both the skills and resources of your NGO and its stakeholders, and the needs of your area. While there are many possible next steps, the following five are most likely, based on Maher's experience. A full list of Maher's 24 projects is included in an appendix, with more information at www.replicatemaher.wix.com/tools.

- Village awareness sessions
- Self-help groups
- Production center

- Family assistance (food, clothing, etc.)
- Village development projects

Village Awareness Sessions

Maher offers a wide array of awareness programs in rural and tribal villages to help people improve the quality of life for themselves and their families. Sometimes a whole village may be invited, or sometimes a subset, such as women. Generally Maher staff lead discussion of a topic with the invited group. Often an outside expert is invited to speak as well. Information may be presented through street plays, lectures, camps, exhibitions, and other methods. Topics have ranged from health and hygiene to inter-caste unity, from the importance of educating girls to the evils of alcoholism, from legal awareness for women to occupational opportunities.

Self-Help Groups

The aim of self-help groups is to promote financial growth in villages through education, community investment, and loan programs. Maher staff recognized that village women often do not have sufficient resources to meet the needs of their families. It is common for poor rural people to be charged high-interest loans from banks, resulting in debt that is difficult to repay. Self-help groups encourage financial independence through education, savings, member loans, and affordable loan repayment. Additionally, Maher has found that family problems decrease as members become more self-sufficient.

Self-help groups may be a next step after developing relationships through a series of awareness meetings. Social workers (and sometimes housemothers) do the outreach, start-up (explaining the purpose, rules, and structure of a self-help group), and support for these groups. As village members sign on and participate, they not only save but also learn communication and conflict resolution skills, leadership and organizational skills, group decision-making skills, and more. Eventually these groups can take on broader purposes than just promoting financial growth.

**Self-help group meeting
with Sister Lucy**

Production Center

The women who come to Maher are destitute and facing overwhelming problems. They worry about their own futures, and about their children's education and futures, which in turn affects their minds and bodies. Handwork is a time-honored way to help quiet people's minds through activity, and teaches them marketable skills as

well. Teens also benefit from learning skills and developing a strong work ethic.

Maher began its production center with one full-time staff person who develops the product lines, teaches the women and teens, procures all the raw materials, and arranges for sales of the finished goods. As the center grew, more staff were added.

Items made at Maher and at other similar sites include cloth bags of differing sizes for purses, schoolbooks, and mobile phones; candles; greeting cards; and food products.

Family Assistance

As noted earlier, some families can be stabilized simply by providing some food or financial assistance to alleviate poverty. Then they can send their children to school, and the family can remain peaceably together. Keeping families united is always preferable if the family can be stabilized. Strengthening families is a core part of Maher's mission.

Maher social workers handle all the family assessments, arrange the needed assistance, and track the families' progress. Sometimes this arises in the course of working with women who flee to Maher, and sometimes families apply directly to Maher for assistance. Maher budgets for this assistance annually. For example, about 20 families can be supported in this way for a total of about

Rs. 500,000 per year (about US$ 7700), including basics such as wheat, rice, dal, and oil, as well as a social worker salary. Support might also take the form of clothing or repairing a roof.

Village Development

Maher may be in a village to work with a family where the wife ran away with her children seeking their safety. During the process of reconciliation, Maher works respectfully with family and even neighbors. In this way, staff members develop relationships, noticing other needs in the village to improve life for other women and children, but also for the village as a whole. For example, if the women have to go a long way for water, then Maher might offer to build a well. Or if there are very few jobs and little access to work, Maher might begin a self-help group for the women to pool resources to help each other solve problems. Even now with all their experience, Maher staff never go to a village or a family and start in with solutions; they listen, they observe, they "see how it is." What do the villagers think they need most? What do they think their challenges are? With what do they need help? What solutions have they tried, and what happened? What other solutions or actions are they thinking about? No assistance is offered by Maher in a "one size fits all" formula, without this learning and listening. Projects might be as varied as boring a well, establishing a kindergarten, installing a solar hot water tank, training villagers in a variety of knowledge and skills, or building toilets for the local school.

Final Advice from Sister Lucy and Others

- You must have vision—be clear about what you want to do and why.

- Do your homework first.

- Know the cultural and legal environment in which you will be working.

- Form the legal entity that allows you to operate, before you start anything else.

- Visit many projects (different Maher homes as well as non-Maher organizations); stay long enough to really "feel" and know the pluses and minuses of each.

- Network with similar organizations and like-minded people.

- Consider the requirements of your location—a city is vastly different from a town and from a village, and the homes will be different in each.

- Find good staff.

- Test the waters; be willing to start small, learn, and then grow.

- Have unflinching optimism:

- There will be many obstacles, and you need to be able to come up with an alternate plan and keep moving.

- You will help many, but not all who need it. Pay attention to what you *can* do instead of the staggering need.

- Hold deep faith—or you will worry to death.

- Remember, this is not work—it is a lifestyle!

Parable

A young woman is walking along the sea's edge after a large storm. Hundreds and hundreds of starfish have washed up on the beach and will die. She stops, picks one up, throws it back in the water; takes another step or two, picks up another and throws it back in the water, and so on. A man comes along and asks her why she is doing this. She can't possibly save all the starfish, he points out—it's a waste of time! She picks up another starfish. As she is throwing it back into the sea, she looks at it with a smile and says, "I made a difference to *this* one!"

"Never doubt that a small group of thoughtful, committed, citizens can change the world. Indeed, it is the only thing that ever has."
— *Margaret Mead*

Closing Prayer
May the light of your soul guide you[28]

May the light of your soul guide you.

May the light of your soul bless the work

You do with the secret love and warmth of your heart.

May you see in what you do the beauty of your own soul.

May the sacredness of your work bring healing, light and renewal to those

Who work with you and to those who see and receive your work.

May your work never weary you.

May it release within you wellsprings of refreshment, inspiration and excitement.

May you be present in what you do.

May the day never burden you.

May dawn find you awake and alert, approaching your new day with dreams,

Possibilities and promises.

May evening find you gracious and fulfilled.

May you go into the night blessed, sheltered and protected.

May your soul calm, console and renew you.

---

[28] John O'Donohue, *Anam Cara: A Book of Celtic Wisdom* (Retrieved 9-10-2013 from http://www.poetry-chaikhana.com/Poets/O/ODonohueJohn/Maylightof/index.html)

Acknowledgements

First and foremost I am grateful for Sister Lucy coming into my life and my heart. I am grateful to the delightful women, children, staff, and trustees of Maher who opened their doors and their hearts and shared themselves and their personal stories with me. And thank you to Will Keepin and Cynthia Brix for introducing me to Sister Lucy and encouraging me to take on this project (which scared the daylights out of me!)

Heartfelt thanks to those who spent hours with me, patiently explaining all the details of running Maher (and SOFKIN), sometimes having to explain, and then explain again: Sister Lucy, Father D'Sa, Chaya Pamula, Hira Begum Mulla, Athena Nair, Sidart Kurias, and so many more. To the housemothers and social workers who showed me Maher daily life, and to Hira and Athena who translated many a conversation for me as it was occurring, and to the office staff (Sabita, Stella, Jenny, Ancy and others) who patiently pulled up files, provided endless copies of records, details, and photos. To the Maher youth leaders—especially Mangesh, Gaus, Amol, and Nandu—who were ready to send me photos or files or whatever I needed whether I was at Maher or home in the US writing. Any inaccuracies in the details here are entirely the fault of this author.

I also want to thank some of the Friends of Maher from around the world who got involved in providing data, perspective, reviews of chapters, or photos from your experience of, and love for, Maher. Some of these folks are: Bernie Hill of UK, Jenny Draxlbauer of Austria, Lucia Kaposi-Krause of Germany, and, from the US: Barbara Whitmore, Mikaela Keepin, Penny Harris, Sue Inches, and Pam Jensen. Some of Jenny Draxlbauer's photos are in this book or on the website, as well as her short videos of Maher life. Also, thank you to friends Babette Welch for her help designing the spreadsheets, including instructions for their use, that are in full detail on the website; and Sarah Walsh for setting up the website, the Facebook page, and showing me how to use them.

Thank you too, to my soul sister Deborah Adele for her encouragement that I could indeed do justice to this project, and that in fact it was my work to do. And thank you for the suggestion of the closing prayer to this book when I asked! Thanks go as well to my mother for supporting several stages of the work, such as helping to sort out workflows and leadership ideas.

My ability to complete this project sits on a base rich with varied work, educational, and life experiences, and teachers, in India, the U.K, and the U.S. To name a few: Dr. Rita Weathersby, mentor from graduate school, who sat with me to discuss the leadership chapter; Edwin and Sonia Nevis, among the founders of the Gestalt Institute of Cleveland where I began to really be able to "see" individuals, couples, families, and groups; to Judith Hemming, who introduced me to Family Constellations and seeing and working systemically and nonjudgmentally; to Mataji who helped me to find myself, and to really see India; to Sister Lucy who helps me to see with my heart, and finally to the rock beneath it all—the lineage of beloved Swami Rama. I bow in gratitude to you all.

Appendix A

Maher's Rainbow of Services

Maher began with its focus on battered women and children (the first two projects below, and the focus of the current volume). As Maher grew and learned more about the root causes leading to women's and children's need for Maher, other projects were born. This process continues even now: in late 2013 Maher opened its first home for destitute old men. Additional information regarding all of these projects, including staff roles, budgets, and examples, will be gradually added to the book's website. These will be updated as new information becomes available.

MAMTADHAM: Home and programs for women in distress. These women live in the children's homes, perhaps as new arrivals with the older mostly college-aged girls, or later as housemothers in any one of the 24 or more children's homes. Maher provides shelter, health and safety needs, childcare, counseling, support for family reunification, and vocational training. Women gain self-esteem, confidence, and skills and purpose for a new life—at home, at Maher, or on their own.

KISHOREDHAM: Home for orphans and children from broken or deeply poor homes. These homes are in cities, villages, and tribal areas. Maher provides for their basic needs of nutritious food, clothing, shelter, and education, but also for their emotional and spiritual wellbeing, with programs in yoga, tae kwon do, music and dance, nonviolence, and more. The overarching goal is to help develop these children into leaders and part of creating the new India of Maher's vision.

VATSALYADHAM: Home for mentally disturbed women, most rescued from the streets. Maher provides basic needs plus psychiatric treatment, counseling, medications and other healing therapies. A large garden is on site and many find solace helping to raise flowers and vegetables. Some even become able to return to their families or even work. (Three children's homes share space in this building, and both the women and the children benefit from the shared living spaces.)

SUKH SANDHYA: Home for destitute aged women. Housed adjacent to the home for mentally disturbed women, the aged women participate in as many of the activities and programs as they are able. Additionally they often play a positive role as grandmothers for the Maher women and children living on-site.

AASHAI: Home for expectant unwed mothers. While at Maher these young women learn hygiene, nutrition, childcare, and nonviolent communication. After they deliver, they may choose to give the baby for adoption and return home, or to remain at Maher, even raising their child if they so choose. (This project is also housed at Vatsalyadham where there is medical care, "grandmothers" and activities to support these young mothers, often mere children themselves.)

USHALYA: Kindergartens in villages and remote areas. Through the kindergartens, children learn the hygiene and study habits needed to attend school. These also provide a way in to villages and slums to help Maher develop relationships with the women and children.

VIDYALAYA: Tutoring classes for students primarily in slum and tribal areas whose parents are illiterate and unable to help their children with their homework. This program allows children who otherwise might fail and dropout of school to succeed.

PREMALAYA: Crèches or day care centers for children of day laborers who would otherwise be either left home alone or taken to the fields with their parents. Maher provides a safe environment, nutritious food, activities, and periodic health check-ups.

EKTA: Free provisions to poor families to help keep families united and their children in school. Assistance includes food, clothing, shelter, school fees, or medical expenses for "catastrophic" issues.

AADHAR: Job placement for village women and youth. Maher has developed relationships with local factories and is known now as a source for good, reliable domestic help.

DHNYANGANGA: Provides libraries in villages and remote areas to foster reading habits and helps improve literacy for children and adults.

KALASAGAR: Open school for dropouts or others who missed out on an education. In coordination with the National Open School program, Maher provides text books and tutoring so children and adults can pass exams equivalent to 4th, 7th, and 10th standard exams. After passing the 10th standard exam they may attend college and university courses.

PARISHRAM: Center for vocational training and production. Residents of Maher learn skills, work ethic, and earn money making a variety of items such as stitched bags, greeting cards, jewelry, candles, incense, and curries. Residents earn a proscribed rate for each piece they complete. These products are sold to companies and to friends of Maher around the world.

PRAGATI: Rural outreach and awareness programs. Maher offers a wide array of awareness programs in rural and tribal villages to help people improve the quality of life for themselves and their families. Topics have ranged from health and hygiene to inter-caste unity, from the importance of educating girls to the evils of alcoholism, from legal awareness for women to occupational opportunities. Case example below.

SWACHATA: Building of toilets and vermiculture pits, and biogas-making facilities. This project supports general household and community cleanliness.

SWAVALAMBAN: Self-help groups for women, men, and youth. Self-help groups encourage financial independence through education, savings, member loans, and affordable loan repayment. Additionally, Maher has found that family problems decrease as members become more self-sufficient. In addition to saving, members learn about communication and conflict resolution skills, leadership and organizational skills, group decision-making skills, and more. Sample loan projects: purchase a sewing machine to start a tailoring business, dig a bore well, buy a goat or a cow. Case example below.

TANTRAGYAN: Technical or vocational training for youth. Instruction may be through a Maher social worker, or draw on outside expertise. Participants may be trained as kindergarten teachers, para-social workers, caterers, tailors, electricians, and more.

LOKMANGALA: General outreach and public welfare programs during acute crises. Maher provides a variety of support to people and communities during times of natural disasters such as floods, earthquakes, and tsunamis.

VIDYADHAM: Education and training support for outstation children (such as college and university students from Maher). Maher provides housing, care, and general support for older children to complete their education and training so they may become financially stable.

KARYA MANDAL: Administration and management of Maher work. Now housed in its own building in Pune, this project includes collecting and maintaining all the records, reports, and data of all the other projects, financial obligations, public relations, etc.

ADIWASI KALYAN KENDRA: Welfare activities for tribal people. Maher develops relationships with these exploited people, teaching them their rights, and helping to improve their lives.

GAMAT SHALA: Daycare and nutrition for the children of brick kiln workers and slum children. Literal translation: play and learn.

Two examples: a village awareness meeting and a self-help group meeting
Note: these are both based on the notes of Maher volunteer Mikaela Keepin.

A village awareness meeting

Several Maher social workers traveled to a Maher children's home in a village called Shirur. While most of the children were at school, the space was used for what Maher calls an "awareness meeting." The people of Pardi Wasti (a nearby slum village for a tribe at the very bottom of the caste hierarchy) were invited to the Shirur Maher center. They were promised a free meal and blankets if they sat through the meeting. Social workers took turns addressing the crowd for about five minutes each. The topics covered general human rights and the rights these people have as a community in the Pune area. Then three guests spoke. One was a lawyer and two were doctors. With this meeting, Maher intended to get the Pardi Wasti people used to hearing about their rights, their responsibilities, and their options when it comes to healthcare and legal aid. This meeting was seen as the first of many. Sister Lucy explained that people need to hear the same things over and over and to see some results before they start really listening and taking action.

After the meeting came the promised free meal. The housemothers of Shirur brought large steel pots filled with freshly prepared rice, vegetables, and dal to the ground behind the meeting room. The visitors sat in a circle while Maher boys dished out the food onto steel plates. After people finished eating, they returned to the meeting room to receive their blankets. Two of the social workers distributed wool blankets. A few of the people in the crowd began shouting and soon most of the people were shouting, making dramatic gestures with their arms and hands. Some ripped blankets out of other's hands. It was tense and loud in the room, but not threatening. Sister Lucy later explained that these incredibly poor people learn to fight for what they have. If they fail to ruthlessly look out for their own backs, they will likely find themselves cold and hungry. She advised the social workers to bring extra blankets next time to help avoid such a crush.

Mikaela noticed one woman remained eating. She sat cross-legged, supporting a small child in her lap. Her fingers brought food to her mouth and bites to the baby's mouth, in turn. A Maher social worker spoke to the woman and then reported that the child in the woman's lap was her seventh baby. She was 22 years old.

A self-help group meeting
There were 12 women sitting on the floor of one of their living rooms, forming a crescent-moon shape. About half of them had small children in their laps. Maher's social worker for this self-help group, sat on the floor as well, facing the group. Notebooks were retrieved and data was recorded. Rupees were collected and placed into an envelope, to be taken to their bank by the designated group member. The host of the evening's meeting served chai and water and supplied a basket of toys for the children. The 45-minute meeting included lots of talking and laughing and head-wagging.

After the meeting, the social worker explained that there were 35 self-help groups in that neighborhood. She attends each of their monthly meetings, and is a resource to all the groups. One woman proudly invited the group to view her small beauty shop, begun with a loan from her self-help group. The entryway was an estimated seven feet high by five feet wide. It was one in a series of entranceways in its building, with a steel, garage-like door that rolled up into a track along the ceiling. Inside there were two small rooms, one in front of the other. The first was a shop, filled with beauty products and household objects and other random knickknacks. A pair of parlor chairs sat in the second room, where the beauty parlor magic happens. Her husband was her only employee. While showing the group her business, the woman beamed with satisfaction in her accomplishment.

Appendix B

RELIGIOUS SYMBOLS*

Om: According to many Hindu mystics and philosophers, God is beyond human words and forms. Silence in the presence of the Absolute is considered better than speaking. The uttering and recitation of Om is a stepping-stone to silence. Therefore, a Hindu often begins and ends his prayer by using the mystic monosyllable Om, which stands for the symbolic representation of the Supreme Being in Hinduism.

Dharmachakra: Gautama Buddha, after his enlightenment, became the great teacher who set in motion the wheel of dharma. The symbol of a many-spoked wheel with a dot in the centre signifies the soul's ultimate liberation from the cycle of birth and rebirth. The wheel may also symbolise a constantly changing universe, the impermanence of everything in the world, and that this journey in search of dharma is an on-going process.

Swastika: Jainism follows the religious path established by Vardhamana Mahavira. Swastika is a primitive symbol in the form of a cross with equal arms with limb of the same length projecting at right angles from the end of each arm, all in the same direction, and clock-wise. The word swastika is derived from 'swasti' or well-being, luck and consecration.

Kara: The steel bangle represents Sikhism which is the evolved product of three primary elements – the devotional system taught by Guru Nanak, the structure of Punjabi society and the period of Punjabi history from Guru Nanak to the present day. The five emblems of the Khalsa (chosen race of soldier-saints committed to five principles) are Kesa, Kangha, Kacch, Kirpan and Kara.

Crescent: The Crescent and the star is used widely to designate Islam. Some scholars allege that the Crescent was adopted as a distinctive mark by the Muslims, in consequence of the Hagira, or flight of Muhammed from Mecca to Medina having taken place at the time of the new moon, when it appears in the form of a Crescent. As the crescent moon gives light to the weary traveller on the hot sands of Arabia, Islam also gives solace to the weary people and guides them towards Allah, the Supreme God.

Cross: The principal symbol of the Christian religion – a cross is beyond doubt the widest used of all Christian symbols. For Christians, the cross is a sign of evoking a historical event basic to the history of salvation: the crucifixion and death of Jesus at Calvary. The sign of the cross is made at liturgical functions, over persons and things.

Star of David: Star of David is the symbol of Judaism. The six-pointed star is formulated by two equilateral triangles that have the same center and are placed in opposite directions. It is a dynamic and positive symbol of Judaism.

Bow and Arrow: Bow and arrow is one of the oldest and most used weapons with its origins lost in paleolithic times. These weapons were used by hunters, warriors and people in pursuit of archery as a sport. We can reasonably argue that in prehistoric times too, the hunting and food gathering people had the mental ability to conceive ideas, which can be described as primordial religion.

Fire: With a history of some three thousand years, Zoroastrianism is one of the most ancient among living religions. It takes its name from its founder, Zaruthushtra. He recommended meditating before the only basic symbol of the religion – fire.

* Source: Maher files

Hammer and Sickle: The prophetic ideology of Marx has found dynamic growth and acceptance because it promised heaven on earth. Marxism did not fail to generate creative tensions between Christianity and the State. Yet, both Hammer and Sickle contributed to the purification of Christian ideologies and practices. The two classes of people namely factory workers (hammer) and peasants (sickle) should emerge into a timely conflict with the oppressors and this will create a society of humans with equality and peace.

Yin and Yang: Taoism, the religionphilosophy founded by Lao Tse that traces its roots further into antiquity than any other Chinese belief, has for long utilised this symbol of gracefully bisected circles as its basic symbol. The belief is that there are two primary forces constantly at inter-play in the cosmos; one is the passive female principle, Yin (black) and the other active male principle, Yang (white). However, there is no conflict between these complementary forces.

Our inspiration originates from...

Is God so small to be possessed by one religion?

Appendix C

Guidelines for Visiting Maher and Additional Resources

Maher has many visitors who come for a variety of reasons. Many want to experience what they have heard or read about Maher, to experience the magic firsthand. Others want to learn what can be done to help the world's poor and oppressed, including how to replicate Maher's success near their own home. Still others want to offer their skills and time to Maher's work. Still others come simply because they are moved by the stories of the women and children of Maher, and by the dedication of Sister Lucy. No matter the reason, every visitor is inspired and touched deeply by the atmosphere of love, compassion, and joy at Maher.

The best way to truly experience Maher is to go for several weeks to several months as a volunteer. Opportunities for volunteering are varied including doing activities with the women and children of Vatsalyadham, teaching English or computer classes to teens, painting buildings, or helping with office computer work. Students seeking internships are also welcome although these are not arranged by Maher. *All guest, volunteer, and internship positions must be approved by Maher before the person makes the journey to India*. All guests are expected to honor cultural sensitivities in dress and demeanor.

If you are interested in visiting Maher, or if you would like to serve as a volunteer or apply for an internship, you may contact Maher via email. Write, explaining your situation and what you are seeking to do. Maher may refer your inquiry first to a Friend of Maher in your geographic area. You may also initiate this inquiry through this book's website or Maher's website.

Contact addresses:
Email Maher   Maher@Maherashram.org
Maher website   www.maherashram.org
Book's website   www.replicatemaher.wix.com/tools

Additional Resources
Dignity from Despair Face Book page   www.facebook.com/NewEnglandFriendsofMaher
  - Tips, ideas, comments from readers and those implementing all or parts of this book! Also events when Sister Lucy is in the United States.

Swayam   www.swayam.info/index.htm
  - This is a Kolkatta group working to End Violence Against Women. They offer day programs plus a great deal of research on women and violence in India.

SOKFIN's website   www.sofkin.org/home.asp
  - Photo gallery and other information and ideas

Half the Sky Movement   www.halftheskymovement.org
  - Founded by authors of *Half the Sky* (cited here) and supporting work internationally with networking, tips, training videos, and more.

Note that the website supporting this book will be maintained and updated with additional information, tips that come in as new Maher-inspired projects start up, and other useful information as it is suggested.

Appendix D

Note to Western Readers

Sir John Templeton said, "Self-improvement comes mainly from trying to help others." Maher demonstrates this truth that is now being born out in research. And Jonathan Haidt (a psychologist at University of Virginia) has shown in his research that "sustained happiness comes from a connection to something larger—a greater cause or humanitarian purpose."[29]

In the West, social service organizations tend to focus on the courts, legal determinations, and financial settlements, often only tangentially helping women and children pick up the pieces and make new lives. Court processes almost always take much longer than the three to six months women can live in a refuge or shelter. Maher takes a different approach and offers new ideas about how to serve and bring about change. While legal and regulatory systems may limit direct application of the approaches Maher is free to use, there is much to be learned. Our mindsets may limit us more than our regulations and red tape.

Sister Lucy also found that halfway houses where shelter, food, clothing were provided was not enough either. Women *survived* but they did not *thrive*; they did not transform themselves as do the women of Maher.

One of the most profound wisdoms of Maher lies in healing through helping care for other women and children. I talked to many women who shared their stories of grief, rage, and helplessness, and the discovery that the way out was working at Maher helping others. These women are now radiantly happy and full of confidence that they can manage their lives and care for their children and grandchildren. They received no payments or settlements or "justice" from their abusive husbands or in-laws. They simply moved on.

And the children: this author has watched Sister Lucy work with children who have been on the streets and in trouble. I have seen that she never gives up on them. She holds expectations that they can overcome these challenges and live good lives. She structures their time with chores, learning, and activities. Her door is always open to any child needing support.

How might "women healing women" work in the West?

Maher's practice of "women healing women" is unique relative to the West. In the West, (as in India), most shelters are licensed for short-stay homes. Often these women are just as traumatized as are the women who come to Maher. They too need more time and space to heal. Yet it is rare that we think these women can help others like them, until *after* their lives are all put back together. This is an error for two reasons: 1) resources (at least in US) are so scarce that women rarely get all the help they need from overwhelmed social service agencies and volunteers—their peers may be their best source of support; and, 2) more importantly, what Maher shows us is that helping others keeps these women outwardly-focused, engaged in a community, and boosts their self-esteem as they give to others. Indeed Maher demonstrates

---

[29] Nicholas D Kristoff and Sheryl WuDunn, *Half the Sky* (NY: Vintage Books 2009), 250.

that helping others is *how* these women heal, instead of something to do later, once they *are* healed.

Example: This author visited a model American women's shelter where there was space for three to five women and their children for short-term (three months) stays. The women were all juggling jobs, childcare, court cases, and more. Yet even though they shared housing, they lived and ate separately, with no arranged communal time, shared meal preparations, or childcare. Each woman was on her own. Social workers were there mostly during the day, when the women were at work and the children at school. Their caseloads included many more clients than the women residents.

It is incredibly important for women who were treated as if they were stupid, lesser humans, or worse, to experience themselves as strong, capable, helpful, wise, and loving. The housemothers at Maher all talk about how they have achieved so much more than they thought they were capable of, how good they feel about themselves, and how happy they are now, even though they work very hard. It is this inner healing that allows them to, for example, forgive parents or in-laws so their children have the opportunity to know their grandparents.

Be creative: how can we take the key principles of Maher, such as communal living for as long as needed, housemothers caring for women and children supervised by social workers, all learning values and skills for nonviolent living? Instead of thinking how that is not the western culture, or what governmental regulations would make it hard, or how to raise funds; think about what we *can* do!

Additionally, since the abuse of women crosses all layers of society, many previous victims have professional skills and resources that can be a great help to newer victims. Many of these women, as well as their friends and family members now sensitized to these issues, want to help. Skills of women in legal aid, courtroom lawyers, forensic accountants, early childhood development specialists, and more can be tapped into. Again, even after starting a new life, healing needs to happen. Helping others who have experienced similar abuse and loss is part of that healing.

The bottom line is that there is much we can do to bring the wisdom and love of Maher to our own back yard!

> *It's in our interest to take care of others. Self-centredness is opposed to basic human nature. In our own interest as human beings we need to pay attention to our inner values. Sometimes people think compassion is only of help to others, while we get no benefit. This is a mistake. When you concern yourself with others, you naturally develop a sense of self-confidence. To help others takes courage and inner strength.*
> *--Dalai Lama*

Index

CPSIA information can be obtained at www.ICGtesting.com
Printed in the USA
BVOW06s2359031214

377637BV00020B/505/P